VINTAGE

R.D. KARVE

Anant Deshmukh is a researcher, critic and the biographer of social reformers of Maharashtra, including Shridhar Pant, Shridhar Balwant Tilak, Dinanath Dalal and R.P. Paranjape. He played a crucial role in mapping R.D. Karve's life and bringing out his biography. Having spent over twenty years teaching, Deshmukh's research includes that of nineteenth-century Maharashtra and literary criticism. He has published forty-five books across genres, including travelogues and short-story collections.

Nadeem Khan has been a teacher of English since 1973, retiring as associate professor in 2010. He was the founder and director of the Western Regional Centre of the Indian Institute of Mass Communication (IIMC), Ministry of Information and Broadcasting, from 2011 to 2018. He has translated several books, mainly from Marathi into English. His translation of Avadhoot Dongare's *The Story of Being Useless* won him the 'Valley of Words' (VoW) award in 2020. His translation of Savita Ambedkar's autobiography, *Babasaheb: My Life with Dr Ambedkar*, published by Penguin Random House India in 2022, is a national bestseller.

ADVANCE PRAISE FOR THE BOOK

'To me, R.D. Karve was the quintessential example of a rationalist thinker with a scientific mindset. His tireless advocacy for family planning was a solitary and arduous endeavour ahead of its time. As a society, we failed him by not recognizing the significance of his mission or supporting it. My decision to make *Dhyaasparva* (An Era of Yearning), a feature film on his life, was a personal tribute, a gesture of redemption for the lack of recognition he received during his lifetime. All through the film-making, I was haunted by one question: Where did he find the resilience to defy convention and fight for his cause? This book too is a form of reckoning the complexities of his legacy and our collective silence. Can we muster the courage to fight our own battles with his passion and fervour?'—**Amol Palekar, actor, director, producer, activist, painter and author**

'Some people are so far ahead of their time that they drag the rest of us into the future: R.D. Karve was one such. Like his father Maharshi Karve before him, he paid a heavy price for his heterodox views. In R.D.'s case, it was a lifetime of work on sexuality and birth control, taboo subjects even today, let alone in nineteenth-century Maharashtra. Anant Deshmukh's deeply researched biography details his unconventional mind and his struggles against the times he lived in. As a not-so-distant relative of R.D. Karve, I found Deshmukh's biography of this unsung hero a revelation. Nadeem Khan's fine, seamless translation will take this singular character to an even larger audience'—**Urmilla Deshpande, co-author of *Iru: The Remarkable Life of Irawati Karve***

R.D. KARVE

The Champion of Individual Liberty

ANANT DESHMUKH

Translated from the Marathi by

Nadeem Khan

VINTAGE

An imprint of Penguin Random House

VINTAGE

Vintage is an imprint of the Penguin Random House group of companies
whose addresses can be found at global.penguinrandomhouse.com

Published by Penguin Random House India Pvt. Ltd
4th Floor, Capital Tower 1, MG Road,
Gurugram 122 002, Haryana, India

Penguin
Random House
India

First published in Vintage by Penguin Random House India 2025

ISBN 9780143475323

Typeset in Minion Pro by MAP Systems, Bengaluru, India
Printed at Replika Press Pvt. Ltd, India

www.penguin.co.in

MIX
Paper | Supporting
responsible forestry
FSC™ C016779

Contents

Foreword

Prof. Raghunath Dhondo Karve, known as R.D. or simply 'Ra Dhon', was a maverick, a rebel and a social revolutionary born ahead of his time. Had he been born in England, he would likely have gained international recognition as a genius, an iconoclast and a fearless crusader—championed and celebrated by the likes of Bertrand Russell and George Bernard Shaw.

In the timeframe of history, Karve was ahead of Russell. Russell's path-breaking and socially confrontational book *Marriage and Morals* was published in 1929. Karve's landmark challenging magazine *Samaaj-swaasthya* was started in 1925. Both Russell and Karve faced protests, social and professional boycotts and even a series of court cases filed against them.

Karve stood firm in his conviction that most of the practices regarding marriage, sexual relations, moral restrictions, taboos and conventional 'wisdom' were unscientific, irrational and mostly harmful to the overall physical and mental health of the individual and of society. It was inevitable that the conservative ('Sanatani'), Brahminical, self-styled monitors of morality and even politico-legal authorities would rise against Karve. He was sacked from his job as professor and was prevented from getting any assignment. This privileged and powerful class rose in one voice to suppress and even punish Karve for his audacity in challenging the age-old, religion-sanctioned customs and entrenched social mores.

Russell, too, faced isolation, boycotts, persecution, and prosecution—first at the hands of Victorian moralists and later by the entire political class in both England and the United States. There was even a campaign to prevent his entry into the US. Some of his books were banned. He was removed from City College of New York. A Catholic judge made the observation that Russell was 'morally unfit' to teach. Russell suffered the onslaught with stoicism and the courage of a prophet.

Both strongly advocated sex education, rejected the notion that homosexuality was immoral or antisocial, questioned conventional ideas of marital fidelity, pushed for easier access to divorce and demanded greater availability of birth control devices, among other reforms.

Karve was a pioneer of the birth control movement, advocating family planning even before it became a subject of discussion in Europe. His campaign for family planning and birth control began in 1921. In 1923, he published *Santaji Nigamananda*, a book on birth control—six years before Russell entered the debate.

Prof. Karve launched the magazine *Samaaj-swaasthya* in 1927, by which time he had already established himself as a staunch advocate of birth control, sex education, women's autonomy in sexual matters and the study and treatment of venereal diseases. He argued that the rise in sexually transmitted diseases stemmed from widespread ignorance about sex and insisted that sex education should begin at the school level.

The conservatives argued that Karve was promoting social permissiveness, encouraging women to be promiscuous and even encouraging extramarital and premarital sex. Criminal cases were lodged against him for promoting adultery and free sex. Russell had said, 'Marriage is for women the commonest mode of livelihood, and the total amount of undesired sex endured by women is probably greater in marriage than in prostitution.'

Karve expressed similar thoughts and was in fact accused of irresponsible advocacy of infidelity, even prostitution. Dr Norman Haire and Dr Havelock Ellis were well known in England as radical sexologists. Karve sedulously followed their writings and recommendations. As the British orthodoxy rose against Russell, so did Karve have to face the ire of the 'Sanatani' Brahmins in Maharashtra (mainly in Pune).

Numerous criminal and civil cases were slapped against him that created a lot of controversy. Charged with vulgarity, Karve had to defend himself as a social health activist and communicator. In one of his cases, no less than Dr Babasaheb Ambedkar came forward to defend him in court.

His intellectual and philosophical relationship was with Dr William Robinson, a New York-based physician and scholar in sexology who had studied the subject of sex, homosexuality and marital sex in multiple dimensions. It is not as if Karve was not supported by anybody. There were high-profile intellectuals and celebrities like Wrangler R.P. Paranjape, historian G.S. Sardesai, Shakuntala Paranjape and, of course, his father Dhondoji Karve and his half-brothers.

'Ra Dhon' was not only an activist in an exceptionally turbulent field but also a man of music and literature. He counted Ustad Abdul Karim Khan among his acquaintances. Having lived in France and immersed himself in European—mainly French—literature, he translated Guy de Maupassant's stories into Marathi. These literary pursuits complemented his primary mission of instilling rationality into society's sexual mores.

By and large, there was little social acceptance of his ideas among the masses and even among the so-called intellectuals of his time. He remained a lone fighter. Born on 15 January 1882, Karve died almost unsung in 1953, at the age of seventy-one. His wife, Malatibai, had died nine years earlier in 1944. R.D.'s state of penury and his self-respect were of such an order that, despite having a bunch of loyal siblings and friends, he carried her corpse from the hospital in a handcart.

However, this has been the plight of most social reformers, idealist rebels and revolutionaries. As Albert Einstein has said, 'Great spirits have always encountered violent opposition from mediocre minds.'

I take this opportunity to congratulate Anant Deshmukh for bringing alive this forgotten trailblazer after assiduous research, to Nadeem Khan for his efficient translation of Deshmukh's Marathi book into English, and to Penguin Random House (India) for undertaking the commendable charge of familiarizing the readers of English with this forgotten hero.

Kumar Ketkar
Author, journalist and
former member of the Rajya Sabha

Preface

The nineteenth century was momentous not only for Maharashtra but also for India. In 1819, the Marathas lost the third Anglo–Maratha war, and most parts of India were left in control of the British East India Company. Peshwa Bajirao II's territories were annexed to form the Bombay Presidency. The British had a progressive outlook and believed in scientific advancement; Britain had established several universities, the printing press had been with them for centuries, the telegraph had been invented and it would soon get appended to the postal services. There was a steady stream of inventions and discoveries that improved the quality of life for the common man in Britain and secular life occupied an important place in their culture.

The natives of India presented a contrasting picture. Their ancient culture was anchored in spirituality and ridden by superstition. Society was resistant to any effort at scientific change and advancement. Only a small, privileged section had the right to education, and that too was circumscribed within the framework of religion.

Those few of the privileged classes, who attended university, saw glaring inadequacies in their native culture, and strove to remove them. For example, people like Jyotiba Phule, Dhondoji alias Anna Karve and Karmaveer Bhaurao Patil made relentless efforts to spread and popularize education, especially the education of women. Orthodox society raised obstacles at every step, but these trailblazers could not be deterred.

Among the stormy and controversial personalities of Maharashtra at the time was Raghunath Dhondo Karve (1882–1953). Raghunathrao carried forward the legacy of his father Dhondo Keshav Karve of undertaking seminal social reform; nevertheless, the area and range of his work were different. Our society often expects children to follow in their father's footsteps, but he did not care about this notion. He writes, 'The idea of children following in their father's footsteps is not at all acceptable to me because this will not lead to progress. It is not difficult to see, however, that we have behaved according to the great example that our father has set for us. It has never been Anna's opinion that children should keep doing the things their fathers have done.'

Raghunathrao studied the subjects of birth control and the science of lovemaking with great dedication and propagated his ideas, backing his thoughts with action. For the purpose of providing scientific information to the people on this subject, he wrote two books, *Santati Niyaman* (Birth Control) and *Guptrogaapaasoon Bachaav* (Prevention of Venereal Diseases). Raghunathrao wanted to enlighten people, and he began publishing a monthly magazine called *Samaaj-swaasthya* (Health of the Society). This magazine survived for twenty-three years and four months. The last issue was written before he passed away and published immediately after his death.

The thoughts that Raghunathrao propagated through this magazine were too radical for the society of his time. The orthodox raised obstacles to his work and filed cases against him in the court of law. Three such cases were in fact heard and he was convicted twice, but they did not deter him at all. His commitment to the cause he had espoused was immense. He received ample support for his mission from his wife Malatibai, friend Shakuntala Paranjape and a handful of others.

The importance of his work began to be realized only after Indian Independence and it even began getting recognition from the State. There were also some people who made deliberate efforts to stop the credit of his pioneering work from going to him. After his death, interest in his public image and in his social work and the importance of his work began gaining recognition from 1970 to 1990.

In due course, biographical articles on him like 'Upekshit Drishta' (Neglected Prophet) by Divakar Bapat in 1970 and *Ra. Dhon. Karve* by Y.D. Phadke in 1981, gained prominence. Later, M.V. Dhond wrote three different articles on him in the second edition of *Jaalyaache Chandra*. Mangala Athalekar too devoted a chapter on Raghunathrao in her book *Maharshi tey Gauri*. Thus, information on him became increasingly available. Of particular significance was the scholarship and integrity of Y.D. Phadke, combined with his penchant for research and his commitment to biographical writing. As a result, his biography *Ra. Dhon. Karve* has been successful in winning the approval of readers and scholars. M.V. Dhond gathered information on R.D. Karve through interviews with his brothers Dr Shankarrao, Dinkarrao, Bhaskarrao and his friend Shakuntala Paranjape.

Raghunathrao has also left behind plenty of biographical material in his own writings. Dhondo Keshav Karve, affectionately addressed as Anna, has been generous with information in his autobiography, *Aatmavritt*, based on which Divakar Bapat created a short sketch. Y.D. Phadke made use of the material and sources provided to him by Haribhau Mote and filled in the details on the strength of his scholarship and disciplined writing. M.V. Dhond interviewed Dr Shankarrao, Dinkarrao, Bhaskarrao and Shakuntalabai to weave their memories into words.

Much historical research still needs to be done to gather more information on Raghunathrao. Gopal Krishna

Gokhale, Nelson Frazer, Poltier, S.K. Kolhatkar, B.V. Varerkar, M.G. Rangnekar, Shakuntala Paranjape; they were gurus, senior well-wishers and friends in that order. Their remarks on Raghunath and articles written on the occasion of the many functions that happened during Anna's lifetime will have to be searched out; Raghunath's own writings on them will have to be read. If the writings of family members Shankarrao, Dinkarrao, Bhaskarrao and Iravatibai become available, perhaps light may be shed on their mutual relationships. For example, Raghunathrao's articles—'What I Think About My Father,' 'The Echoes at Home: The Other Side of Renouncing Selfishness,' 'My Experiences with Anna'—help us understand the relationship between Anna and Raghunathrao.

Research keeps throwing up new, different, untouched, unseen and therefore unused material. Whether it is a biography or history, when new source material becomes available, when a new perspective arrives, new writing is necessary. Perhaps, the last word in many areas of life can never be written. That was why I was drawn towards doing a biography on Raghunathrao.

I have made an effort at capturing in this book the 'new' that I believe has emerged from my readings. I hope that this book will not only correct the discrepancies and lacunae that I noticed in the writings of some of the earlier biographers, but will unveil some new aspects of the personality of this extraordinary man.

Early Days

Birth and Murud Days

Maharashtra saw a change in the political scenario in the first two decades of the nineteenth century. The rule of the Peshwas ended and the English usurped power across India. This had an extraordinary impact on life in Maharashtra. Our spiritualistic, static culture came in contact with, and had to live alongside a western culture that laid emphasis on earthly life and had a scientific attitude. Though they were just a handful, the Englishmen came upon us as rulers, and we benefitted from it. Our traditional lifestyle and our *chaaturvarnya*[1] system came under assault. The communication tools, the expansion of schools, offices and the arrival of textile mills caused fundamental changes.

Earlier, the Brahmin class would travel to Wai, Nashik, Poona and Kolhapur to study the holy books, while the lower castes would train themselves in the professions into which they were born.

Bombay came into prominence in the British period and became the marketplace of trade and commerce. People of all castes and creeds began converging there from all corners of the country to make their fortune. The Bombay University also began in 1857. Around 1830, steamboats began to ply on the Konkan coastal strip. The Konkan is basically a land of intelligent people, but it was groaning under the curse of poverty. Therefore, the youth began travelling to Bombay for education. Balshastri Jambhekar, Ramchandra Gopal Bhandarkar, Dhondo Keshav Karve were among these youngsters. Around 1869, the textile mills started in Bombay. The poor, simple farmers and the labour class of Konkan began moving to Bombay in the hope of finding themselves employment in the mills, in offices and in the police department.

In those days, Bombay had Elphinstone College, while Pune had Deccan College and Fergusson College. Youngsters began arriving from different regions of Maharashtra and when they couldn't find accommodation in the township, they would live in the hostels provided by the colleges.

The picture we get of Dhondo (Anna) Karve from his early days in his autobiography *Aatmavritt* matches this scenario. He hailed from a village called Murud near Harne and had come over to Bombay for his education. Even before he left for Bombay, he was married to a relative named Radhabai, in 1876. On 14 January 1882, Radhabai gave birth to a son who was given the name of Raghunath. Anna received his BA degree two years after the birth of his son. This obviously means that while he lived in Bombay for his education, Radhabai lived in Murud.

While he was in college, Anna lived in a hostel along with a close friend, Narhar Balkrishna Joshi. Anna writes about him in *Aatmavritt*:[2]

> The reason why my friend Narhar Balkrishna Joshi left such a deep imprint on me was that he had some extraordinary qualities. A bare five or ten minutes of conversation with him would reveal his intelligence and brilliance.

Anna treasured Narharpant's company, but Narharpant left the hostel and took up lodgings in Girgam where he began living with his family. He then proposed to Anna that he should also bring his family over and they could live together. Anna accepted the proposal and brought over Radhabai and Raghunath to constitute a joint family.[3] Thus it happened that Raghunath's earliest years were spent first in Murud and then in Girgam, Bombay.

Anna experimented with Raghunath's education when he was in Konkan. He writes,

> I used to feel that it was not right to have children sitting inside a class room for hours at a stretch. Accordingly, we decided to teach our son Raghunath at home instead of sending him to school. Radhabai would teach him between her chores. Then, for a year or two we had a teacher visiting home to teach him for an hour. When he was eight years of age, it was decided to put him in a school. But then the thought came that since he had not been taught in any proper sequence, it would not do to send him immediately to school. All the weaknesses that had remained because of not having attended a regular school would first have to be removed. We thus thought that instead of being put into a school, he should be put in charge of my childhood friend Balkrishna Savant Achval. . . . After staying with him for a year or a year and a half, Raghunath did well in his Standard V and was then brought over to Bombay.

Radhabai was alive when the thread ceremony of Raghunath was performed. Anna wanted to perform this ceremony rather differently so that he could cut expenses, which required the consensus of his parents and his wife. He writes,

> The circumstances of our family had improved. During this period, the time arrived for the thread ceremony of our son Raghunath. Even the poor get into a lot of expenditure for this

ceremony, which I didn't like at all and I thought this to be a good opportunity for setting an example. . . . It was decided that the ceremony would be performed as per my desire. I got great support in this matter from my childhood friend B.V. Achval. He too had to perform the thread ceremony for his son, which he decided to do along the same lines as me. Our friend Kashinath Kane worked as a teacher in Mahim, Bombay, and we managed to perform the function in his house for fifteen rupees. I contributed two hundred rupees and Achval came up with a hundred to make a total of three hundred which we gave over to the Murud Fund.

Radhabai returned to Murud where she fell ill. Anna wrote a number of confidence-building letters to her during her illness. But she passed away just as the monsoons arrived. Anna, unfortunately, could not be with her during her last days. He later married Narharpant's widowed sister, Anandibai, better known as Baya.

Joint Family Experiment and a Lost Childhood

Raghunath's childhood was spent in a joint family with Anna and Narharpant. At a tender age, he witnessed the discussions that the two of them would have, their intellectual growth and the influence that Narharpant had on Anna. However, Raghunath did not emerge with a favourable impression of Narharpant because of his attitude towards children. He was a disciplinarian and believed in licking kids into good behavior. Raghunathrao was destined to suffer his tyranny. This is what Baya Karve writes about her brother's (Narhari's) nature in her autobiography, *Mazhe Puraan,* (as translated from Marathi):

A number of parents believe in a similar kind of tyranny for disciplining their children. They brag that disciplining means opposing anything that the children say, at least for the time being; in never immediately accepting what they have to say. But experience says that this kind of disciplining spoils the children; they surreptitiously begin to do the very opposite of what their parents tell them to do.

Based on his own experience, this is what Raghunathrao had to say about his childhood:

'*Ramya tey baalpan, deyee deva phiruni*' (Oh that charming childhood, bring it back to me, oh god.) There are two lies in this statement: one is god and the other is the charm of childhood . . . . The memories that I carry of my childhood carry no happiness at all.

This is what Shakuntala Paranjape has to say in this matter:

The demon who took the plan (of joint family) in hand subjected everyone, particularly the children, to terrible maltreatment . . . thrashing them like animals, making them starve, making them eat filthy stuff . . . . Nobody got away from this person's clutches.

Prof. M.V. Dhond writes that the Karve brothers referred to Narharpant as a 'sadist'. Raghunathrao writes of Narharpant, 'If this gentleman had a special quality, it was not being of use to others; he was mainly concerned about how he could make use of others for maintaining his grandeur and dominance. . . . He would stretch himself unnecessarily even for acquiring even trivial gains.' In a certain interview,

Raghunath talks about Narharpant and says, 'That friend of his (Anna's) appeared to us children as a demon. Stealing if we were hungry; we could only steal if we were hungry and wanted to eat. I was so terrified of this man that I was afraid of even talking to my father.'[4]

Y.D. Phadke writes, '. . . Surly and ill-tempered, Narharipant had strange methods of delivering punishment. . . There would be beatings at the slightest excuse.' The internal relationship between Raghunathrao and Narharpant needs to be carefully studied.

On the occasion of Raghunathrao turning seventy, his contemporary and friend S.S. Navare has written:

> Both the Raghunaths (Raghunathrao Karve and R. P. Paranjape) later became great believers in rationality. While some credit for this goes to Anna's reformist tendency, a good bit of the credit goes to Anna's brother-in-law— Baya's brother—Narharpant Joshi's disposition.

When Navare wrote this, Raghunathrao was alive and he was very likely to have read this. Since there has been no contradiction from him to Navare's statement, it is likely that he agreed with it.

As a Student in Pune

Anna shifted to Pune with his family when he got himself a job as the professor of Mathematics in Fergusson College. While Raghunath went to school, Anna lived in Pune township. In the interim, Baya had gone to Nagpur to complete her course in nursing. The inspiration had, of course, come from Anna. During this period, Anna, Raghunath and Parvatibai Athavale's son, Nana,[5] lived together. Anna has written about his memories of those times:

During the absence of my wife, I managed the household affairs myself. There was my eldest son about thirteen years old and Parvatibai's son about nine. We cooked our food, washed our dishes and cleaned other utensils and swept and coated our rooms with cow-dung slurry. We were living at that time in a small house in the Fergusson College Compound. The boys were of course of great help to me.[6]

Regarding Raghunathrao's school life, his classmate at New English School Senapati Bapat wrote, 'in New English school, we were together in the same division of Standard VII. Brilliant in Mathematics. His father Sant [sic] Karve mathematician, he [too a] mathematician.' This means that Raghunathrao was regarded as an intelligent student in school and Mathematics was his favourite subject.

In the second half of the nineteenth century, the father of the house was held in awe and his behavior was very stern. It can be said that in the beginning, Anna too behaved with Raghunath in a similar manner. He may not have been an extreme disciplinarian, perhaps, but it certainly cannot be said that he enjoyed an intimate relationship with Raghunathrao, at least in the earlier days. Later, he began to feel that he should give some attention to the motherless boy.

As things stood, he was being bombarded from all sides with criticism for having married Bayabai. He recognized the importance of the remarriage of widows, and he got drawn into that mission. He kept this mission in the forefront for the rest of his life. He had made a firm decision that while holding his job at Fergusson College, he would devote the rest of his time to social work, and that was when he found the direction in which he would move forward. As was to be expected, the scope of this activity went on increasing with every passing day. Looking around for people with similar values and similar dispositions, getting into consultations with them, giving them a full idea of his undertaking, making an effort at bringing detractors around to the extent possible, trying to get financial help from wherever possible for creating an organization and running the campaign for women's emancipation, meeting concerned persons, explaining to them the importance of the movement and getting donations, keeping a close account of revenue and expenditure—were activities that Anna had immersed himself into. Baya had to take over the responsibility of looking after the family. It is possible to imagine the kind of childhood that Raghunathrao would have had in these times. Circumstances would have become a little more palatable with the arrival of his half-brothers Shankarrao and Dinkarrao, but it impacted his disposition. He became self-absorbed and reserved. He developed an inferiority complex on account of being swarthy in complexion. He began to believe he was ugly and that people did not want to speak to him and therefore he should not speak to them either. He turned to books and spent most of his time reading and it became a passion. But for all of his reading, he failed in a subject like history. That was when the father and the teacher in Anna woke up and began paying personal attention to him. This is what Anna has written in *Aatmavritt* in this context:

> I myself prepared the History and Geography lessons and began teaching them to him. I gave special attention to Mathematics, got him to solve question papers for the past ten or twelve years and checked them out for him. Fortunately, the tutoring showed good results and he stood first in class. Later, when he sat for his Previous exams, I again got him to solve papers of the past ten years and he passed in the first division.

He then took admission in Fergusson College, but his experience there does not appear to have been very satisfying.

He believed that he should have got into a better college, but
his suspicion was that he had been admitted there because his
father was a member of the management committee. He was
given a scholarship for the first few years, but when he was
in the second year of his Master's degree, the scholarship was
withdrawn, because of which he had to discontinue his college
education. In this context, he has written somewhere:

> Actually, I should have received a good scholarship in
> college. But the people who ran the college had this fear
> that if the smarter students were not given scholarship, they
> would leave and join some other college. Their calculation,
> therefore, was that instead of being given to the children of
> the Management Committee, it was better given to others.

Bayabai also felt that the children didn't receive any help from
Anna. She wrote:

> The children too didn't receive any preferential treatment
> from him. The preference shouldn't be undeserved, but when
> it is deserved, shouldn't it then be given? It was only fair for
> Raghunath to have received the fellowship at Fergusson. But
> it was on account of Anna staying silent that he didn't get it.
> Even if his people stood the risk of losing, he would never
> make demands that were legitimate.

But there is no doubt that his stay at Fergusson College set the
direction in which his life would move. He submerged himself
into the subjects of birth control and sexology. There was his
curiosity, his study of books available in the library on these
subjects, and the realization that these kinds of books were not
readily available in either English or Marathi. There's a strong
probability that his young mind would have noted the openness
with which these subjects were discussed in the French culture

and the availability there of books and periodicals. The period from 1899 to 1903 that he spent in Fergusson College and its hostel, therefore, turned out to be quite important.

In the College Hostel

He was seventeen when he joined college. Anna writes, 'I had never had the opportunity of staying in the residency of my college. I put my son there so that he could benefit from it.' Raghunathrao also provides the following information on this matter: 'As a reward for having stood first in the matric examination, I was put into a hostel.' Besides, circumstances were not such as could ensure that he would have got along with Baya Karve.

It is important to know who else was in college during this period. The Pune of those times was famous as the 'mother city of education'. Around the year 1904, Ram Ganesh Gadkari was trying to get himself an education in this college. Besides, people from reputed, rich families from all over Maharashtra—even married men—would come to Pune. Raghunathrao cleared his BA in 1903 and the first year of MA in 1904. He had to abandon his Master's programme due to lack of money. He was twenty-three then. In the prime of youth, his curiosity about women, his attraction towards them, his curiosity about a heterosexual relationship and the desire to learn more about the subject had begun to simmer. He was witness to the illicit relationships between his contemporary young men and women, married and unmarried, the 'gift' of venereal diseases about which they could not talk to anyone and for which nobody knew remedies and their consequent mental and physical agonies.

'My efforts in this direction had begun in 1901,' he has written somewhere, 'because I knew of a few students suffering from V.D. and some others who had one child every year.'

In the *Samaaj-swaasthya* of December 1936, he wrote, 'Some of my student acquaintances of thirty years ago kept pictures of nudes, some of them were married, some visited prostitutes, some masturbated and indulged in other unnatural acts. This has been going on since ancient times.' With regards to students from colleges in Bombay and Poona (and those who have returned from a stay abroad), he noted:

> It is untrue that college students stay away from their wives for one year; staying away for three and a half months is true. That they live as celibates is also untrue. The notion that students going abroad for studies live as celibates is only our imagination. Nobody, however, admits to such things on returning.[7]

He was of a timid disposition. There was nothing that happened in his personal life that would have got him so strongly interested in studying these subjects. He writes, 'I had never had a relationship with any woman before my marriage . . . on account of my timid nature. I cannot say how it would have been if I had not been so timid.'

Another important information that Dr Dinkarrao gave to Prof. M.V. Dhond during the interview was that Anna was quite taken in with using birth control and used whatever was available during those times. Besides, Anna would have open conversations with his children on these subjects. It could have been on account of all these factors that Raghunathrao stumbled upon his mission in life.

This is what he says about exactly when he began studying this subject, 'My study of the science of lovemaking had begun about ten years before I got married.' Since he got married in 1911, he would have begun these studies in 1901, that is during his Fergusson College days.

Training for the Profession of Teaching and
Actual Teaching

A diploma in teaching was essential for becoming a teacher and a facility for acquiring this diploma had just begun in Bombay. Thinking it worthwhile to get himself that training, he came over to Bombay in 1906, the year the training college was established, and secured admission.

Detailed information on those days can be found in the articles he wrote for *Manorama*. He came into contact there with the principal, an Englishman named Nelson J. Frazer. During the early days, Principal Frazer was not very well disposed towards Raghunath, but his inherent intelligence and sustained interaction changed his opinion. During this period, he would have felt a keen desire to learn French so that he could pursue his studies on sexology. Or, perhaps, having developed a close bond with Principal Frazer, he would have discussed his obsession with him and received counsel from him. On his advice, he went to Elphinstone College to meet Peltier, who was a French professor there. Peltier also offered private tuition in the language. Raghunathrao would have been delighted at the signs of the fulfillment of his desire after meeting Peltier. He began learning French with great diligence and soon acquired sufficient competence in the language.

Soon, however, he informed the professor that he could not continue the tuition anymore because he didn't have the resources to pay him Rs. 7 per month. But Peltier was so delighted with his student that he not only waived off the tuition fees, but also insisted that Raghunath join the French Club. He went around telling other students that Raghunath was his favourite. He was bound to have given his student appropriate help and guidance, and would certainly have given Raghunath books on heterosexual relationship, venereal diseases, and birth control, and provided him with plenty of advice on the books and magazines he should study. Raghunathrao applied himself to the subject with diligence.

Raghunathrao equipped himself with the qualification for a middle school teacher in good time and found himself a job in Bombay. But the headmaster turned out to be corrupt and covertly—and sometimes, even overtly—suggested that Raghunathrao visit his house and bring him gifts of expensive clothes. Raghunath, however, was not the kind to buckle. When the headmaster began giving him trouble, he decided to teach him a lesson. He first took leave and sent the headmaster advance intimation through the post. Finally, left with no other alternative, the headmaster accepted that the two could not get along with each other and advised him, 'You apply for a transfer; I shall endorse it.' Raghunath was thus transferred to Solapur.

Raghunathrao did find some contentment in Solapur because he established a good equation with everyone. For one, the headmaster there was a straightforward person. He liked Raghunathrao's work and his disposition, which allowed the teacher to settle in comfortably. The other thing that happened was that whenever the Patankar theatre group came visiting, its owner would stay in the same lodge where Raghunath had his room. Thus, the two got to know each other and Raghunath would always be invited to attend their shows. Raghunathrao would even write for them. The owner of the theatre group was very fond of tamasha, the popular Marathi group dance with lewd overtones. Whenever he went for a tamasha show, he would always take Raghunath along with him. Raghunath, thus, had a great time in Solapur. In due course, a vacancy opened up at Elphinstone College for assistant to the professor of Mathematics. Raghunathrao's application was supported by a very strong recommendation from the headmaster. This was how he returned to Bombay, with extremely pleasant memories of his stay in Solapur.

Marriage

During this period, he fell in love. In 1900, Gangu Gode arrived at Anna's institution along with her two sisters for education. This girl, also called Malatibai, later became Raghunathrao's wife. Anna has made a reference to Malatibai at two or three places in *Aatmavritt*, which give us his perspective of her. The piece given below comes before his description of how Anaath Baalikaashram (Hostel for Orphan Girls) became Mahila Vidyalaya (Women's School):

> Around that time, a courageous person from Ratnagiri wrote a letter: 'I have three girls aged 14, 12 and 10. The eldest is a widow, while the younger two are unmarried. It's my desire that I should send these three girls to your *aashram* for education. I shall not be able to offer much financial support, hence much of the burden will have to fall on the *aashram*. If I send the widowed girl alone, the chances of the girls getting a good match disappear under the circumstances prevailing here. Please think over this matter and advise.'

On receiving the letter, Anna himself travelled to the gentleman's village in Konkan and met the girls and was impressed by their native intelligence. It was only after going through this process that Anna decided to bring the girls over to the ashram. The three girls came over to Anna and gave his mission a new dimension. He gained the perspective of not limiting his work to the welfare of widows but expanding it to include the all-round development of women. Thus, the education of women gained importance. The arrival of the Gode sisters gave Anna direction for his future enterprise. The girls were truly smart and bright. Whenever an important guest arrived in Anna's house, he would have the girls appear before them. They would respond to questions with great confidence and competence.

The guests would be thrilled at their responses and donate liberally to the ashram. Anna, therefore, developed a special affection for them.[8]

Once, the girls accompanied the family to Murud during the holidays. It got to be very convenient, since their village was just a little further ahead. The eldest of the girls was sufficiently educated and took over the responsibility of getting her brothers educated as well. Later, around 1916, she got married to Prof. D.L. Sahasrabuddhe who taught at the Agriculture College in Poona. Prof. Sahasrabuddhe was awarded the title of Rao Bahadur. P.C. Patil, in his autobiography, *Mazhya Aathvanee* (My Memories), mentions that after the Agriculture College was established in Poona, Sahasrabuddhe was among the people who had graduated along with him in 1906.

The third among the girls was Gangu Gode. When they came over to the ashram, she was just ten years old. She passed her matriculation in 1907 when she was seventeen. Till then, at least, she had connections with the Women's Education Society of the Hinganes. Later, her intimacy with the Karve family increased. Recounting his memories, Dr Shankarrao told Prof. M.V. Dhond in 1979:

Theirs was a love marriage and I was witness to it. In the year 1909, we of the Karve family went to Murud along with the sisters Banu, Rangu, and Gangu. These girls lived in the *aashram* and their village was quite close to Murud. Spending the day in the town and travelling at night—this was our programme for those six–seven days. During the night and dawn time, we—Anna, Appa, Gangu, Rangu, and I—would walk. It was during these walks that Appa and Gangu got close to each other and they informed Anna about it. Anna wrote to Gangu's father and their marriage was fixed.[9]

On 14 January 1911, Raghunath turned thirty. This means that
the wedding would have taken place within a year of 14 January
1911.[10] Similarly, it is reported that Anna got Gangubai's
father to give a written agreement saying that he would get his
daughter married when she was twenty-one. I have never come
across any writing that endorses this agreement. Similarly,
there is no evidence for the statement that 'Malatibai and
Raghunathrao had agreed that they would not have children'.
In 1908, Raghunathrao was employed as assistant to the
professor of Mathematics at Elphinstone College. Before that,
Malatibai had passed her matriculation in 1907 and, as Anna
writes, she had studied up to Previous in Fergusson College
for a year. Sometime between 1909–1910, Raghunathrao told
Malatibai that he loved her. He was by then a highly educated
man working at Elphinstone College with dreams of a good
future. He was Anna's son, came from a reputed family and
earned a handsome salary working in a significant area of
women's welfare. All of these thoughts would certainly have
gone through the mind of Malatibai (then Gangu Gode)
and she must have been excited to become the wife of such a
man. In 1909, they fell in love. Malatibai was slightly dark in
complexion with delicate features. Raghunathrao's mother had
passed away when he was eight and he wasn't close to Bayabai.
Besides, he was timid in nature and thus not given to start a
conversation with anyone. Against this background, he would
have appreciated Malatibai's company and liked her nature.
Their love for each other led to their marriage. After living in
Poona for some time, she left with Raghunathrao for Poona.

2

Professor R.D. Karve

In 1908, Raghunathrao was appointed to the post of assistant to the professor of Mathematics in Elphinstone College and he held that post till 1917. He was, of course, not idle during this period. It was in his nature to help students out with their problems. He wrote a book out of this experience titled *Ganitaacha Ek Bhag* (A Section of Mathematics). In the book he writes, 'While I was teaching in Elphinstone College, since there was no good book on a certain section of Geometry, I wrote a book myself and that's the reason why it's present everywhere.' His study of the French language was proceeding very well alongside. He wrote a farce based on another French farce that was published under the title 'Don Bahirey' (Two Deaf Persons) in the monthly magazine, *Manoranjan,* of the time. It was around this time that C.D. Deshmukh had taken admission in the college. 'In the year 1914, R.D. Karve joined as Professor of Mathematics', he has written in his autobiography. He didn't much care for Karve's teaching, but the two would meet on the tennis court, since Raghunathrao was interested in the game. When he first came to Bombay, he lived in Parel but later moved to Girgam. He would visit Peltier's house along with Malatibai and occasionally go to the French Club or to the theatre. During this time, Malatibai had found a job as a teacher at the Chandram High School in Bombay.

There was no prospect of getting a promotion in Elphinstone. If he wanted one, he would have to leave Bombay, because there weren't as many colleges then as there are now. There were government colleges only in the western belt of Bombay, Pune and Ahmedabad. A college was due to open in Dharwad in 1917, and the probability existed of his going there on promotion if he wanted it. The dilemma that Raghunathrao got into, therefore, was staying on with Malatibai or accepting a promotion. There is a strong probability that Malatibai had helped him resolve the dilemma. Carrying dreams in his heart, he joined the Karnataka College in Dharwad as assistant professor of Mathematics.

Karnataka College, Dharwad

The Department of Education had given permission to Dharwad College to hold first year and inter classes. Once these classes got going, there was a possibility of getting permission for higher classes. With a promotion, Raghunathrao obviously got a pay hike too and worked at Dharwad from 1917 to 1919. During the first year of college, he had S.K. Ksheersaagar (who later gained fame as a critic), A.K. Priyolkar (who earned a name for himself as a professor of Marathi and a researcher) and P.B. Gajendragadkar (who became the Chief Justice of the Supreme Court of India after Independence) as his students. This is what Ksheersaagar has written about Raghunathrao:

> When I got into college, Prof. Karve would imitate his celebrated *aatey-bandhu* [father's sister's son] Wrangler Paranjape. He applied pomade to his long moustaches and turned them up, always dressed in European clothes, kept on hurriedly scribbling mathematical steps on the blackboard with his back turned to the students for the entire period.

He had thus become an object of interest for the fresh first year students. Our Kannada classmates had created imaginary names for all the professors to fill out the initials. R.D. was thus filled out as Rudrappa Dudbasappa.

If we ignore the relationship error between Wrangler Paranjape and Karve, the rest of Ksheersaagar's observations are important. It is also important to note that Ksheersaagar had clarified earlier that he was not fond of Mathematics, and it appears that he had Wrangler Paranjape as his ideal. What Ksheersaagar did was exactly what Priyolkar avoided doing; also, the information he has given about Raghunathrao's teaching abilities appears to be incorrect:

> Prof. Karve had no teaching skills. I, at least, couldn't understand a word of what he was teaching. Other students would also have been similarly placed. Complaints against him reached the Principal *Saheb*, with the result that a gentleman named Charles Saldhanha was appointed in his place. I don't quite remember whether this appointment was made in the first term or in the second term.

Priyolkar's memory had obviously deserted him. Charles Saldhanha was appointed to fill in for Raghunathrao when he had taken leave and gone on a furlough to Paris. In this context, Raghunathrao wrote, 'When I took leave in 1917 for going to Paris for further studies in Mathematics, the person named Saldhanha who replaced me was less than me in education and experience.' Therefore, things were unlikely to be as A.K. Priyolkar describes. One thing, though, becomes clear: Raghunathrao hadn't created a good rapport with the management, his colleagues, or his students at the Karnataka College. Besides, his taciturn, reserved, and self-absorbed disposition would also have worked against him.

The management, therefore, would have formed a rather negative opinion about him.

The Karnataka College had just begun and in due course of time it would grow. Therefore, not many days had passed since he had been appointed assistant professor of Mathematics. As and when the college grew, the chances of being made professor of Mathematics were strong.[1] He should have worked there with greater diligence and shown the patience of taking things as they came along. The management had not advised him to improve his qualifications therefore the decision to learn more Mathematics would have been entirely his. One can understand his desire of possessing the highest degree in his area of study, but his obstinacy about wanting to acquire that degree—particularly when circumstances were not felicitous—is intriguing.

Departure to Paris for Higher Studies

While Raghunatharao was at Karnataka College, he started collecting money for going abroad. He writes,

> Later I did my M. A. and after working for thirteen years I made a trip to Europe at my own expense. With my salary not being much, I could not have managed it even then; but I was the paper valuer for the entrance examinations for a few years and I could manage to save that money to give me the funds.

His entire focus during those days had been to go to France for further studies and he had begun correspondences with Bombay Province's Department of Education for that purpose. His efforts bore fruit, and the department granted him a year's furlough. If his intention behind going to France was to acquire a PhD, it is impossible that he would not have known that a year's furlough would be thoroughly inadequate to do so. He would, perhaps have calculated that if he did manage to get admission for a PhD programme, he could then apply to the department for an extension of leave; if, perchance, some obstacles arose, Wrangler Paranjape—who was then the minister of education and was Anna's friend—could resolve the problem. Hence, he left for Paris as soon as the leave was approved. He has written no memoirs of his stay in Paris, his experiences at the university there, nor about the sea voyage that people undertook those days.

When a reader asked him what the Diplome d'Etudes Superieures was and whether he was a PhD, he responded saying that it was a diploma awarded by the University of Paris and it meant a diploma in Higher Education. He said that he had 'acquired this diploma which is considered higher than a master's degree and lower than a doctorate. I am not a PhD.'

B.V. Warerkar said in an article in *Manorama* that Raghunathrao had gone to Paris for his PhD. Dinkarrao Karve echoed the opinion in his interview with Prof. M.V. Dhond. He said, 'Appa was fond of living well. He was collecting money for making a trip to Paris. He had wanted to stay there for three years so as to earn himself a PhD, but because of the inadequacy of funds, he had to return with just a Superior Diploma.' Y.D. Phadke has written in this context, 'From there (Dharwad) he went to Paris in 1919 on a year and a half's leave. After earning a higher diploma, Diplome d'Etudes Superieures, in Mathematics, he returned to India in 1920.' What we can gather here is that nobody says anything about the exact state of affairs in this matter. Since Raghunathrao too has made no mention on this topic in *Samaaj-swaasthya*, the mystery remains unsolved.

He has mentioned in an interview about going for a PhD and the circumstances in which he had to return. This is the information he gives:

> I had gone to Paris then for a doctorate. I wanted to write my doctoral thesis in a year's time, but the Professor under whom I was working was not agreeable to that, because he himself had worked for three years for passing that. Hence he did not like the idea of my getting this concession. The other professors had given their approval, but those approvals were of no use. The approval has to come from the Professor under whom one is working and he was loath to approve of a one-year period for me. He deliberately ignored the fact that I was an M. A. I felt sad that I had to come back without a doctorate despite possessing the ability to acquire one.

Y.D. Phadke doesn't appear to be right when he says that Malatibai was with Anna's organization while Raghunathrao was in Paris, because she herself has said: 'I passed (matric) in 1907. After that, there was no contact left with the institution and the direction of the institution's education changed too.'

Promotion Denied

While Raghunath was in Paris, the Dharwad college was given recognition for junior and senior classes. It was the responsibility of the college management to make arrangements for the students who had taken admission in those classes. Since Raghunath was not there, they appointed Prof. Saldhanha to the post. As Saldhanha was junior to him in experience, Raghunathrao's friends informed him in Paris about it. Raghunathrao inferred that not only had the management ignored his due right for promotion, it had humiliated him by promoting a person junior to him. Flaring up, he sent a continuous stream of letters and telegrams to the management and the government.

Anna himself has written on this episode:

> Even while he was in Paris, he had written stinging letters to the authorities. This criticism did not serve any purpose, and he had to join duty at Deccan College on his return. Since the rules demanded that a person should work for at least six months after returning from furlough leave, he was not in a position to submit an immediate resignation. To compensate for this injustice, the government gave him the job of a teacher of Mathematics in Gujarat College, Ahmedabad. But by doing so, it perpetrated a new injustice. A person who had joined just a couple of years earlier as a lecturer but was lower in qualification was given a salary of three hundred rupees, while Raghunath, who was appointed to the post of a professor was given two hundred and fifty rupees. Believing that he couldn't work at a place where such injustice was perpetrated, Raghunath not only resigned from his job, but also published the reasons for his resignation in the Bombay Chronicle.

Resignation from Government Service

The letter that Raghunathrao wrote while resigning from the government college, outlining the reasons behind the resignation, is given here for the reader's information:

To

The Secretary to Government,
Education Department.

Sir,
I have the honour hereby to resign my appointment for the following reasons:

1. Grave injustice has been done to me by the appointment of Mr. Saldhanha to the Professorship of Mathematics at the Karnatak College, Dharwar.

2. His alleged [sic] better qualifications and experience are purely imaginary. I have shown in the representation I sent to you in February last that the real qualifications and experience are in my favour. I must explain that the reason given for my supersession was that it had become necessary to appoint better qualified and more experienced men, and so an MA in Physics was apparently preferred for the Professorship of Mathematics!

3. The University Committee which inspected the college on the occasion of its being made a first-grade college have placed on record a remark, showing clearly that they agree with me in the above statement; and this remark is obviously made by the present Minister for Education, the only mathematical member of the committee.

4. In spite of this expert opinion, Mr. Saldhanha was appointed to the Professorship on Rs. 350/- a month and I was transferred to the Deccan College to an inferior post on Rs. 200/-.

5. No notice was taken of the representation I made about this in February. I do not even know if it has been forwarded by the D.P.I. (I have since received a reply to the effect that nothing better than my appointment at Ahmedabad could be done.)

6. A further insult has been offered to me in my appointment to Professorship at the Gujrat College at a ridiculous salary. The previous incumbent, Prof. Swaminarayan, was getting Rs. 300/- a month and I am appointed on Rs. 250/-.

7. Even Prof. Saldhanha who superseded me, although he is not even an M. A. in Mathematics, is given Rs. 350/- a month and I am given Rs. 250/- in spite of the fact that besides the Bombay MA, I have taken the Diplome D'Etudes Superieures from the University of Paris, which ranks above the MA The latter is apparently considered a disqualification.

Under the circumstances, and notwithstanding my more than fourteen years of service in the Department, I find it incompatible with my self-respect to remain any longer subject to the caprices of any D.P.I. who chooses to recommend my supersession on the strength of mysterious qualifications [sic].

I am aware that the Civil Service Regulations require me to serve till the 31 August 1921, inclusive as I returned from Combined Leave on the fourth of February. I am willing, under protest, to serve till that date if necessary, but I have the honour to request that I may be relieved on that day at the latest if it is not convenient to relieve me earlier. I hope this will be considered sufficient notice.

I beg to remain etc.
(Sd) R.D. Karve
Prof. Maths, Gujarat College

Raghunathrao resigned from his post as professor of Mathematics from the government college. He was working at the Gujrat College, Ahmedabad, where he had been transferred from Deccan College, Poona. 'I was in Gujarat College when I resigned. The principal of that college, Robertson, was notorious for his rancidity. "How much more are you likely to earn after leaving this job?" he asked. I responded calmly, "Who knows? I may earn ten times as much."' He writes further, 'My salary then was Rs. 310/-.'

When he resigned from his post, his relationship with Wrangler Paranjape suffered some strain. Shakuntalabai made an effort to repair this damage. She writes:

'When Appa put in his resignation, my Appa was the Minister for Education. Looking at the injustice that had been done, he instructed the Education officials to not accept the resignation and requested Appa (Karve) to withdraw his resignation. He also assured him that as soon as the next post emerged, it would be given to him and the injustice shall be corrected. But then, later, when Appa (Karve) suddenly saw in the *Gazette* another Professor's name placed senior to his, he flared up and wrote to the Senior [education] officer why his resignation had not been accepted. The officer was left with no choice except to accept the resignation. He held this permanent grouse against my Appa (Wrangler Paranjape).

At Wilson College

After resigning from the college, Raghunathrao tried his hand at private tuitions, but couldn't succeed. He began writing books in Marathi and English on birth control and started a centre for offering guidance on birth control. But there was not enough money to be made there. Around this time, Principal Wilkinson recommended Raghunathrao's name to Mr McKenzie, the principal of Wilson College. The college was run by a mission, which meant that it was independent. A post was vacant there for a part-time lecturer of Mathematics. Raghunath took up the position in 1922 and later was appointed a full-time professor of Mathematics in 1924.[2]

'The question of what should be done now arose within four months of resigning. I had earned a small reputation of being a good teacher, so I managed to attract a few tuitions . . . . After a year of giving private tuitions, I was called over by Wilson College and appointed on a part-time position on a salary of Rs. 200/-,' Raghunath writes outside of *Samaaj-swaasthya*. In an article called 'Samaaj-swaasthyachi Samaaj Seva' (The Social Service of *Samaaj-swaasthya*), he writes, 'While taking up a professor's job with Wilson College, I had told them in clear terms that I would be committed to them only to the extent of my work and do whatever I chose to do the rest of the time.'

All that this means is that in 1922 he got the job of a part-time professor. In 1924 he was appointed full-time professor and was in due course made permanent on the post, it appears. In other words, during those days, Raghunathrao was busy with a number of things: his job at Wilson College, the beginning (and perpetuation) of his work on birth control, the dissemination of information on this subject in society, its propagation through writing books in Marathi and English, writing articles in magazines, and such like. During this period, his younger half-brother Bhaskarrao had come over to Bombay for doing his BT course, which was a two-year-course in those times. In the first year, he lived with Raghunathrao. His expenditure was borne by Anna and he got to observe Raghunath and Malatibai from close quarters for that period.

Article in *Kirloskar Khabar*

Everything was getting along thus when suddenly a sequence of events led him to resign from Wilson College. A small article of his appeared in the August 1925 issue of *Kirloskar Khabar* titled 'Amaryad Santati' (Limitless Progeny). Since Kirloskarwadi fell in the Aundh state, somebody brought this article to the notice of Jacob Bapu, the political agent of the state, who thought it utterly inappropriate that this kind of article should be published in a magazine in their state. Believing that the article was written by Anna, he sent a letter to him making enquiries about it. Anna forwarded it to Raghunathrao. Keeping in mind the political weight that Jacob Bapuji carried in those times, Raghunathrao should have settled the issue then and there; instead, perhaps because of excessive self-confidence, he began arguing with him through correspondence.

Giving details of the circumstances in which he had to resign from Wilson College, he has written:

> The reason is that *Kirloskar* asked me to write an article on birth control and published it. When the well-known Jacob Bapuji of the state and a few others saw that article, they wrote to Balasaheb Pantpratinidhi that the publication of articles on such subjects in their state was not proper, hence steps should be taken. Balasaheb did not know me and still doesn't, but he knew my father. Mistaking him to be the author of the article, he wrote to my father, saying that many complaints were being received on my article, and that he should please come over to have a look. When that letter came to me, a clarification had to be made that the article had been written by me and that Prof. Karve of Pune had no connection with it. On his side, Khan Bahadur got details about me, where I lived and so on from the editor of the magazine and got two of my books delivered to him by V.P.P.

Resignation

Under pressure from Jacob Bapu, the management of Wilson College had to institute an inquiry into Raghunathrao who also wrote in his article 'Maazhe Prachaarkaaryaateel Anubhav' (Experiences of my Propagation) that:

What they say seems to suggest that the sahebs were not aware that I wrote on such kinds of subjects. In fact, they should have known about it because Professor McClean, the other professor of Mathematics, had called me and the second teacher Mr. Agashe over for tea and discussion had happened on it. Perhaps he had not told McKenzie Saheb about it.

The conversation between Raghunathrao and McKenzie finally happened in the manner given below:

As soon as Principal Saheb received the letter from Jacob Bapu, he told me, 'Birth control goes against our religious principles. Professors of this college should not be supporting it. Whatever you may have written, let that be, but now you will have to stop it. It is our desire that you should stay in college.'

I told him clearly, 'You will find as many people to teach Mathematics as you want, but there is nobody ready to do the propagation work. Since I consider it as important, I shall continue to do so.'

He had not expected this answer from me. He said, 'This matter needs to be placed before the senate of the college. But you will have to resign.'

Then, looking at the catalogue, he asked me more questions. 'Birth Control, well, okay. But why this prevention of venereal diseases?'

I replied, 'If diseases must not be prevented, what, then, should? No diseases are desirable.'

He said, 'These diseases are a punishment for evil deeds.'

I responded, 'So, they shouldn't be treated?'

He then said, 'Hmmm, there's medicine here for impotence too. Why? Is sexual desire something to be encouraged?'

I replied, 'There are things inside the ovaries about which we may not know. Nature definitely has some use for them. They also help a person keep enthusiasm alive.'

Since we could find nothing but disagreements, the interview stopped there. Overall, the college authorities showed great courtesy in this matter. They gave me six months of salary, provident fund and all, and McKenzie Saheb wrote a letter to me in which he mentioned, 'I hold you in respect for the tenacity with which you have held on to your undertaking.'

Raghunath has also criticized the college administration wherever he found it necessary. But when there was criticism against the running of Bible classes and a demand for closing such classes, his sympathies were with the college. He has written:

It will not do to forget that it's the missionaries that run Wilson College, and they have to beg for funds from religious people in Scotland for running the institution. The religious people give them funds for disseminating the religion, not just for providing education. And if we notice that there is no other dissemination of religion except the Bible classes, then it is quite easy to understand why Bible classes have been made compulsory. (1940, p. 165)

This, then, was how Raghunathrao first lost his government job and then his role of professor at the missionary college. After this, he never worked in any college anywhere.

Notes:

- In Indian civilization *samudragaatu sweekaarah kalauh varjya* means that we should not cross the seas. Till the previous century, this injunction prohibited foreign travel. Whoever flouted this injunction was required to perform penitence after returning to the homeland. With the arrival of the English and the change of rulers, considerable leniency arrived in the observance of religious injunctions and the natives began making foreign trips. To begin with, the proportion of kings, princes, feudal lords and the men with the money was larger. Sayajirao Gayakwad of Baroda, the prince of Rajkot, the son of Shahu Maharaj of Kolhapur, are those who crossed the seas. When education began spreading in the Bombay province, scholarships began being offered for higher education. Students began travelling abroad, particularly to England, for getting good quality education for the ICS and law. Dr Anandibai Joshi and Dr Shridhar Vyankatesh Ketkar went to the US for studying medicine and sociology, respectively. Raja Ram Mohan Roy, Rango Bapuji, Lokmanya Tilak, Gopal Krishna Gokhale went abroad on political missions. The children of barrister Krishnarao Gopal Deshmukh, Shripad Babaji Thakur, Dr Atmaram Pandurang Tarkhadkar went for studies to England. (The only exception was Anna;[3] she went abroad along with her brothers.) Pandita Ramabai went to England to change her religion. She later went to America to be present at the convocation ceremony of Anandibai Joshi. Moti Bulasa had the opportunity of going to England to study the 'One God' sect, but because his wife passed away because of an illness during the journey at Aden, Vitthal Ramji Shinde got that scholarship. While Pandurang Chimnaji Patil went to England for higher education after graduating from the Agriculture College, Pune, Shankarrao Kirloskar went there for studying painting.

The greatest honour for a mathematician is to go to England and come back with a Wrangler's title. Raghunath Purushottam Paranjape had acquired this title. In his autobiography titled *Naabaad 84* (84 Not Out), he has given a list of fifteen persons who became wranglers from 1892 to 1909. At least three of that list are Maharashtrians: Paranjape, Gharpure and Bhide. This list can be extended. The main point here is that for becoming an ICS, barrister, or wrangler, the brighter students preferred to go to Oxford or Cambridge. Those who truly wanted to master Mathematics would always dream of becoming wranglers.

• Raghunathrao has described his experience at Port Said in an issue of *Samaaj-swaasthya* as follows:

'On way to Europe, one always meets tricksters who want to sell pictures or some spurious things at the Port Said harbor. As soon as the buyer takes the sealed packet over, the cry goes up that the police is coming; the buyer pockets the packet, pays the money demanded and rushes to his boat. On opening the packet, he is always disappointed.'

He has drawn a sketch of his experience of a red-light area in Paris in his story-like article 'Ghamand Jirli' (Pride Collapses). It is likely to be based on his observations there. At a certain place he writes, 'I am not a moneyed person . . . . I just about managed to scrape together enough money to come here for my studies. I cannot afford to fall into such shenanigans.'

Criticizing Raghunathrao's ideology and his social work, Dr K.B. Lele has said that Raghunathrao observed the free man-woman relationship in France and was much impressed by it. His effort was to bring about the same kind of thing in India. This criticism is ill-founded. Raghunathrao has never painted pictures of the free life of France in iridescent colours.

3

Jobs in Other Areas

The Nairobi Episode

Shankarrao did his MBBS from Grant Medical College in Bombay. This is the information that Anna gives on this matter:

> Later, during the World War, he joined the Medical Corps in the army. He worked as an army doctor on the Afghanistan frontier, Iran, and Mesopotamia. After being released from there, he set up private practice in the Kenya Colony of Nairobi and he has found good success in this venture.

He gained considerable renown and did notable work for the Indians settled there. He participated in social and political life to the extent possible. He and his wife Revatibai were also interested in the theatre. As a part of the cultural activities, they acted in a few plays. They were financially well-off too.

Shankarrao was Baya's eldest child and was born in 1894, which means that he was twelve years younger than Raghunathrao. They were half-brothers and carried a lot of affection for each other. Baya writes, 'I feel very satisfied that at least in his interaction with my boys, there was no half-brotherly attitude.' There would be a stream of visitors in Raghunathrao's Bombay house. References to this matter can be found in the writings of Anna, Iravatibai and Shakuntala Paranjape. It was in the early days of October 1925 that Raghunathrao resigned from his post of professor of Mathematics at Wilson College. During this period, he looked around for private tuition from Kolaba to Parel, but he couldn't get adequate numbers. Raghunathrao loved to live in style, which was difficult to manage in Malatibai's salary. He was going through a rough patch in life and he even thought of driving a taxi to make money.

Dr Shankarrao got to hear of these things and was upset at the state of his elder brother. He decided to call him over to Africa and sent him the money for the travel expenses. Accordingly, since there were no third-class or second-class tickets available in April 1926, he travelled first-class to Nairobi. His stay in Nairobi was short; somewhere between five and six months.

Three Matters

He did three important things there.

1. Application to the Department of Education Turned Down

The first was that he had applied to the school education department. That was his main area of interest, and he was equipped with adequate qualifications for a job there and had plenty of experience as well. He also had the support of barrister Phadke who enjoyed considerable heft in the executive council. But there were no signs of landing a job there.

'The reasons why he had to resign from his jobs in India— those were the exact reasons why Raghunathrao would not get a job in Africa, is the observation that Y.D. Phadke makes. The reason why he had resigned from his government job was the injustice that had been perpetrated upon him; besides, he had nailed the lies of the authorities in no uncertain terms and the reason why he left his job in Wilson College was that his work on birth control did not fit in with the policies of the institution. In Nairobi, however, there was no question of getting into any argument with important people; as for the work on birth control, that wasn't why he had gone there. Hence Phadke's observation is misplaced. There had to be a far more important reason somewhere. Raghunathrao himself, however, had a clear opinion on why he did not get a job in the school department in Nairobi, which he mentioned in an article. He states:

The other reason why I did not get a job there is this: when I was studying mathematics in Paris where I had gone on a furlough in 1919, a 'Khilafat deputation'[1] had come to Paris then. Since I had not had news from India for a long time, I went for a few of their lectures along with other Indian students only out of curiosity. The spies assigned to keep an eye on Indian students sent this information to the British Council, from where it went to the Department of Education. I had not been involved with any political movement till then. But how would the government settle for a person who went for political speeches? The government in Nairobi is British too; so, from their perspective it was an offence. However, a friend of mine named Barrister Phadke was in the Executive Council there and the government had not wanted to cause him offence. Therefore for the next five months it just kept me hanging with the response: 'No vacancies', till at last, I lost patience and walked away.

This is what he writes in another article:

Barrister Phadke there was a member of the Law Council and
he carried weight in the government. I had known him for
many years. But with a written complaint lodged against me
by the Department of Education, that came to be of no use.
After waiting for five months, I myself met the authorities
and asked them why this was happening. I demanded a clear
'yes' or 'no', but the response I got was that there was no
vacancy. I understood what that meant and returned home.

The fact is that Raghunathrao had ruined his prospects by
being present in the Khilafat Deputation meeting. This episode
even impacted his later writings in that he did not write on the
political scene of those times. For one, the cases of obscenity
against him had left him drained; for another, Malatibai's state
of health during those days had made it impossible for him to
do anything. However, when he did feel excited enough to write
on the political scene of those times, he would write under a
pseudonym. Such, then, were the reasons for his not getting a
job in Nairobi.

2. Editor of The *Democrat*

The second important thing he did there was to write for an
English newspaper called The *Democrat* run by a gentleman
named Acharya. Raghunathrao got the opportunity to write
for it and Shankarrao supported him. In this context, he has
told Prof. M.V. Dhond, 'I had helped him get into journalism
by finding him a place in the *Democrat*. Their editor was on a
two-month leave, which gave Appa the opportunity to do the
editor's job. My thought was to buy off the newspaper and give
it over to him.'

Raghunath himself has given the following information:

While I was in Nairobi, I got an opportunity to write a political article. A gentleman ran a newspaper called the *Democrat*, and claiming that he presented the viewpoint of the Indians, he would collect donations from them. Actually, there were enough advertisements and subscriptions, so there was never any need for donations. But since the Indians there had decent earnings, they would donate. While I was there, a certain gentleman went off on a tour. Finding me at a loose end, they requested me to do a bit of writing and I accepted. Therefore, as per my usual habit, without carrying any fear of anyone, I started presenting the status of the Indian people in the clearest manner. But my articles began giving the editor cold feet. My articles were not published with my byline but as editorials. The day on which he returned, he got my article removed from the printing machine after the page had been made. He then came and met me and said, 'If these kinds of articles start appearing in my paper, how will I get advertisements from Whiteway?' I responded, 'In which case, your purpose is to get advertisements and donations and not to present the position of the Indians here.'

More or less the same kind of matter has appeared in an article in the February 1944 issue of *Samaaj-swaasthya*. When a reader voiced his desire to hear his 'opinion on politics in India and abroad', Raghunathrao's response was:

These articles of mine frightened a few of my well-wishers here and they telegraphed me to 'return immediately' without assigning any reasons. I thought that there was a job opportunity here; it had become more or less certain that I would not get any job there.

Y.D. Phadke elaborates on 'a few of my well-wishers' by quoting a line from a private letter, which reads, 'those articles having reached here in India too, some of my friends and relatives feared that the African government would throw me into prison and on their advice, my wife sent me a telegram and called me back.'

Earlier too, he had written several articles on various topics, but the style he had adopted for writing the editorials on social and political issues in the *Democrat* was sharp, biting, hard-hitting and critical. He later used the same style to the hilt for the rest of his life for demolishing his opponents. Therefore his experience of writing the editorials in the *Democrat* came to be of great use later and can be counted among his gains.

What meaning could be derived from these episodes? While in Paris, Raghunathrao used to attend lectures of the Khilafat Deputation. Since these lectures propagated thoughts against the British rule in India, the organizers, the speakers, as well as the audience were blacklisted by the British government. It may be recalled that when Raghunathrao had the opportunity of writing editorials in the *Democrat*, he had not fought shy of criticizing the British government on behalf of Indian citizens. It would not be surprising if the British government in Kenya found a similarity between the information, they had been provided about Raghunathrao and his articles from Nairobi. The government authorities would certainly have decided that if such a person were to be employed, he would not hesitate to generate public opinion against the government in Nairobi and build public organizations. Believing that providing a job to such a person would be the equivalent of creating another opponent to the government, the authorities there would have decided to oppose barrister Phadke's pressure and refuse him a job. Raghunathrao was well aware of what had happened in Paris. He had come over to Nairobi in desperate financial straits after winding up his household. Therefore, when he got the opportunity of writing in the *Democrat*, he should have wielded his pen with some restraint. Earlier too, Raghunathrao had brought upon himself the misfortune of winding up his household by defiantly telling the Wilson College administration that 'birth control is my field of activity'. However praiseworthy this devotion to one's mission may be, it had the potential to destroy personal and family life. He should have therefore had the patience to reduce his diatribe and move cautiously. But this discretion he did not possess since he was temperamentally impetuous. Dr Shankarrao has told Prof. M.V. Dhond that at the time of resigning from the government college, Wrangler Paranjape had advised him to 'take it easy'. Here too, his impetuosity gets underscored. Raghunathrao could not get a job as a journalist in South Africa because of Acharya's selfish perspective of looking at a newspaper.

3. Surgical Operation

The third thing that Raghunathrao did during his stay in Nairobi was that he got a vasectomy performed upon himself. In 1926, sixteen years since his marriage, he had turned forty-four years of age, when it was neither possible for him to have children nor to raise them.

Right from the beginning, he had been using various means of birth control, but they were not altogether dependable. His financial situation wasn't satisfactory either. Besides, he had no desire for children. He had always nursed doubts about whether he would be able to bring them up properly if he happened to have children. Of course, he did not believe in extending his lineage either. On account of all these reasons, he had made arrangements in India for undergoing vasectomy, but he couldn't find a doctor. When he went to Nairobi, he asked

Dr Shankarrao to perform the surgical procedure which he did. 'I performed that surgery,' Shankarrao told Prof. Dhond.

> In the year 1923, . . . he was forty-four years of age. His age had advanced, he had no job and Gangu hadn't been keeping well either; hence he had wanted to get himself operated. But when he told me that no doctor in Bombay was willing to perform this operation, I decided to do the operation myself. This I did with the help of my friend, Sorabji.

Raghunathrao has made one solitary mention of this in *Samaaj-swaasthya*: 'During that period I got the birth control operation performed upon myself.' Nothing can be said about whether there had been discussion of any kind on this topic between him and Malatibai.

In this context, responding to a reader's question, these were the thoughts he expressed in the June 1949 issue: 'Neither of us had any yearning to have a son. So many people want a son for religious reasons. So many of them want an heir. Neither of the two of us was religious.'

Raghunathrao had gone to Nairobi with the hope of getting himself a job. But he returned disappointed after having spent about five or six months there. Thus ended the Nairobi episode of his life.

In the Bombay–Bahrain Company

He returned from Nairobi either at the end of October or in the first half of November 1926. But he couldn't find himself a job here. Finally, in December, he got himself a job as an administrative assistant in the office of Prof. Peltier's son. Obviously, his acquaintance with the professor helped.[2]

Anna has written in this context:

Even before he went to France, he used to know French well. After going there, he had to use French for all transactions; This got to be of great help in fetching him a job. There is this firm by the name Bombay–Bahrain Company that deals in pearls and jewels. Its office is in the *Times of India* building. The manager of that company is a French gentleman named Rosenthal. He was in need of a private secretary or a personal assistant who knew both English and French well. Raghunath has been doing this job for about a year and a half now.

Anna has got the name of the company right. Considering that the manager there, Mr Rosenthal, was a Frenchman and Raghunath could read and write French quite proficiently, the two should have got along well; but this did not seem to have happened. One reason could be Raghunathrao's basic disposition. It can also be said that, perhaps, Rosenthal did not have the temperament to understand Raghunathrao. When Raghunathrao had earlier worked as a teacher in schools and colleges, he would, perhaps, have liked the atmosphere there. Whatever time was left after holding classes, he could plough into his personal work—propagating birth control—and reading and writing. Circumstances in the Bombay–Bahrain company were different. For one, he had to work for eight hours straight from nine in the morning to five in the evening. Very often he would even be required to stay on beyond duty hours. He writes:

But for a good six or seven months in a year – that was when the saheb was in India – there would be no holiday on Sunday either. One had to work from nine in the morning till such time that the saheb felt like working. For the other months, however, there would be holidays like the other clerks had.

Later, when the business crashed, a number of clerks were dismissed; which meant that their work had also to be done, thus making the workload limitless. Sometimes one had to sit typing letters right up to nine in the evening. Such being the case, it would have been impossible to manage beyond a few months.

He would certainly have considered this kind of life as an imposition. From Mr Rosenthal's perspective, it wouldn't matter that Raghunathrao was a visionary, or the first person to work in the area of birth control. He was just a private secretary like managers have in offices everywhere. Raghunathrao might not have been willing to accept these realities of life and the result would have been that whilst he needed the job because of difficulties at home, he would surely have felt like resigning at the earliest possible opportunity. The consequence was that he avoided mentioning the name of this firm in any of his writings.

Resignation

Raghunathrao has expressed these thoughts in the editorial of the June 1933 issue of *Samaaj-swaasthya*:

The monthly completes six years with the publication of this number. The job on the basis of which I managed to run the magazine for the first four years – I resigned from that job on May 1. This is the third time in my life that I have had to resign from my job for the sake of retaining my dignity. Having arrived at the conclusion that I do not possess the virtues or the defects that are needed for retaining a job, I have decided not to sweat much about finding a job – at least for now. How long I can hold on to this decision remains to be seen.

The meaning here is quite clear. The Bombay–Bahrain company had been absorbing losses and employees were being dismissed, thus increasing Raghunathrao's workload. He wasn't getting along with Rosenthal either. Information on why differences arose between them and how Raghunathrao had to suffer humiliation has lately come to hand. In an interview with H.V. Desai, Raghunath said in this matter:

> I can never tolerate humiliation. Since I had worked as a professor earlier, I was not used to somebody shouting down at me. Since our saheb was particularly habituated to shouting down at people, I abandoned the thought of working for him and left that job.

Like any self-respecting individual, he resigned from that job and walked out with his head held high. The language of this statement is extremely telling. A clear idea of his own faults having become apparent, his self-esteem was also hurt. Earlier, when he had resigned from jobs, he had always wanted to get back into another job. In 1933, he was fifty-one years of age, and finding a job was much more difficult. Besides, he would have slowly begun to understand the nature of Malatibai's illness and the gravity of the situation. It was as a result of all these things that he would have decided not to look for a job anymore. And so, his job at the Bombay–Bahrain company turned out to be his last one.

Thus, when he resigned from his job for the sake of his dignity, he did it with the firm decision that from 1 May 1933, he would never take up another job. Actually, Malatibai's illness had crippled her. She would somehow drag herself around the house with the help of a stick and do whatever work she could. When even that became impossible, she was left with no choice except to lie stretched out on her bed. After resigning from the government college, Raghunathrao had opened up a centre in the Parel area for the convenience of the citizens to give advice on—and to provide the means for—birth control. For the purpose of making medicines and facilities available for people of other towns, he had started the Right Agency. The sale of medicines and articles for birth control and the fee for the advice given through the agency were not enough to run the household. Besides, Malatibai's medicines were expensive. Considering these desperate circumstances and no source of income, his decision to resign from the job would have to be regarded as extremely courageous. However, since he had worked for six years and six months, he could do a few things. That increases the worth that this job held for him.

4

Samaaj-swaasthya: Earlier Life and Writings

Anna's Example and His Love

The first page of the autobiography of Maharshi Karve, *Aatmavritt*, carries a dedication note that reads as follows, 'This autobiography is dedicated with lots of love to the divine young boys and girls who strive for the welfare of the country.' Through this dedication, Maharshi Karve declared his admiration for youngsters who had got into the field of social work. He had taken notice of the weaknesses that existed in the institution called the 'family'. He had seen with his own eyes among his close relatives and friends how, in the absence of birth control concepts, they had allowed their progeny to multiply without restraint and let increase the number of mouths that needed to be fed. Since they had not thought through the consequences of the responsibilities that came with this uncontrolled proliferation, they had been reduced to desperate straits. Many families had been brought to utter despair and destitution with the untimely death of the breadwinner of the house. Maharshi had even experienced this distress to some extent, and it had left a mark on his personal life.

Anna appears to have contemplated the likelihood of his own progeny when he set up home with Bayabai. He had taken note of the accepted norm of those times that a subject like birth control could not be discussed in public and had accepted the norm; but he was aware that although women's education and birth control seemed different subjects on the surface, they were really two sides of the same coin. As it was, he had invited criticism by getting sucked into the whirlwind of the controversy over remarriage. He had been trying to garner acceptance of his work and was sure that society would be able to digest his thoughts little by little. Hence, perhaps, he would not have wanted to rattle public sentiment further by talking publicly on the subject of birth control and decided to stay silent on it. Even so, he had taken care that there was a four to five-year gap between his sons Shankar, Bhaskar and Dinkar. This would obviously mean that he had not only realized the importance of family planning quite early, but also used whatever resources were available then to put those concepts into practice. As the children grew up, this topic was discussed quite openly before them. It is reasonable to assume that consciously or unconsciously these concepts would have impacted Raghunath. Perhaps, it was during this time that a seed would have been sown in his mind that social work could be done in this very unusual area. It appears that the ordinarily reticent Raghunath did have discussions with intimates like Anna, Shankar, Bhaskar, Dinkar, Wrangler R.P. Paranjape, Shakuntala Paranjape and his wife Malati. His thoughts seem to have found total acceptance with some, partial with others. Some gave silent consent, while others actively supported him. Malatibai accepted his ideas with all her heart because she loved him deeply and firmly believed that if circumstances around her had to be changed, there was no surer tool than birth control. Anna, however, lived by the precept of *swadharm nidhanam shreyah*, which meant that he was willing to lay down his life for his own area of work, but would not want to dabble in Raghunath's area, about which he did not have much knowledge. This position suited his temperament too. Nevertheless, his father's heart would have been gladdened that his son had deliberately adopted his area of work and, uncaring about losses, and had opted for a life of struggle. That was why, perhaps, though he was not a sentimental man, he has dwelt quite a bit on Raghunathrao in his writings. He has even gone beyond: he has recorded a brief but deeply-felt opinion on his daughter-in-law Malatibai who was helping her husband in his mission. His affection cannot but be more starkly evident there. Thus, there is a background to Raghunathrao's life mission of birth control, unusual for the society of those times in all respects. It is also clear that the roots of this choice lie in Annasaheb's articulations on this subject and his own conduct in practical terms.

R.P. Paranjape

Raghunathrao's expectations from both Anna and Appa (Wrangler R.P. Paranjape) are quite visible, more so from Appa. Since Appa was the minister of education at the time, Raghunathrao had quite naturally expected him to help in the matter of the government college. However, Appa did not want to be accused of nepotism and while he did make efforts at finding a solution, it was not enough to save Raghunathrao's job. Even earlier, when Raghunathrao was in the Karnataka College, Wrangler Paranjape's recommendations had not been taken into consideration. It was natural, therefore, for Raghunathrao to carry some grievance against Paranjape, but he wasn't bitter.

Regarding the work of birth control that Raghunathrao had taken in hand, Paranjape wrote in a letter of 1925:

> Let me tell you that I regard your propaganda about birth control as of vital importance to our country and wish you every success. I am glad you are thinking of starting a journal

about your subject . . . But birth control is perhaps too limited
in scope and will not at present appeal to large numbers.

His words affirm his genuine feelings regarding Raghunathrao's
enterprise. Raghunathrao published the first issue of *Samaaj-
swaasthya* on 15 July 1927, in which he gave extracts of
Wrangler Paranjape's above letter. Besides, Anna has himself
written, 'He had been toying for a long time with the plan
of bringing out a monthly for propagating his ideas.' This
means that Raghunathrao would discuss his plans with both
Anna and Appa.

From 1938 onwards, Wrangler Paranjape's daughter
Shakuntala can often be seen writing in *Samaaj-swaasthya*,
propagating Raghunathrao's work and coming over to Bombay,
with her daughter Sai, to stay with Raghunathrao. 'Many people
enjoyed his hospitality,' she writes in this context. 'I too was
one of them.'[1] Over and above this, when, after Raghunathrao's
wife Malatibai had passed away and he was living a solitary and
impecunious life, Shakuntalabai would call him over to Pune
to live in her house. All these incidents militate against the
notion that Raghunathrao was prejudiced against Appasaheb
Paranjape.

Birth Control: Work and Writing

Raghunathrao began his work on birth control in 1921 and
wrote a book titled *Santatiniyaman* in 1923. It was an effort to
try and make people understand the importance of the subject,
and public opinion was not quite ready to respond positively to
such new reforms.

Back in 1911, when Raghunathrao got married to Malatibai
in Pune, he invited his friend Abdul Kareem Khan for the
occasion. As they sat for the communal dinner, he even quoted

a *sloka*. At this, the Brahmin community imposed a fine of Rs. 150 on Anna, which he paid. Thus, Raghunathrao was very clear that a subject like birth control was difficult to tackle, but equally essential.

It is important to know what Anna himself thought about the subject. When he expresses his opinion on *Samaaj-swaasthya* in the early part of his *Aatmavritt* in 1928, he also mentions Raghunathrao's work on birth control in the following words:

> After giving careful thought, whatever information he considers as beneficial for individuals and for the society to possess, he has been propagating fearlessly and without bothering about anybody's opinion and has been suffering great discomfort on account of that. I cannot but admire his resoluteness and his readiness to face the hardships that he shall have to bear as a consequence.

Anna and Raghunathrao, therefore, were people of independent opinions; hence it was impossible that their opinions would match every single time. Regarding the differences of opinion Anna had with Raghunathrao, he said, 'I am not in agreement with a number of opinions that Raghunath holds; at the same time, I don't even approve of publicizing them all the while.' But he was inclined to express his 'admiration' for the sincerity he saw in Raghunathrao for applying himself to the task at hand. For a person who ordinarily wrote with a lot of balance, his use of a phrase like 'cannot but admire' indicates that Raghunathrao had won his father's heart through his abilities; this is an emotional father expressing his pride, but with restraint. One can constantly see the love that Anna bore for Raghunathrao. When the author from Baroda, Kashibai Herlekar, had wanted a copy of *Santatiniyaman*, Anna himself took the trouble of sending it to her. 'About a month ago, your father sent me the book *Santatiniyaman*,' she wrote to Raghunathrao in her letter of 22 July 1925.

S.K. Kolhatkar's Opinion

Around this time, Raghunathrao sent copies of *Santatiniyaman* to a number of reputed people, expecting a suitable response and other necessary action from them. Two of the biggest names in the world of [Marathi] literature during those days were S.K. Kolhatkar and N.C. Kelkar. Kolhatkar had written an article called 'Sudamyaache Pohe urf Sahitya-battishi', a light-hearted criticism of the satire emanating from society. Raghunathrao would have noted his natural inclination towards reform.

Acknowledging the receipt of Raghunathrao's book, Kolhatkar wrote to him in English:

> The copy of *Santatiniyaman* that you have been kind enough to send to me is duly received. I thank you for the handsome present.
>
> I have read part of the book and I have no doubt that it is both useful and interesting. Though it is a scientific book I find a vein of humour running through it – a vein that was also present in the play that appeared some months back in the 'Manoranjan'. I would like to read more plays from your pen.

Along with his appreciation of the book, *Santatiniyaman*, he has also taken notice of the writing style. Raghunathrao always made use of Kolhatkar's comment while advertising *Santatiniyaman* in the magazine *Samaaj-swaasthya*.

N.C. Kelkar's Inability

N.C. Kelkar was the editor of *Kesari.* Raghunathrao might, perhaps, have believed that a few positive words in the *Kesari* on *Santatiniyaman* would help him in his work. Kelkar, however, sent back a cautiously worded note:

> Read your book. However, discussions on vulgar [*graamya*] thoughts related to the vulgar areas of bodily needs [*shareer-dharma*] are better held in privacy or secrecy . . . . Hence, I feel bad that I can do nothing beyond sending you an acknowledgment of receiving the book.

Despite Kelkar's response on birth control, Raghunath's resolve of bringing about public enlightenment on this topic did not wane at all.

Riyaasatkaar's Encouragement

When the first case against *Samaaj-swaasthya* was heard in 1931, Riyaasatkaar Govind Sakharam Sardesai had stood witness for Raghunathrao. Raghunathrao has made the following mention in his advertisement for *Samaaj-swaasthya*:

> Riyaasatkaar G. S. Sardesai writes, 'From the nation's perspective, this subject chosen by Shri Karve is not at all deserving of revilement. In this context, the present turmoil in our life can be dissipated only when efforts to reform society are made through gathering scientific information.

In this context, Riyaasatkaar had expressed his opinion in two articles under the title of 'Stree-Purush-Samaagaman'

(Man-Woman Conjugation) written in *Manoranjan* in October and December 1907. He had, therefore, shown courage to write on this subject much before Raghunathrao had.

Our society was not quite ready to talk or write about the subjects of birth control and the science of sexual intercourse. The fact is that these subjects are an inescapable and essential part of human life and scientific information on these areas should reach the whole strata of society. However, the ultra-orthodox class in society completely stifled any discussion on these subjects under the guise of propriety. In contrast, a tendency began to take root of sneakily reading such articles to satisfy one's curiosity. Raghunath firmly believed that he would be able to convince people about the position of his work in society and its need for and importance of conserving society. He believed that the opposition of conservative people would dissipate little by little; that society would finally be able to digest his thoughts and his work. In this context, he has written:

> The first thing I did after gaining my freedom after resigning in 1921 was that I wrote two books in English, titled *Family Planning* and *Protection from Sexually Transmitted Diseases*. I had always known that my thoughts were not likely to be appreciated by everyone. That was why I gifted copies of my books to very few people . . . sent one to Anna. After having read them, he informed me that he didn't find much that was objectionable in *Family Planning*, but he didn't like the thoughts expressed in the other book. He felt that if people could find such an easy cure for diseases, they would go astray and indulge their passions. This was the exact objection that the principal of Wilson College raised four years later. Then, of course, I left him [i.e. the principal] speechless, but this time I did not get into an argument with Anna. However, three months down the line he told me on his own, 'After some thinking I find your thoughts right.'

There is no truth in the statement that there was a distance between Anna and Raghunathrao, and he often repeated Anna's greatest virtue. He said that those who changed their opinions with changing circumstances and changing times and talked accordingly, are great people and Anna possessed this virtue. Raghunathrao had faith in people who created thoughtful opinions in society. He believed that the opposition to his thoughts and deeds would dissipate bit by bit.

Raghunathrao had been studying this subject since his college days; he had also firmed up quite early on his decision to get into this kind of activity. However, he wanted to do social work in his spare time and he had been waiting for an environment that would support his plans. That was why, after returning from Paris and resigning from his government job he thought that the suitable time had arrived for his work and he began accordingly. Before 1921, despite possessing information and knowledge on the subject, he hadn't felt like starting some such thing. Talking about why and in what circumstances he started his work after being relieved from his government job, he says:

> It would be wrong to say that if the eventuality of my leaving the government job had not happened, this propagation work would not have happened. But even if rational people like me do not gain satisfaction by believing in *yadabhaavi na tadbhaavi; bhaavi chetratada nyaacha*[2] as people who believe in god and destiny do, when seen from the scientific perspective, we will have to agree that a certain event happened because it was not possible for it to have happened in any other way.

Bhaskarrao Karve's Pleasant Memories

In 1925–1926, Bhaskarrao Karve came to Bombay to do his BT and stayed with Raghunathrao. The age difference between these brothers was twenty-one years. This is what he has written about the opportunity he had of living with his elder (half) brother and sister-in-law:

> For the purpose of working in the Hinganes' school, requisite qualifications were needed; hence I took admission in the Secondary Training College in Bombay in the year 1925-26. It was the only training college of those times. There was no problem about staying because Appa [Raghunathrao] was there, so I obviously lived with him. Since both Gangutai and Appa were happy to have me, I was well settled. As a child, I had never had the opportunity to spend time with him, but this year I had it in abundance. He had lost his job at Wilson around this time and he was searching for another occupation. The 'Right Agency' had been started as a centre for propagating family planning and for selling medicines for the prevention of sexually transmitted diseases and resources required for birth control. It was on account of Gangutai's job that their household was somehow running, hence it could not have been convenient for me to stay with them for a year; but on the other hand, since it was just the two of them living there, there was no crunch for space. Also, since it was Anna who covering my expenditure, they had no problem accommodating me. Since I was always conscious of not being a nuisance to anybody, I would always look for opportunities for being of help. I developed considerable closeness with Gangutai and Appa and the year went off well.
>
> Appa was by nature a man of few words and talked only when there was need for it. He was always busy in work. Occasionally, when he had the time, he would sit alone playing chess. He would play this game with a foreigner through correspondence. Conversation with him, therefore, was quite rare. Gangutai was an open person, but she too would mostly be busy with her cooking, other household

work or with her job-related work. In spite of all that, a bit of
conversation would happen with her. A few years later, when
I came with Anna for meetings of the Women's University,
I would meet with the two of them.

Later, in April 1926, Raghunathrao went to Nairobi to
Dr Shankarrao in search of a job. The BT course during those
days was for two years and 'practical experience of teaching in
some recognized secondary school was required' during the
second year. He decided to gather this experience in a school
of the Camp Education Society of Acharya P.K. Atre and hence
returned to Pune. But he has delineated here only the time that
he spent with his elder brother in 1925.

After Raghunathrao lost his job at Wilson College, he
decided to become a taxi driver. Highly educated people would
never think of getting into this trade, but it was quite in character
with him to make this choice. Prof. M.V. Dhond has examined
the temperament that led him to this choice:

> Why would he have chosen the meanest of mean trades?
> Well, a taxi driver is not required to talk much with his
> passenger. Carry him where he wants to be carried, that's all
> there is to the work. Even the fare does not have to be spoken
> out; the meter shows it. No occasion comes for haggling
> about the fare.

However reasonable Dhond's analysis sounds, it doesn't quite
match with the facts. It does not happen that there is never any
occasion to get into an argument with the taxi driver either over
the fare or over anything else.

It is true, of course, that Raghunathrao was by nature a
reticent person. In a letter he wrote to one Ravindra Kelkar of
Goa, he says, 'It's quite difficult for me to strike an acquaintance

with someone because of my rather aggressive nature. I write absolutely freely in a letter, but when I meet someone in person, I don't talk much. At least, I don't talk, perhaps, till I am made to do so.'

Dhond's assertion that Raghunathrao wanted to become a taxi driver because of the single reason of being reticent sounds like an exaggeration. During that period, teaching was the main source of livelihood for him, but he was being made to resign. He was unable to get enough private tuitions and given these circumstances, it was necessary for find a means of livelihood. He would not have seen this trade from the perspective of 'mean' or 'prestigious'. Raghunathrao himself writes on this issue, 'The question now was of earning my wherewithal. It was impossible to survive by selling contraptions for family planning or books on it. I was not getting tuition either as I used to before. Hence I decided I would get into the business for six months.'

From all this it appears that he had decided to learn to drive a car as a means of earning a livelihood.

Writings in *Yashvant* and *Vasundhara*

After 1925, Raghunathrao would likely have developed a close acquaintance with the editors of the magazines *Yashvant* and *Vasundhara* because his articles began getting published in both. The two translated stories 'Gulaam' (Slave) and 'Seemaanchaa Baap' (Simone's Father) and also an article 'Vivaahaachi Aadhunik Kalpana' (The Modern Conception of Marriage) were published there. They are likely to have been his first articles to be published here, because this remark can be found in the 'Editor's Comment': 'There are a few families in Maharashtra of which most members are devotees of literature. Shri Tatyasaheb Kelkar, Shri Tatyasaheb Kolhatkar, Shri Annasaheb Karve—the desire is to bring out a compilation of the articles of the members of these families in *Yashwant* one day or the other.' The editor seems to have expressed this desire keeping in view Raghunathrao's articles that were published in the issues of *Yashwant* that followed.

During the period 1930–1940, M.G. Rangnekar edited a few periodicals, including *Vasundhara*. A specialty of *Vasundhara* was columns like 'Aamchi Collejey' (Our Colleges), 'Prasiddh Vyakteens Shela-Pagotyaacha Aheyr' (Felicitating Famous People with Shawls and Turbans), 'Paahuney ani Aatithya' (Guests and Hospitality) and many others of this kind. One such column was 'Maazhyaa vadeelaanbaddal Malaa Kaai Vaatate?' (What do I think about my father?) An article on this topic was written by Raghunathrao in which he stated that he considered family planning as a more important issue than widow remarriage and women's education.

It appears that Raghunathrao enjoyed friendly relations with Rangnekar. News on the propagation and publication of *Samaaj-swaasthya*, news on the penalty of Rs 100 slapped upon Raghunathrao in the *Samaaj-swaasthya* case, a jocular remark on what Prof. R.D. Karve would say on the birth of Tukoji Maharaj Holkar's third daughter, an introduction to and recommendation for Raghunathrao's book *Aadhunik Kaam-Shaastra* (The Modern Science of Sexology) in the book review column of 'Paahuney Aani Aathitya'—are evidence of the friendship that existed between the two. Besides, the probability cannot be denied that the articles written in the column 'Aamchi Collejey' on Elphinstone College, Wilson College, Deccan College, and Karnataka College were written by Raghunathrao.

Also, the articles 'Shankarrao Kirloskar' (Kirloskarwadi), 'Pativratya-rakshanaasaathi Amaanush Upaai' (An Inhuman Remedy for Protecting Fidelity Towards Husband), 'Does the Hindu Community Need Family Planning?', and 'Nudity is Good for Health' were published without a byline, but it was only Raghunathrao who could have written them. The piece that follows is taken from 'Nudity is Good for Health' and is in complete consonance with his opinions:

> Clothes stunt the human body. If the human animal were to live in a state of nudity, the person's body would grow strong and robust. The reform-loving West has implemented this concept immediately. Germany has taken the initiative and even established a Nudist Club. When some of the most reputed leaders of society are members of this club, why talk of others? We feel surprised that the unusual and illegal reforms mentioned above are being endorsed through the auspices of this club, but there is really nothing surprising about it. It is their practice to bring reform everywhere, whether it finds favour or doesn't, whether it is decorous or indecorous. There is nothing novel, therefore, if they have brought about these strange, unusual reforms and put them into effect.

In a letter that he wrote to Raghunathrao in September 1931, a reader had this to say—'The thoughts that you put forward so courageously in *Vasundhara* a few days back: a wandering minstrel has woven them into his kirtans and cast abusive aspersions on you.' There is mention in the letter of his article in the *Vasundhara*.

There is a strong probability that while he wrote a few rare articles under his name, most of them were anonymous. This again throws light on the relationship that existed between Raghunathrao and Rangnekar.

Raghunathrao translated the French author Guy de Maupassant into Marathi extensively. An independent list published in *Samaaj-swaasthya* identifies thirty-one stories. A story of this author, titled 'Claire de Lune', was published under the title 'Pavitr Mandir' (Holy Temple) in the issue of 16 July

1932. The probability of it having been done by Raghunathrao cannot be denied.

A series of articles under the title 'Aamchi Collejey' was run in *Vasundhara*. People who had information on some of the important colleges of those times in Greater Maharashtra would write about those colleges. The information provided on colleges like the Karnataka College, Dharwad College, Fergusson College, Pune College, Wilson College, Bombay College, Gujarat College, and Ahmedabad College makes for interesting reading. For example, here is some information related to Wilson College:

> The intimidating Prof. McClean teaches Mathematics. His expressive eyes, strange nose, and manner of talking put a scare among the students. Graphs and Statistics are his favourite subjects and they have been dumped upon the first year. Earlier, Prof. Karve and Agashe used to teach it, but presently Prof. Kashikar teaches it.

The reference to Professor Karve is quite revealing here. It should be noted that the writer does not provide either positive or negative information on Raghunathrao. Another person would have supplied information on Raghunathrao and his colleagues, Raghunathrao and his teaching, and the circumstances in which Raghunathrao had to resign. Besides, Professor M.D. Altekar was teaching Marathi in the same college. Raghunathrao was always critical in the column 'Sharadeche Patr' (Sharada's Letters) of *Samaaj-swaasthya* on Altekar's book, or a lecture delivered by Altekar or any article of his published in some magazine. This is what is found on him in an article published in *Vasundhara*:

> The famous author Altekar is a professor of Marathi literature. It's impossible for him to teach without the use

of beautiful puns and humour. When he talks, he can do so in fluent Marathi. One day, I casually went and sat in his class. 'Mukteshwar' had yet to be started. This was how he introduced Mukteshwar: "Mukteshwar's mother's name was Leela. It appears from this that people of earlier times were fashionable. Where else would such a romantic name have come from?"

The description here does not talk about Altekar's competence but is an oblique criticism. The probability is that it was written by Raghunathrao.

The column 'Shelapagotyache Aheyr' in *Vasundhara* was written under the pseudonym Chanakya which has mentions of Shankarrao Kirloskar, Govindrao Tembe and B.V. Warerkar. Raghunathrao had known all three gentlemen very well. Besides, he had written on them in *Samaaj-swaasthya* for some reason or the other. He had an editor-author (Shankarrao–Raghunathrao) equation with Kirloskar. His relationship with Warerkar was that of a close friend who was more or less the same age as him. Raghunathrao was well-acquainted with classical music and was contemptuous of the harmonium as a musical instrument. Hence, as a person who knew the instrument, he often wrote critically on Govindrao. The remark on Shankarrao Kirloskar may be read closely, 'We writers who have spent an entire lifetime in poverty feel a particular regard for you who have successfully brought together mutually exclusively things like writing and livelihood.' And again;

Kirloskar's livelihood does not depend upon his magazine. His real provider is his plough and the monthly he publishes for advertising his products is merely for his satisfaction. Also, because it is a business magazine, *Kirloskar* has received great support from the business community and helped it

settle down nicely. Therefore what is the surprise if he pays
his writers?

He also wrote, 'For appreciating his strategy of inviting four
reputed writers every year for a tour of Kirloskarwadi and thus
making permanent friends of them . . . .'

This displays his grouse that the editors of other magazines
did not have these privileges. Any reader would know that
whenever he has made mention of Shankarrao in *Samaaj-
swaasthya*, he has harped on this theme.

Raghunathrao expressed his opinion on 'biographical' and
'autobiographical' writings at three or four places. In them,
he has emphasized the hazards of writing about the personal
lives of people. The sentence that occurs in an article published
in *Vasundhara* about which Govindrao Tembe expresses the
same thought goes like this: 'It is improper to write something
disrespectful about a person during his lifetime.'

Raghunathrao wrote an independent article on B.V. alias
Mama Warerkar. He also expressed his affection for Warerkar in
a number of places in *Samaaj-swaasthya*. Raghunathrao would
find Mama's novels to be top-notch and he often said that after
Haribhau, for him, Mama was the best novelist. In an article
on Mama Warerkar that was published as a part of the series
'Prasiddh Vyaktis Shela-Pagotyaacha Aheyr' in *Vasundhara*, the
author writes:

> It's the same soppy story in the matter of novels. I have
> heard every man and woman in every house sing praises
> of '*Vidhva-kumari*', '*Chimani*', '*Daawataa Dhota*' or '*Godu
> Gokhale*' and say that each one of these novels is extremely
> lachrymose. But whenever somebody writes an article on
> Marathi literature, he is always found writing platitudes
> for Prof. Phadke or Prof. Waman Malhar. It's as if out of

all of Warerkar's novels, not one novel has left any trace of
memory on the writer's heart and yet P. Y. Deshpande's one
single novel – '*Bandhanaa-palikadey*' – has been praised to
the skies.

It appears from the paragraph that other than Raghunathrao,
nobody else felt any connection with either Mama Warerkar or
his writings.

Besides, the contents of articles like 'Vivaahaachya
Chamatkaarik Chaaliriti' (The Strange Traditions of Marriage),
'Pativratya-rakshanaasaathi Amaanush Upaai' (An Inhuman
Remedy for Protecting Chastity), 'Parismadhye Daaaridryaachaa
Phera' (Poverty in Paris), 'Afrikeyteel Jadu-tona' (Black Magic in
Africa) and 'Bhikaaryaanche Shahar—Vienna' (Vienna—a City
of Beggars) would have graced the pages of *Samaaj-swaasthya*.
Thus, it can be said that Raghunathrao wrote anonymously for
Vasundhara frequently.

Participation in Meetings and Conferences in Bombay

Raghunathrao had adopted Bombay for his centre of operations.
In the early days, he maintained cordial relations with the
editors of magazines there, but as differences of opinion arose
with regard to his favourite subject, distance between them
increased. However, he found himself very much at home in
the Bombay Marathi Sahitya Sangh and the Asiatic Library.
His biographers say that he would arrive at the Sahitya Sangh
a few minutes before their programmes began, take a seat in
the last row and leave as soon as the programmes were over
without speaking to anyone. Towards the end of 1937, a three-
day conference was organized jointly by the Bombay Marathi
Sahitya Sangh and the Bombay Marathi Granth Sangrahaalaya
on the topic 'Aajkaalchi Marathi Neeyaatkaalike' (The Marathi

Periodicals of Today). A report on the conference appeared in the monthly, *Jyotsna*:

> . . . Prof. Gajendragadkar, Shantabai Kashalkar, Dajisaheb Tulzapurkar were in the chair. Literary scholars well-known for one reason or another – Mama Warerkar, Prof. Karve of '*Samaaj-swaasthya*', Navare of '*Prabhaat*', Shri Gadre of '*Nirbhid*', Shri Purohit of '*Navaa Kaal*', Shri Tamhane of '*Navaa Manu*', Bhailalji Pendse, R. M. Athavale of Thane, Shri and Sau. Yamunabai Herlekar, Prof. M. D. Altekar, Prof. Vasantrao Naik, Shri Varde and others – delivered enlightening lectures on the subject chosen for the conference. Prof. Karve stated that obscenity does not reside in words but in the minds of the readers and – as with God – it cannot be defined. Saying that obscenity very much exists in words, Shri R. M. Athavale criticized Prof. Karve in many other areas. For instance, he said that Prof. Karve did not have the slightest idea of logical and scientific thinking . He stated as evidence that not merely every issue, but every page of '*Samaaj-sudhaarak*' (he meant *Samaaj-swaasthya*) was full of illogical and unscientific statements. He, however, conveniently omitted to say why and how he found them illogical or unscientific. It was never revealed to the audience whether all the articles of '*Samaaj-swaasthya*' went through Prof. Karve's hands in his role as the editor or a proof-reader.

It can therefore be said that to the extent possible, Raghunathrao clarified the nature of his work in literary forums. Secondly, there were many like R.M. Athavale in the community who displayed extreme unhappiness over his work. Thirdly, writer Chandrashekhar implies that V.R. Dhawale's articles in *Jyotsna* is that Prof. Karve's articles in *Samaaj-swaasthya* are mostly translations. Lastly, Mama Warerkar was an intimate friend of

Raghunathrao about whom he had written reams upon reams in *Samaaj-swaasthya* when he was caught in controversies. Despite being present there, it appears that he did not express his opinion on R.M. Athavale because Chandrashekhar would certainly have mentioned it.

Raghunathrao, however, hit back at R.M. Athavale at the appropriate time. Athavale delivered a lecture on family planning and related topics in the Vasant Lecture Series in Pune, on which the following comment was published in *Samaaj-swaasthya*:

> Even when they do not know about the resources available for family planning, a number of writers and speakers are in the habit of flaunting their opinions on the subject. From the manner in which Shri R. M. Athavale got after common sense with a hatchet in the Vasant Lecture Series at Pune, it does not appear that he has any knowledge at all on the subject. The organizers of the Lecture Series had, perhaps, brought him in for entertainment. If this was indeed so, then they need to be congratulated.

5

Launching *Samaaj-swaasthya*

Dr Robinson and Dr Ellis

Dr William J. Robinson was a celebrated physician in New York. Sexology had been his special area of study and many years of contemplation; he also ran a journal dedicated to this subject. Since Raghunathrao was a regular reader of the journal, he had become quite familiar with Robinson's thoughts and work. He would certainly have been deeply influenced by the man and his ideas, and they would have impacted his personality too. The visible impact of this influence could be seen in the inspiration he drew from the articles in the journal to begin his own work, particularly work related to *Samaaj-swaasthya*. He acknowledges the source of his inspiration in unequivocal terms when he writes:

> As I had resigned from my job at Wilson College for the purpose of propagating my thoughts, it was imperative that I got it started as soon as I had made arrangements for my wherewithal. When I found the magazines of those times unwilling to print my articles, I decided to start my own magazine . . . . I had wanted a broad-based magazine in which whatever subjects I wanted could be accommodated; I got

this idea from Dr. Robinson's journal and similar journals in
France. I particularly wanted to propagate modern thoughts
on sexology. I finally settled on the name 'Samaaj-swaasthya'.

However, since this article was published in a magazine other
than Samaaj-swaasthya, his indebtedness to Dr Robinson
remained unnoticed. He has also written, 'The late Dr. Robinson
from America was a writer who applied logic to every subject
in this manner and he too ran a journal single-handedly, as
I do. (I got my inspiration from him.)' Dr William J. Robinson
was the first to state that students doing medicine should be
taught the use of contraceptives. Dr Phadke has written,
'Raghunathrao has often referred to Dr. Robinson by name and
used his opinions and writings in Samaaj-swaasthya.' There is
no indication here, however, of even a semblance of a personal
equation between Raghunathrao and Dr Robinson.

Since Dr Robinson lived in New York, it is impossible
that they could have met. However, Raghunathrao regularly
wrote to foreigners and his subjects ranged from chess to
cancer among women. Nothing can be said on whether the
two corresponded with each other, but Raghunathrao would
unfailingly give translations of Dr Robinson's articles to his
readers in Samaaj-swaasthya.

Raghunathrao would exploit the doctor's articles for
Samaaj-swaasthya by publishing their translations and quoting
from them for either supporting his own arguments or for
demolishing the arguments of others. Alongside, he would give,
wherever possible, information on the man and his writings.
For example, here is his remark in the April 1935 issue of
Samaaj-swaasthya: 'Dr Robinson has written a small book on
the atrocities committed by Hitler.'

Dr Robinson passed away in March 1936. Raghunathrao
was not sentimental. In fact, when his wife Malatibai died, he
did not bother to inform the readers of Samaaj-swaasthya.

So, it was only in exceptional cases that he mentioned the deaths of a few select people, like Shripad Krishna Kolhatkar and Luigi Pirandello, and of course, Dr Robinson. In the April 1936 issue of *Samaaj-swaasthya*, he published the translation of an article titled 'The Consequences of Masturbation'. Under the title is mentioned 'From the Journal of William J. Robinson'. In the footnote of the same page is written: 'We are deeply grieved to announce the recent passing away of this world-renowned scholar.' This remark was not a formality because in Dr Robinson, he had met a co-religionist, a friend and a guide. In the correspondence section of *Samaaj-swaasthya* of May 1937, he wrote: 'Another American scholar has passed away recently. Read what Dr Robinson has to say . . . .' This can only mean that emotionally and intellectually, Raghunathrao had become one with the intellectual world of Dr Robinson.

Dr Norman Haire and Dr Havelock Ellis lived in England and never practiced as physicians. Despite living in the ultra-orthodox atmosphere that prevailed in England, they did a minute study of sexology and wrote a number of books on the subject which, instead of being published in England, were published in America. Even during those times, they were regarded as experts on the subject. Their philosophy was based upon the concept that sex and food are natural needs. Their very first book on sex was declared as obscene, but later their concepts gained recognition; one of their books was even taught as a part of the curriculum. Raghunathrao had made a serious study of the books of Dr Robinson, Dr Ellis, Dr Norman Haire and Sigmund Freud. He would also reproduce the thoughts of Ellis to the readers of *Samaaj-swaasthya*. In an article called 'Ellis and Freud', he introduced the readers to the work of these two scholars. Dr Y.D. Phadke writes:

Raghunathrao has also made occasional references to Havelock Ellis. Havelock Ellis published his renowned

book *Studies in the Psychology of Sex* in six volumes. Ellis
was in the forefront in the scientific study of the problem
of homosexuality. He had also studied closely the subject
of sexual perversities. In Volume Six of his work, he has
discussed nudity, prostitution, sexually transmitted diseases
and such other subjects. Ellis had mounted a spirited attack
on the mouldy perspective of Christianity.

Phadke also mentions the love affair between Ellis and
Margaret Sanger—the American woman who in 1915
established a clinic for birth control. Ellis and Raghunathrao
had close ties.

Raghunathrao wrote an article titled 'Vyabhichaaraacha
Prashn' (The Question of Adultery) in 1931, against which a
case was filed for obscenity. A second case was filed in 1934,
claiming that the correspondence in *Samaaj-swaasthya* was
obscene and a third case was filed in 1939. As a consequence,
for a decade beginning from 1931, along with other articles,
he started writing and publishing articles like 'Obscenity and
Law' and 'Law and Social Reform'. From May 1939 onwards,
he started declaring forcefully at the start of every single issue
that 'Obscenity is not a quality that rests in writings, pictures
or other things. It is only a quality of the mind of the accusing
person.' Dr Y.D. Phadke has made a note of this.

Acharya Atre gave a definition of the word 'obscene' in the
Sahitya Sammelan of 1939. This is what Raghunathrao wrote:

> In the opinion of people like Havelock Ellis who have
> devoted their entire life to the study of sex, 'obscenity' is not
> a quality of any writing or anything; it is the quality of the
> mind of the person who makes the accusation of 'obscenity'.
> It is a kind of flaw of the mind. A strong evidence of this
> is that every person has a different definition of 'obscenity'.

Atre says, 'Any literature that creates bad thoughts about the sexual process is obscene.'

Thus, by writing about Atre's definition of obscenity, he seems to be clarifying the source of the sentence that was printed in bold letters on the first page of every issue of *Samaaj-swaasthya*. This means that Raghunathrao had taken the sentence from Havelock Ellis.

I have devoted my entire life to this work so as to gather information not only on unwell people, but on healthy ones too. Most of the time, doctors have to deal with unwell people and often they cannot even see what a healthy person is like; hence they are not able to throw proper light on this question. I have tried to search for the truth and think freely upon it with an open mind. Even if I have not been able to solve the mystery of sex, I have arrived at the firm conclusion that the only single way of resolving it is honest thinking.

Raghunathrao has translated from Ellis in his article, and his own role was no different.

In 1936, Raghunathrao had written an article titled 'Stree-Purooshaanteel Laingik Bhaavanaateel Bhed' (Difference in Feelings on Sex Among Men and Women). He had taken Havelock Ellis's pronouncements as his basis for the article. He mentions this in the second half of the article under the subtitle 'Havelock Ellis Yaancha Nishkarsh' (The Findings of Havelock Ellis). This makes it quite clear that the writings of Dr Robinson, Dr Ellis and others had given direction to his own mission and he often quoted these scholars. A reader had written to Raghunathrao, 'It may be said that except for your magazine and a few of your books, there is no literature on sensuality in Marathi. Hence, if scholars like Havelock Ellis, Bertrand Russell, Norman Haire, Freud, etc., can be translated,

it will be a boon for Marathi readers.' Raghunathrao not only
published this letter in *Samaaj-swaasthya*, but also expressed his
opinion: 'I have written my books on the basis of these books.
Translating them is an expensive proposition, but there can be
no doubt that it would be extremely useful.'

To summarize: Raghunathrao started and ran a clinic
for birth control from 1921 onwards, wrote on sexually
transmitted diseases, family planning and the 'Uninhibited
Man-Woman Relationship' from 1923 onwards, and
started and ran the monthly *Samaaj-swaasthya* from 1927.
Raghunathrao could do all this work that ran against the
winds of time because his foundational knowledge on these
subjects was very strong and the writings of Dr Robinson
and Dr Ellis had adequately prepared him for it. The result
was that he was never disheartened despite the obstacles
in his way.

Circumstances That Brought About the Starting of the Magazine

Kirloskar Khabar was a progressive and forward-looking
magazine published from Kirloskarwadi. When it requested
Raghunathrao for an article, he sent an article titled 'Amaryaad
Santati' (Unlimited Progeny) which was published in the
August 1925 issue. After that, when he sent an article titled
'Vinay Mhanje Kai?' (What is Humility?), the editor returned
it to him without printing it. There were some other magazines
during those times that were ultra-orthodox, and they would
not publish Raghunathrao's writings. Therefore, around 1925,
he thought that instead of being dependent on other periodicals,
he should start his own for propagating his views. It appears
that he got into discussion on this issue with his near and dear
ones. Even before Raghunathrao, Gopal Ganesh Agarkar had

written in his article 'Stree-Daasya-Vimochan' (Redemption of Women from Slavery), 'With the passage of time, methods can be developed for men and women to have sex without having unwanted babies . . . .' An unwritten injunction existed during those times that nobody should either talk or write about this subject. Raghunathrao had, of course, written two books in Marathi titled *Aadhunik Kaam-shastra* and *Gupt-rogaapaasoon Bachaav*, but there was no magazine that was devoted to this subject. He had therefore wanted to bring out a magazine that would deal not only with this subject but also cover all other important aspects of life. This was an extraordinary thought because, for one, even learned people of those times would not themselves write on this subject; for another, most magazines were unwilling to publish writings on this subject by others. In an article written somewhere else, Raghunathrao has recounted his experience:

> When an advertisement for an English book on birth control was sent to Ramanand Chatterjee for publication in the 'Modern Review', he wrote back, saying: "Please do not send anything to us from now onwards." Later, writing a Marathi book on the same subject I sent it for a review. It came before the reviewer K. Apte. He gave the book an extremely adverse review, which brought the book a lot of free publicity. The *Kesari* of Pune did a similar thing. They also returned the advertisement that was sent to them. A letter was sent to Shri N.C. Kelkar that even if there was a difference of opinion on the book, there should be no objection to accepting advertisement requests. A copy of the book was also sent along with it.

Besieged with unfavourable responses, Raghunathrao considered bringing out his own independent magazine.

Wrangler R.P. Paranjape had written the following letter to him from Bangalore on 9 October 1925:

All—or almost all—difficulties [in] the way of progress in India are due to religion putting its nose into everything. Nothing can be discussed from a really nationalistic standpoint. What do you think of enlarging the scope of your journal a bit and call it the 'Rationalist', [so] that you may include other subjects on [sic] which you are interested? A section can be set apart for birth-control and other allied subjects. But birth-control is perhaps too limited in scope and will not at present appeal to large numbers.

Wrangler's thought had already been given shape with the publication of a magazine called *Reason* by some intellectually oriented youngsters. He had remained closely connected with this magazine and its organization.

Referring to Wrangler Paranjape's above letter in an article, Raghunathrao wrote:

But even that was not satisfying. I had wanted a magazine that was broad-based enough to accommodate whatever subject I wanted. Dr. Robinson's journal and similar journals in France had put this idea into my head and primarily I had wanted to present modern thoughts on sexology. Hence, finally, we firmed up on the title *Samaaj-swaasthya*.

In another article, he wrote:

Instead of getting after literature that only educates or entertains, I felt that there were important things to be told to people and that they must be told at whatever cost; hence I decided to bring out this magazine.

The Beginning of *Samaaj-swaasthya*

Raghunathrao was already over forty-four years of age when he joined the Bombay–Bahrain Company. Prior to that, he

had spent fifteen months being jobless and would naturally
have heaved a sigh of relief at landing a job. With financial
support having arrived, he immediately began publishing
Samaaj-swaasthya. However, Malatibai's ill-health flared up
in 1928 and her medical expenditure increased. Besides, while
he was in the company, he was required to visit the Gulf of
Iran along with Rosenthal Saheb. Thus, in 1919 he went to
Paris; in 1925 to Nairobi on the invitation of his brother Dr
Shankarrao, and from 1926 to 1932 he visited the Gulf of Iran
along with his boss. During his lifetime, therefore, he travelled
to three foreign countries.

Samaaj-swaasthya came out with its first issue on 15 July
1927. Its size was 7" X 5" and remained the same till the last
issue of November 1953 that was published after his death. The
earliest issues carried the image of a lighthouse on the cover.
Later it carried the sketch of a naked woman, and still later, of
a number of naked women. The number of pages would keep
fluctuating. For the twenty-six years and four months of its
existence, it would be put into post on the fifteenth of every
month. He was a disciplined person by nature anyway, but also
had as his ideal the discipline that was observed by the magazine
Kirloskar. In 1944, the Second World War caused Depression
across the world and prices began to soar, causing a shortage
of newsprint. This impacted *Samaaj-swaasthya* too, making the
already slim magazine slimmer. The result was that the August–
September–October issue was required to be published as a
joint issue. Except for this one anomaly, *Samaaj-swaasthya* was
always published on time.

In its inaugural issue, Raghunathrao laid down the objectives
and policies of the magazine in the following words:

> The objective of this magazine is to hold discussions on the
> physical and mental health of individuals and of society and
> what we should do about maintaining it. There are certain

subjects which other journalists hesitate or fear to discuss in print, however important they may be. As ordinary readers find it extremely difficult to get information on those subjects, our intention is to remove those difficulties. Our information shall not be of philosophical nature only, but it will be practically useful. The word *kaam-shaastra* has been misused, but we are compelled to use this word to mean 'a scientific examination of the sexual urge'; there is no reason, therefore, for anybody to take offence on this point.

The path that Raghunathrao had chosen was difficult. He rustled up this magazine with the purpose of educating the masses and for that he was always required to scrape and scrounge for funds. If a magazine has to run, the editor must have an entire team of writers available. Like-minded writers must be brought together so that there is never a shortage of articles. Raghunathrao believed he should have various kinds of writers available to him and all these writers should be compensated for their efforts. He believed that since he was not in a position to pay them, he had no right to ask them to write. In spite of knowing this, Bhaskarrao Jadhav, Madhavrao Bagal, Sahridaya Mahad and a few others would send their articles voluntarily, which Raghunathrao published in *Samaaj-swaasthya*. Shakuntala Paranjape also offered invaluable help in this matter. Raghunathrao would write most of the matter for the magazine himself. Along with his original writing, there would also be articles translated from French.

To underline the message that truth is always naked, he decided to print pictures of naked women on the cover. But Raghunathrao has written that the managers of many printing presses would refuse to accept such pictures despite being offered money in advance.

Bombay Vaibhav, the printing press of the Servants of India Society established by the late G.K. Gokhale had agreed to print our magazine (not for free); but when its manager R. Dewale saw our manuscript, he said that our opinions were far too revolutionary and refused to print it. As a result, we could not get the print quality we had wanted, and the publication was delayed too. And the members of that Society consider themselves liberal.

The same issue says that 'even a backward magazine like the monthly *Manoranjan* refused to carry our paid advertisements.' Thus, even during its early period, the managers of printing presses as well as the owners of contemporary magazines refused to cooperate with Raghunathrao. Even after it started getting published regularly, it had to confront many obstacles. It was quite understandable that opposition should come from the ultra-orthodox with their mildewed ideologies; but it doesn't appear that those who considered themselves progressive were much in favour, or that Raghunathrao gained any active support from them.

The fact is that during those times nobody talked much about heterosexual relationships, sexually transmitted diseases, and certainly never wrote on it. There was just one autobiography of Nana Phadnis that talked about his extra-marital indulgences, but that was clearly an exception. Our culture had Rama as a paragon of virtue and fidelity to one woman; but that never meant that all men were embodiments of virtue. Our great writers have admonished, 'Never give your books, money or woman to another; if you do, they rarely come back; and even if they ever do, they return in a wrecked and contaminated state.' These great writers would have felt the need for this admonition only because of what they saw in the society around them, surely.

In *Mrchchha-katika*[1], the depiction of courtesan Vasantasena and the married man Charudutt can be taken as representing reality. When Tukaram counselled, '*parviya naari rukmai samaan*' (A woman not one's own is sacred), he was talking in the context of prostitutes. Also, when the heroine of a *laavani*[2] expresses her sexual passion by telling the young, shelter-seeking traveller that her husband is out doing guard duty and her mother-in-law at home suffers from night-blindness, it sounds quite natural. All of this obviously means that heterosexual relationships have always existed in society, but they cannot be expressed openly, resulting in incurable diseases that are suffered in silence. This would happen on quite a large scale. Raghunathrao had himself seen such people in the hostel during his college days. That was when he had realized the extreme need for creating public awareness on the issues of sexually transmitted and other incurable diseases as also on the alarmingly burgeoning population.

Dr Robinson and Margaret Sanger in America and Marie Stopes, Norman Haire, Ellis and others were either pondering over this subject scientifically or had actually opened clinics for dispensing advice and treatment. In our parts, there was nobody either offering scientific guidance or even writing about it. This was the vacuum that Raghunathrao tried to fill by bringing out his magazine *Samaaj-swaasthya* and by starting a birth-control centre at Parel earlier.

The Pictures on the Cover

The first few issues of *Samaaj-swaasthya* carried the picture of a lighthouse on the cover page, but later pictures of nude women were being published, particularly sketches. Artists were often not willing to do sketches of this kind. Some of these pictures were done by the famous artist V. Sinnarkar. Giving information on these pictures, he has said,

Raghunathrao would call me over to his house at night and give me some magazines published in English and French. They carried countless photographs of naked women in various postures. He would then ask me to do a sketch of one of those photographs. This was how the pictures were made. It was all done in a hush-hush manner, meaning that Raghunathrao took care that his neighbours were oblivious that we were drawing sketches here.

From 1938 onwards, Raghunathrao began to bring out a bigger January issue of *Samaaj-swaasthya* in which he printed several pictures of nude women. They were also taken from foreign magazines.

The pictures that Raghunathrao printed were always branded as obscene. Compilations of the magazines of those times are even now available in some libraries; the pictures on their covers and inside, like in the Diwali issue—sometimes black and white and sometimes colour—were of an uninhibited nature. But there is no indication of any accusations of indecency. Some examples include the picture titled 'Oleti' (The Wet Girl) done by Thakur Singh for the cover of the magazine 'Ratnakar' or the picture of a half-naked girl standing in a lake with a pot, published on page 120 of the Diwali issue of *Mauj*. It carried a line from Prof. V.G. Maidev: 'Oh, you beauty with your fake anger and fake modesty, carry this x x x x home then'. There was a nude picture of young Miss Percy Henderman titled 'In the Realm of God' that appeared on page thirty-four of the 1934 issue of Sanjivani and Kumari Alu Mukadam's picture titled 'Semi-Nude Snake Dance' in the special edition of *Pratibha* in 1935. The cover of G.T. Madkholkar's book *Swair-Vichar* (Wild Thoughts) is also of the same kind. The picture of a semi-nude young girl titled 'Pushp-Dhanva' done by the painter R.B. Kelkar and published on page five of the second issue of *Sanjivani* in

1936, as well as the pictures on pages 56–58 of a 1932 issue of *Yashvant* were titillating too. There is no record of anyone squeaking a word against these magazines or their editors. The controversy against 'Oleti' can be seen as the only exception. Therefore, the general perception that *Samaaj-swaasthya* was replete with nude and semi-nude pictures is not supported by facts. Around 1940, a friend of Kusumagraj named Ramakant Weldey brought out a magazine named *Jeevan* for about twelve to eighteen months. The quality of its paper, its printing and its nude photographs were of the best kind. A reader had asked Raghunathrao why he couldn't give *Samaaj-swaasthya* the same shape as *Jeevan*.

In this matter, the blame cannot rest entirely on the editor because those who created such a hullaballoo about obscenity were found to read such magazines secretly. This has been the attitude of our society. This is what Raghunathrao has said about this attitude:

> This magazine has given precedence to articles related to sex. One of the reasons for giving this precedence is that privately, ninety percent of the people consider this subject as important, whether they want to admit it or not. The second reason is that even those who consider themselves as pure rationalists are not ready to think logically on this subject.

This was essentially a matter of identifying the interests of readers in those times; editors would print photographs (and articles) that satisfied these interests. But nobody can say that Raghunath used them to stir sexual passions of readers or satisfy their unmet desires. He firmly believed that the doors of knowledge could not open unless scientific and critical study was made of every single one of the various arenas of life.

He believed that people contracted incurable diseases in their effort to satisfy their unfulfilled sexual desires while remaining ignorant, superstitious, unhygienic and distrustful of science. Relief from these predicaments could be obtained only by a systematic, scientific study of these areas. That was why he desired, with his very heart and soul, to advertise and propagate this message across the widest cross-section of society.

Bhagirathibai Tamhankar stated, 'By and large, the consensus among the readers of this magazine was that the pictures appearing in it should be kept away from children.' A letter writer endorses this opinion published in an issue during the third year of *Samaaj-swaasthya*. It reads:

> Why should there always be women on the cover page? And that too naked? Do clothes also trigger ill-health? The cover page should have carried a fully clothed (instead of semi-nude or fully naked) woman, because we still haven't become complete adherents of nakedness. If we do, we will have to stay naked too. But even before that, around the beginning of the third year, you had written in the editorial, "authorities hold that semi-nude pictures are sexually exciting. Since exciting sexually is not the objective of this magazine, the pictures on the cover page have been changed to full nude."

Answering the question why Raghunathrao used pictures of only naked women, Shakuntala Paranjape said that he had also printed pictures of naked men on the cover. (However, after examining almost all the issues across twenty-six years and four months, I didn't come across any such picture on the cover or on the last page.) Raghunath informs on this matter:

> A few women have asked why our magazine carries the pictures of only women and why not of men. But pictures

of naked men will have to be given from behind, because I suspect the law may create obstacles. The stupidity, of course, is in the law. In Germany, permission exists for selling magazines containing naked pictures of men and women on the street.

Some readers of *Samaaj-swaasthya* were alert critics and would notice the tiniest change made on the cover. A gentleman named Shantaram Shringarpure lived in Thane. When Raghunathrao delivered a speech in Thane on 17 May 1931, Shringarpure was the chairperson of the programme. He asked Raghunathrao the following question:

> I want a small clarification in the matter of the pictures that appear on the cover page of your magazine and I hope you will give this clarification through your magazine. I am aware of all the information published earlier on these pictures. However, please explain why the relics of womankind's slavery such as bangles on the wrist and *kunkus* on the brow have been retained.

Among the readers of *Samaaj-swaasthya* were a few opponents who articulated their opposition according to their disposition. Some criticized the editor under pseudonyms, and some did so anonymously. 'I am subjected to a lot of sarcastic criticism in the letters,' Raghunathrao has written, 'but since most of the time they do not carry any meaningful argument, I don't think it appropriate to eat up space by responding to them.' Even so, he did not withhold himself from taking cognizance of such letters. These letter writers sent their opinions to other magazines as they did to *Samaaj-swaasthya* too. When

Dr A.V. Ketkar expressed his disapproval of birth control in a magazine called *Bhishagvilas*, Raghunath published a no hold barred examination of the article under the pseudonym 'Another Doctor'.

Samaaj-swaasthya had been created to publicize birth control, sexology and the remedies available for sexually transmitted diseases. Therefore, when Raghunathrao responded to the backward opinions of his opponents, the language he used was straightforward, sharp and aggressive. He would sometimes be oblique too. The renowned Marathi author Dilip Chitre has made the following remarks about Raghunathrao:

> One of the great masters to have lived was the late Raghunath Dhondo Karve. Like all the other Karves, he was eccentric, bizarre, proud, and honest to the point of death. He brought out a magazine called *Samaaj-swaasthya* with the objective of teaching rationality to Marathi people and for removing their ignorance in sexual matters. He did not stop at simply popularizing birth control as an intellectual concept, but even sold the articles required for practicing it. Although he was a professor of Mathematics, he was a thoroughly cultured person in all aspects, highly educated, and progressive. He never aimed for popularity. His language was lucid, unornamented, straightforward. A bit on the dry side. Every one of his articles looks fresh even today, because the dullness of the Marathi brain couldn't possibly have been removed by one single R.D. Karve.

Readers' Responses

The responses of some concerned people are worth noting. Mrs Bhagirathibai Tamhankar has described her experience thus: 'Prof. R.D. Karve is the editor of the magazine *Samaaj-swaasthya*. By and large, the consensus among the readers of this magazine has been that the pictures appearing in it should be kept away from children. We keep it under lock and key. . . .' Girijabai was an author of those times and she too had negative opinions on *Samaaj-swaasthya*. But it appears that there indeed were some thinking women who understood the purpose behind *Samaaj-swaasthya*. This can be gathered from the following news item that was published in the magazine:

'The motion of Mrs. Ramabai Tambe – that every mother should necessarily impart education about the body (knowledge on sex) to their adult sons and daughters – and the second motion of Prof. Kusumavati Deshpande – that all women should have knowledge about birth control – received only one negative vote.'

Among all these, Bhagirathibai Tamhankar's opinion may be taken as representative. The elders at home read *Samaaj-swaasthya* secretly. They either had at least a sneaky curiosity about the articles there or they desired scientific information on the subjects discussed. But they were very alert about not letting the next generation access the information they themselves wanted to garner. But these children, between ages, eleven to thirteen were smart. The issues that the parents had kept under lock and key—'we would read these issues surreptitiously,' says Dr Y.D. Phadke. This experience was not Phadke's alone, but of most people of those times.

The Format of *Samaaj-swaasthya*

Anna writes in *Aatmavritt* in 1929, 'he had this objective for a long time of bringing out a magazine for propagating his views.

. . . He has been bringing out this small magazine called *Samaaj-swaasthya* for the past eight months.'

However much the magazine is called a one-man show, there are articles written by Shakuntala Paranjape, Dr K.B. Lele, Dr Bhaskarrao Karve, Dr Iravati Karve, Dr Dinkarrao Karve, Mama Warerkar, Sahridaya Mahad, Bhaskarrao Jadhav, Madhavrao Bagal and Durga Bhagwat. The magazine had columns, an editorial, letters to the editor, book reviews, 'Sharada's Letters' and 'Griha Karmey' (Household Chores). There were series written on a variety of topics. The editor was also particular about publishing short stories. The pictures appearing on the cover kept changing and often nude photographs of women would grace the inside pages too.

A practice had been adopted of sharing the account statement with the readers at the beginning and end of each year. One can find repeated reminders about the straitened circumstances in which the magazine was being run. If somebody donated money for the running of the magazine, it would be gratefully acknowledged in the next issue. Three cases were filed against Raghunath for obscenity. The details on the episodes were covered under the title 'Aamchyavareel Khatla' (The Case Against Me). The editor also published the 'Aamchya Sattaree' (In My Seventies) and other such autobiographical pieces. Raghunathrao would also tell readers about many other personal things.

Other than the above, the magazine carried columns like 'Ishwarvaad' (Theism), 'Shastribuvashi Samvaad' (Conversation with a Pundit), 'Ajab Kaifiyat' (Strange Circumstances), 'Maanas-Shastrachey Thotand' (The Pretensions of Psychology), 'Satyaani Neeti' (Truth and Ethics), 'Kaam-Vishayak Swatantra Paaya' (An Independent Foundation for Sex), 'Aarya-Sanskrutichey Maasale' (Samples of the Aryan Culture), 'Shetakicha navaa jamaana ani Loksankhyecha Prashn' (The New World of Agriculture and the

Question of Population), 'Taaji va Shili Baatami' (Fresh and Stale News), 'Kaam-Vaasanechi Meemaamsa' (An Analysis of the Sexual Urge) and 'Vyaayaam' (Exercise). There were also articles, translation from the French author Victor Margarine's novels, a few translated articles, a few poems, fillers and other kinds of information. Since Raghunathrao was particularly interested in a wide variety of subjects like literature, music, theatre, cinema, painting, social activism, education and politics, a number of these subjects would find their way into his magazine quite naturally. *Samaaj-swaasthya* strikes out prominently because of being different from other periodicals of those times and entrenched in controversies.

The very first issue carried the objectives and policies of the magazine on clear terms. From the very beginning, it was seen as the mouthpiece of unabashed rationality. Along with carrying discussions on heterosexual relationships, women's independence, equality, sexually transmitted diseases, birth control, etc., it also published opinions on literature, music, theatre and other art forms like the cinema. There wasn't any shortage of litterateurs and politicians during those days. A good number of politicians, in fact, were first litterateurs. But for all that, not much support could be found for Raghunathrao's opinions. His was a serious magazine committed firmly to a certain ideology and his journey was solitary and Raghunathrao had quite deliberately accepted it as his lot.

The paper on which the magazine was printed, the quality of the printing, the transparencies used for the photographs, all of these could barely make the grade. The reason, obviously, was paucity of funds. Its quality did not ever go beyond monochromatic pictures. From January 1938 onwards, issues began getting thicker and carried more pictures, but even so, it never happened that any more than one colour of ink was used for its printing.

Even though it is true that Raghunathrao had a very clear and firm picture of how his magazine should be, he would occasionally be given suggestions on some novelty that could be brought in; if he liked the suggestions and if implementation was possible, he would do it. For instance, it occurred to him— or perhaps, somebody suggested it—that his magazine should carry stories. Accordingly, he began publishing stories from the July 1933 issue onwards. There can, of course, be doubts or differences of opinion about the quality of these stories. *Samaaj-swaasthya* was not renowned for poetry, but it did publish a few poems, as a kind of exception. It also published other literary forms like one-act plays and translated novels. But the single most important but unappreciated piece of literature was book reviews. Even among them, the reviews that Raghunathrao himself wrote were remarkable in terms of both quantity and quality. In fact, for a complete assessment of Raghunathrao's personality, his book reviews as well as reviews of other art forms like cinema and music should be taken into consideration.

He also did stellar work in the areas of translation and transcreation. Since paid contributors were not feasible, he avoided asking for articles. Instead, he filled the pages of the magazine with translations and adaptations of French writings. He would surely have realized that monotony would creep in, but he wasn't left with many choices. If any writer offered his or her writings for publishing without asking for a fee, the matter would be published if it fitted in the framework of the magazine's avowed aims and objectives. That was how he came to publish articles from Bhaskarrao Jadhav, Madhavrao Bagal, Durga Bhagwat, Mama Warerkar, Sahridaya of Mahad, and a few others every now and again. Therefore, the opinion that *Samaaj-swaasthya* was altogether a one-man show is not true. The editorials, correspondence, columns, the discussions

presented in the column 'Sharadeche Patr' and articles that
came in other columns were important pieces of writing.

Because it was modified periodically and run under
extremely difficult financial circumstances, it was different
from magazines of other publishing houses that kept a sharp eye
on quality. Besides, the rising cost of paper, the circumstances
of war and the monthly increase in the cost of printing always
placed severe limitations on *Samaaj-swaasthya*. He would give
close reading to magazines published in Belgaum, Goa, Satara,
Akole, Nagpur, Indore and other urban centres. He would
unfailingly examine the thoughts that either matched or ran
counter to his own and also cross swords with his opponents.
His mastery over Sanskrit—particularly its embellishments and
its meter—was amazing.

Due to its analytical character, *Samaaj-swaasthya* created an
independent and markedly different space for itself in the world
of magazines. While it is true that it was an important forum
for discussing heterosexual relationships, sexually transmitted
diseases and other related subjects, it also laid sufficient emphasis
on the nurturing of artistic proclivities. The editor was clearly
more interested in dispensing knowledge than in providing
light entertainment. In this sense, we may confidently say that
this was the first 'bold' magazine in Marathi. The magazine
Jeevan run by Ramakant Velde had begun imitating *Samaaj-
swaasthya*, where Raghunath also wrote under the pseudonym
'Ku. Shailaja'. Its contents, however, were more inclined towards
obscenity. Raghunathrao wrote a series of articles for *Jeevan*
under the title 'Kaam-Vishayak Swaatantryaacha Paayaa' (An
Independent Foundation for Sex). What can be gleaned from
this is that cheap imitations of *Samaaj-swaasthya* existed then.

In his column 'Granth Sameeksha' (Book Review),
Raghunathrao has, as it were, given a live demonstration of how

a book can be deeply analyzed within eight to ten sentences or two to three paragraphs. A look at the subjects and the types of books he reviewed reveals to us the subjects that were not taboo to him. While reviewing the stories in *Kalyaanchey Nihshwaas* (The Breath of Buds), Raghunathrao showed great felicity in the use of the sociological method. One can't help feeling that greater cognizance should have been taken of his skill as a reviewer.

One look at his list of writings on the subject of literature and theatre gives us information on the areas on which he wrote: 'Purogaami Vaangmaya' (Progressive Literature), 'Marathi Bhashecha Namoona' (A Sample of the Marathi Language), 'Satyachi Kasoti' (The Touchstone of Truth), 'Satya and Neeti' (Truth and Ethics), 'Wamanrao Tadnya Navhta' (Wamanrao Was Not an Expert), 'Warerkaraanchi Badnaami' (The Defamation of Warerkar), 'Na Kelele Bhaashan' (Lectures Not Delivered), 'Tukaramachi Punyatithi' (Tukaram's Anniversary), 'Monna Vanna', 'Marathi Natyaprayogaateel Thadak Chookaa' (Prominent Errors in the Staging of Marathi Plays), 'Yandacha Natya-Mahotsava' (The Drama Festival This Time), etc.

He was a member of organizations like the Bombay Marathi Sahitya Sangh and the Marathi Patrakar Parishad and would make it a point to attend all their functions and write news reports on them in *Samaaj-swaasthya* without fail. He wrote 'Solapurchi Patrakaar Parishad' (The Journalists' Conference at Solapur), 'Belgaumchey Sahitya Sammelan', (The Belgaum Literary Festival), 'Marathi Granthalaya Parishad' (The Marathi Library Conference) and many such articles after attending these programmes, which just goes to show how enthusiastically he participated in them.

Samaaj-swaasthya published stories and the author Sahridaya Mahad took full advantage of it. Apart from him,

Madhavrao Bagal and Mama Warerkar also wrote. But the magazine was not known for the stories it published. In fact, the stories were not particularly artistic either, hovering around the sensual.

The March 1943 issue of *Samaaj-swaasthya* was planned in advance to be a 'Two Wives' special issue. Developments had happened to justify this subject. V. Shantaram, Rajkavi Yashvant, Shankarrao Kirloskar, R.G. Harshe and Mama Warerkar were among the notables who had taken a second wife while the first was still alive. When Prof. N.C. Phadke too married a student of Rajaram College, Kolhapur, named Kamal Deekshit, while his first wife was alive, it had created quite a scandal.[3] Raghunathrao himself had written an article titled 'Why One Wife Is Not Enough' that was published in the magazine *Chitra*. He was aware this was a hot subject and he gathered articles from his acquaintances on this topic and got his sister-in-law Dr Iravati Karve to write an article that did a scientific analysis. He had even advertised in the previous issue as follows:

Next Issue:

A number of people find it depressing that the number is increasing of educated people going for a second wife while the first wife is alive. To show that this question does not have a single side, we have decided to dedicate our March issue to this subject. This 'Two Wives Special' will be published on March 15, as always.

Raghunathrao published a letter to the editor with the intention of entertaining the reader and is an example of the kind of letters *Samaaj-swaasthya* received.

My affectionate greetings to Right Agency.

I would like to inform your agency that Shri Raghunath Dhondoba Karve, who is a well-educated person with an M. A., has been bringing out bad books on *Samaaj-swaasthya* and thus cheating his buyers. I have been one such buyer. I bought a number of issues, but since I could not find anything worth reading in them, they have just been lying around. Therefore, by taking an agency for such bad books unfit for reading, you are cheating your clients.

There being no obscene subjects in the books, nor there being enough information on them, all your issues are filled with vulgar chatting. You may, therefore, inform him that if he has to give information on these subjects, he should give them in full. He must stop this business of pointlessly duping his buyers. The picture on the cover was attractive, but in the inner pages it is just: I went to Pune where I met Sumati and this kind of meaningless chat. Therefore, you must kindly inform this deceitful gentleman immediately (Please turn over) that if there is information to be given, we want it in full and it should be written fully. If there is a subject, it should be completed.

Yours, A Reader.   (March, 1942, Page 300)

'This monthly is read by 30,000 readers.' This information (or advertisement?) appeared on the cover of the October 1931 issue. The later advertisements show upward and downward fluctuations in the number of readers.

The April 1938 issue of *Samaaj-swaasthya* carried information on a change of address, suggesting that Raghunathrao would have changed at least two houses in Girgam. However, he stayed at this address till the very last: Floor 2, Jagjeevan Mansion, 14, New Bhatwadi, Girgam, Bomabay-4. This was where he would counsel people who came to him for advice.

Raghunathrao had firm opinions on matters related to literature and art. His position on stories becomes apparent in the paragraph given below:

> From the perspective of art, short stories written for propagating a philosophy are bad. Two mutually contradictory philosophies can easily be propounded in a short story. The world should be reformed or can be reformed only after it has first been understood. Therefore, artistic short stories fit quite well within our policy. (September 1933, p. 76.)

His unrelenting stance was, 'It is not our opinion that short stories should be written with the purpose of propagating a philosophy. The primary purpose of short stories, plays and novels is to draw an authentic picture of human behaviour.'

While it is true that *Samaaj-swaasthya* was a serious magazine, it did contain plenty of fillers. Whether they were humorous is a matter of opinion, but here is an example:

> 'My wife is an extremely organized person. Nothing ever moves out of place.'
> 'Really?'
> 'What really? Look, you are leaving this *beedi* stub here, aren't you? Come after eight days and you will find it exactly there.'

If one wants to, one may call it the Mama Warerkar variety of humour. In any case, Raghunathrao was good friends with Mama and could have heard it during a visit.

Mama Warerkar wrote an article on Raghunathrao in the monthly *Manohar* in which, addressing Raghunathrao, he requested, 'You should consider writing your autobiography or a book with the title *My Experiences*.' Raghunathrao was not interested in this venture. He has expressed his opinion on biographies/autobiographies in *Samaaj-swaasthya*. 'Facts can very often not be mentioned in an autobiography. Besides, I do not believe that any benefit comes out of it. Diversion, perhaps, is possible. As of now, at least, there is no plan of writing an autobiography.' (May, 1936, p. 343).

> However, about the autobiography, I haven't changed my opinion. If truth is revealed about a person, it can lead to calumny.... There is no scope for speaking the truth about a dead person either, because their descendants can create the farce of hurt sentiments and start complaining.... However, I have this thought of writing about some experiences. In any case, I do not have enough material for writing a complete autobiography. I never wrote a diary. Whatever I did write occasionally is not all that good. The probability of jotting down experiences we shall examine some day.[4]

Malatibai became extremely ill from early 1944 onwards and Raghunathrao had to pay serious attention to her. That would have seriously affected his work in the publication of *Samaaj-swaasthya*. Also, because of the war, paper was costlier. August, September and October were, therefore, testing times for Raghunathrao. When Malatibai became critically ill, she was admitted to Singhania Hospital, Bombay, perhaps after August. As a result, it became impossible for him to bring out *Samaaj-swaasthya* during that period and he ultimately brought out a joint August–September–October issue in October. The information that follows was printed in this joint issue: 'Although this issue mentions August–September–October, it will be considered as a single-month issue. Hence the expiry limit of the subscription has been extended by two months.' This tells us how particular Raghunathrao was about dealings.

And as mentioned earlier, he did not inform his readers of his wife's death.

Compelling Writing

Raghunathrao's desire was to develop *Samaaj-swaasthya* into a complete magazine that would provoke intelligent discussion on all aspects of life. It was obvious that his favourite subjects would be prioritized. But the impression among people was that it was a magazine devoted to subjects related to sex though he frequently tried to bring variety in the content. He added a number of new columns and made extensive use of fillers. He openly shared whatever criticisms the magazine received with his readers. That was the reason why it never turned boring or pedantic. Let us look at how compelling the writings in it were.

Raghunathrao's Poems

Four poems were published in this magazine, of which two were written by Shakuntala Paranjape. In 1931, the ultra-orthodox, particularly from Pune had slapped a punitive fine against the magazine; plenty of verbal battles occurred and finally the matter was taken to court. The poem that follows affirms that when circumstances are adverse, the saintly person and the reformer do not vacillate:

The Reward of the Good Person: सज्जनांचे बक्षीस

जे स्वकार्य सोडुनि जनकार्याकारिता	निंदाच त्यांप्रती बहुत मिळत जगती	कुणी मूढ म्हणति हा सोडुनि स्वहिताला	सेवितो पहा तो कृतघ्न जनतेला || की जनकार्य मिषे स्वहितची हा साधी	जरी नसे असे मग स्वकार्य का बाधी || कुणी म्हणति मतलबी कीर्तिच मिळवितो	मतलबाविणें कधी कोण काम करितो || यश येता ही अपवाद अशे येती	तद भावी तर ते अनिवारचि होती || जो अधिकची ग्रासा सूक्ष्म मुखी घेई	त्या योग्यचि म्हणति शासन ते होई || सज्जनी गुणाला दोषचि जे म्हणति	शोभते तयाला सहजा निंदा ती || हे समजुनि जो जनकार्य शिरी घेई	अक्षय्यम्य यशाते तोचि पात्र होई ||	Those who put aside self-work for public service Calumny they get from the world. Some say: This fool, forgetting self-interest, Seeks to serve an ungrateful public Or: feigning public service he serves himself; Why else would he ignore self-work? Some say: the self-seeker acquires fame Does anyone work without self-interest? When success too brings calumny its absence only increases it. A person who eats with care Even he is considered deserving of punishment Those who consider virtue as vice They love to calumniate everybody. One who accepts public service knowing all this Deserves undying success

The signification of the second line, 'people consider him *moodh*, meaning foolish' was an experience that Raghunath himself had encountered. Vinayak J. Joshi of 92, Somwar Peth, Pune too could not tolerate Raghunathrao's criticism of

Mahatma Gandhi and Rabindranath Tagore; he wrote a letter to Raghunathrao published in the April 1950 issue that read, 'I'll tell you what people say of you: they call you a mad person.' The other accusation on the same lines is, 'Does anyone work without self-interest?' That is: there is bound to be some advantage in social service. This accusation too was often made against Raghunathrao.

Raghunathrao's second poem was published in *Samaaj-swaasthya*:

भय विसरा रे	चिती सन्द्भाव धरा रे || भय विसरा रे	चिती सन्द्भाव धरा रे ||	Forget fear: Always keep goodwill in heart Forget fear: Always keep goodwill in heart
साधु दिसे तरी भोंदू पक्का धुलवुनी लोका घेई टक्का || प्रसंग येतां देई धक्का || तो न बरा रे	त्यापासुनि दूर सरा रे ||१||	Although he looks a sadhu he is a charlatan. He fools people and fleeces them of money He will abandon you in your bad times
संतमहंतहि टे नावाचे | पाहुं जातां कूचकामाचे || वदती तैसे करिति न साचे | बहु नखरे	त्यापासुनि दूर सरा रे ||२||	He is not a good man. Stay away from him They are not saints and monks, only pretenders As you can see, they are useless They do not behave as truthfully as they claim
पीरफकीरहि शोषिती रक्ता | चिपाट बनविति आपुल्या भक्ता }} धर्माचा जणू त्यांचा मक्ता | चोरचि सारे	त्यापासुनि दूर सरा रे ||३||	They are full of drama. Stay away from them Holy men and mendicants suck the blood

समानप्रेमा बांधुनि गाठी | लोकहिताच्या कार्यासाठी || निंदास्तुतिवर लावूनि कांठी | मी तुं हरा रे | सत्यकार्या धीर धारा रे ||४|| काठी टाकुनि द्या धर्माची | डोळसां न ती उपयोगाची || दिशा आंखुनी सत्यकार्याची | भय विसरा रे | चिती सद्भाव धरा रे |५|	They turn their votaries weak and skeletal They treat religion as their monopoly Thieves all. Stay away from them Love all For the work of public weal Disregard censure or praise Abandon this talk of me and you Apply yourself to truthful work Throw away the staff of religion It's of no use to the one who can see Locating the direction of good work Forget all fear. Always keep goodwill in heart

The following was published in the June 1936 issue under the title 'Do Read':

'On April 17, a buyer was charged a rupee more because of a mistake in the billing. We shall reimburse the rupee on production of the bill or on being provided details.'

S.A. Kulkarni of Sangli had sent some money by post which got lost en route to Raghunathrao. Raghunathrao informed Kulkarni, who accused him of stealing the money. In the March 1936 issue of *Samaaj-swaasthya*, Raghunathrao wrote, 'After having resigned from three jobs to preserve my independence and self-esteem, I now find a man who harbours such kinds of doubts about me.'

In sharp contrast was the father of the hard-core atheist N.K. Joshi. Joshi's father considered Rajaramshastri Bhagwat,

the Sanskrit scholar and social reformer, his ideal. With a
spiritualist younger brother who was a disciple of Gondwalekar
Maharaj and Narayan Maharaj, the father decided to donate Rs.
30,000 to the Deccan Education Society. Joshi, therefore, wrote
a letter to Raghunathrao seeking his opinion on his father's
decision and waited for a reply. This information has been
published in the November 1947 issue. To summarize, it is not
true that *Samaaj-swaasthya* carried information only on birth
control and uninhibited relationships.

An Examination of the Column 'Sharada's Letters':

From the issue of July 1932 onwards, plenty of material got
to be regularly published under the title 'Sharadeche Patra'
(Sharada's Letters). It is absolutely clear that the inspiration
behind this column was A.B. Kolhatkar's column 'Vatsalaa-
Vahineenche Patra'. Raghunathrao's creation, Sharada, was an
unmarried, progressive woman who would express her opinions
on sexual relationships fearlessly and freely and stun renowned
people with her thoughts. Due to her rebellious nature and in-
your-face language, many suspected that Sharada was in fact
Raghunathrao. Another reason for the doubt was that she
would always take Karve's side and fall upon his opponents like
a ton of bricks. There were no signals in the articles to suggest
a woman writer. They were knowledgeable, argumentative and
logical. The emotional elements found in women's writings
were altogether missing. It is probable that some readers of
those times would have considered Shakuntalabai as the writer,
but she had quite a different style that was quite evident in her
writings. But most readers were convinced that it was a man
writing under the pseudonym of Sharada, and that man was
no other than Raghunath himself; they were right too. With a
rare exception or two, this column continued right up to the
very end.

The column was so popular during those times that when the magazine *Pratibha* was bringing out its Diwali issue, it expressly invited Sharada to participate in a symposium titled Burkha-Mandalaateel Sadasyaanchi Pratibhela Bhet ('Members of the Burkha-Group Visit *Pratibha*). Sharada responded as follows:

I am not ready to put my name in the Burkha Group, whatever people may have to say about it. Also, I do not write under a pseudonym. As for my letters that get printed in *Samaaj-swaasthya*, I have written them to a married friend who lives in Pune. She sent the very first one for publication without seeking my permission. Since I didn't want to hurt her, I granted her the permission and that is how my letters to her are then forwarded to the editor. I had obviously placed the condition that my entire name should not be revealed. Everybody, therefore, will agree that my case is a little different.[5]

It appears that the readers of *Samaaj-swaasthya* often asked the editor about the identity of Sharada and the editor would duly respond. To one such reader in the November 1952 issue, the response was, 'We do not have a separate a list for subscribers. It is against editorial policy to reveal a person hiding behind a pseudonym.' It was quite an appropriate stand too. A controversy had erupted in 1937 between Rani Anubaisaheb Ghorpade of Ichalkaranji and Shankarrao Kirloskar, who was then the editor of the magazine *Kirloskar*. When Shankarrao exposed Anubai as the person who had written a story in *Stree* under a pseudonym, Raghunathrao protested strongly against Shankarrao's act. While Malatibai Bedekar declared that she was Vibha Shirurkar, Sharadabai never did. When the last issue of *Samaaj-swaasthya*, which had been readied earlier, was published after the death of Raghunathrao, it carried an article

by Sharadabai. Today, however, we can assert with certainty
that 'Sharadabai and Raghunathrao are the same person'.

The question that emerges is, why did Raghunathrao have
to write under the pseudonym of Sharada? He was second to
none in the battle of words, but he wanted to introduce to the
world an educated—and particularly, a progressive—woman
and her revolutionary thoughts on a heterosexual relationship.
Therefore, the role of Sharada had remained vacant—the role of
presenting and endorsing Raghunathrao's opinions (whom she
always addressed as Karve) and calling to account the opinions
of opponents and demolishing them. Raghunathrao's eclectic
and intensive reading and his critical faculty are unmistakably
reflected in her articles. He has written repeatedly that the
objective of his magazine was to make an effort at bringing about
an all-round development of society. He thus got for himself
a forum for expressing his views on his interests that covered
an amazingly wide range: literature, music, theatre, cinema,
education, social reform, political transformation, and much
else. 'Sharada's Letters', therefore, became a column that touched
upon all the issues that unnerved the society of those times. The
following paragraph written by Prof. M.V. Dhond suggests that
he understood the objective of the column perfectly:

> Sharada's Letters may be seen as the cultural history of
> Maharashtra across the twenty-seven years stretching from
> 1927 to 1953, that too recorded by an intellectual . . . . I read
> through those issues of *Samaaj-swaasthya* once again and
> that entire period once again floated before my mind's
> eyes. Dange's definition of laavani as poetry of the pimp;
> Tarktirth's assessment of progressive criticism as 'finding
> Sanskrit equivalents for English words, adding to them
> Marathi suffixes and then trying to get a Russian meaning out
> of them'; Balgandharva's claim that only male actors could

do feminine roles; the Marathification of Hindi things by Kelkar; the boycott of Akashvani by the artistes; Krishnarao Marathe's motion against obscenity; corruption in the matric examination of the university in 1944; the storm that erupted when Phadke, Kirloskar, Yashvant, and Harshe took second wives while their first wives were alive; the controversy on whether Sarasvats were Brahmins, and within this controversy, Krishna Nadkarni's punning when he said, 'Since all Sarasvats were Khare (a surname as well a word meaning "truthful"), the exceptions among them got to be called Khote (a surname as well as a word meaning "untruthful"); similarly, since all Chitpavans were Khote, the exceptions among them got to be called Khare;' . . . What a variety of subjects were covered in it! While this history was happening, the person who stood firm as a rationalist and recorded all of it was Karve.[6]

Dhond did not stop at merely critically examining *Raghunathanchi Bakhar* (Raghunath's Chronicle); he also interviewed Raghunathrao's relatives for *Chaturdhaami* and went on to write an article on him. The observation that he records in the following paragraph deserves appreciation:

He had completely absorbed into himself the lesson from the Gita: 'For friends and foes alike'. Although Sardesai had stood witness for him, when he came out in praise of celibacy, Karve declared him as senile. When the A. H. Gadre who had brought him advertisements sat on a fast, he criticized him as doing it for propaganda. Although Mama Warerkar was his close friend, he did not shy away from severely criticizing Mai Warerkar's magazine *Mahila*. In contrast was the magazine *Kirloskar* that had refused to publish his article, which had led to the birth of *Samaaj-swaasthya*; yet during the celebration of its silver jubilee he praised it fulsomely. Wilson College had compelled him to submit his resignation; yet, when a movement began against the teaching of the Bible in that college, Raghunathrao stood up for the college by saying that it was necessary for the college to do so for the sake of getting help from the church.

Using Sharada as his mouthpiece, Raghunathrao covered a wide spectrum of events in the column, for instance the episode of students gifting bangles to Pune university officials. Raghunathrao was against the harmonium. Quoting psychologist McDougall on mathematicians' interest in music, he wrote with insight into his own musical hobby. He criticized Abdul Karim Khan Saheb for not taking a clear stand on the harmonium. The same was true regarding Indumati Purohit; he was upset because instead of teaching the guitar, she would teach some other instrument. He thought the historian and essayist Tryambak Shankar Shejwalkar was conceited. He vigorously opposed the idea of separate schooling for women and a separate magazine for them. He informs that between Hitler and Mussolini, Mussolini favoured birth control. He found Shyamrao Oke's jokes on the Constitution inappropriate. His favourite aphorism was, 'Religion is the world of imagination and science is the world of facts.' The column gives new information regarding Vishwasrao Dawkhare's plaint on Sane Guruji's suicide. Dr Ketkar, N.C. Phadke, S.K. Ksheersaagar, R.G. Harshe and M.D. Altekar were among his favourite targets of criticism. Sharada's opinion on women was very clear:

If women want to stand in competition with men, they have just one way, which is that they must learn to stand on their own feet. If men raise obstacles in this path, they should smash them down by all possible means. . . . Since only women deliver babies, it is true that some natural limitations emerge; but this is not the fault of the man. Why he should be punished for it is beyond my understanding. (March 1943, p. 233)

Raghunathrao on Literature

Regarding the work of the artist, Raghunathrao says:

> . . . I admit that the job of litterateurs, like the job of other
> artists, is to provide entertainment to the public, not to
> deliver homilies. I believe that trying to use art for the
> purpose of propaganda detracts from its artistic merit, but
> that does not mean that the author does not have the right to
> propagate ideas through the use of the novel.

Satya-Shiv-Sundar (Truth-God-Beauty) was a popular subject
for discussion during those days. The writings of W.M. Joshi,
Kusumavati Deshpande and B.S. Mardhekar discussed these
subjects aplenty. Raghunathrao stated his own position in this
regard in the following manner:

> It was Wamanrao's ideal that truth, ethics and beauty should
> be mutually supportive. The fact, however, is that no two
> among the three are related to each other. Nobody can define
> beauty because it is an individual response. Whatever I like is
> beautiful in my eyes, not in the eyes of others. How, then, do
> truth or ethics connect with it? Ethics is a concept created by
> human beings. If we wish, we may say that it should be based
> upon truth, but that is not how it actually is. Truth does not
> depend upon anything at all.

Raghunath had done extensive reading on Sanskrit poetry,
plays, figures of speech. His recall was phenomenal. He would
never fight shy of pointing out errors in Marathi poetry. 'Poets
have become lazy these days,' he would always say.

He disliked the use of English words in Marathi writing.
Whenever he came across this, he would bring it to the notice of
his *Samaaj-swaasthya* readers. Here is an interesting sample. 'A
magazine is published from Sawantwadi named *Satyaprakash*.

It carries a dialogue between God Indra and Narad Muni, in which Indra says, 'It is a principle of science that water finds its own level,' in which, while the rest of the sentence is in Marathi, he uses the English word 'level'.[7]

He brought to Prof. V.H. Kulkarni's notice the error in the use of the word '*suvar*' (swine).[8]

H.R. Mahajani approved the usage of the word '*card-dhaarak*' (card-holder); Raghunathrao, however, considered it '*dhed-gujari*', a mongrel word.[9]

He points out an additional diacritical mark in Khanderao Trilokekar's poem 'Baa Maharashtra Jaagaa Hoee'.[10]

Raghunathrao's position on stories and poetry of his time was:

A number of scholars have begun to write under the belief that it is all right if a short story is not short; or even if it is not a story. Painting is in a bad state these days. . . . In the same manner, a strange kind of poetry has turned rampant in England–America these days. The tradition of rhymeless poetry in English is quite old, but after that, there is no music left in it either. The trend now is that just because the lines are of different lengths, they should be called poetry. We have also started imitating the trend here and call it '*mukt-chhand*', free verse. . . . Why should they be called poetry at all? (March 1949, p. 218)

Similarly:

A number of people have called poets prophets, called them gods of the world of words. But this, I believe, is mere conceit among the poets. If they had been gods with words, they would have been able to express their ideas in simpler language, and they wouldn't have used mongrel words and cacophonous sentences like Mardhekar. Mardhekar has himself given a very mathematical definition of poetry, which in simple terms means: metaphors, analogies, and similes is poetry; there is no connect with the heart. I do not agree with this definition and I also don't understand why these metaphors and similes should bring incomprehensibility. . . In my opinion, there is only one cause of incomprehensibility: the poet himself is not clear about what he wants to say. A number of people consider this haziness of thought as a virtue; I, however, see it as confusion in thinking.

Y.D. Phadke has wondered whether something unpleasant had occurred between Raghunathrao and Mardhekar. From the perspective of poet and poetic temperament, it was quite clear that there was nothing that could endear Mardhekar to Raghunathrao.

Raghunathrao would participate in several literary competitions. Once, he submitted a manuscript on the topic 'Literary Criticism'. He had read through quite a few English and Marathi books for the purpose. In one of the books it was written, 'The writer says that a critic must have a religious perspective.' This is what he said about that writer, 'This is an excellent example of how stupid religious people are.'

Raghunathrao seems to have carried a marked prejudice for V.V. Shirvadkar and always made adverse comments against him. 'Atre says that *Vyjayanti* is an excellent translation, but the texture of the play has been ruined by changing the father of the hero in the original play to an uncle in the translated version. This is an unforgiveable error.' (September 1951, p. 57)

Here are some more comments:

It is a mystery to me why the Sahitya Sangh has given a contract, as it were, to Shri V. V. Shirvadkar for supplying a play every year. His really good play was just one – '*Doorche*

Divey' (Faraway Lamps), and that too was a translation.
(February 1951, page 164)

These highs and lows have not caused any damage to the
Sangh. From here on, instead of a few persons being allowed to
dominate, everybody should be given an opportunity. Whether
it is a translation or an original play, the decision seems to
be that if it is Shirvadkar, it has to be accepted. It is true that
Shirvadkar is a good writer, but he was the one who messed up
'Vyjayanti'. My opinion is that even the good writers should not
be pampered so much. (September 1951, p. 57)

On Agarkar

He had great faith in and regard for Agarkar's rationality.
Raghunathrao was a committed rationalist and he regretted
that rationalism was not propagated as much in Maharashtra as
it should have been. He also felt proud of being the only person
travelling down the path of rationalism and has repeated this
thought several times:

> Very few people have much idea of what Agarkar has actually
> done. Those who talk in an authoritative tone of voice have
> most of the time not understood Agarkar's thoughts. The
> Sahitya Sangh had invited Acharya Bhagwat to deliver a lecture
> on the fiftieth death anniversary of Agarkar. They couldn't have
> hit upon a worse person for this job because Agarkar was an
> atheist while this gentleman was a spiritualist. He therefore
> fitted Agarkar into the spiritualistic framework. For the death
> anniversary that just went by, Manohar Devdhar wrote an
> article for Loksatta. It doesn't appear that he too understood
> anything at all. This was what he wrote, 'His essays, perhaps,
> will not be as valuable as those of Tilak, Kelkar, Paranjape.' Why
> not? Agarkar's Marathi was more lucid than Tilak's. Kelkar,

of course, does not measure up to him in any aspect. While Paranjape's style has gained popularity, there is no reason to believe that it was better than Agarkar's. (July 1952, p. 23)

What this person has written at the end of the article is quite true: 'Will another reformer arrive who can bring a new vision to Agarkar's reformatory zeal and gain credit for supporting the development of society?' But what has been happening currently is easily noticeable for a person with his eyes open. But a person who considers bob-cut as a movement in the direction of tonsure, how can he see things?

In just one paragraph, Raghunathrao lambasted Acharya Bhagwat and Manohar Devdhar and expressed his displeasure that Devdhar could not see that after Agarkar, he, Raghunathrao, was continuing his rationalist tradition in Maharashtra.

Raghunathrao wrote in the May 1948 issue:

I had lately written that after Agarkar, I have been the one single person to propagate rationalism with enthusiasm. Some found this statement boastful, but at least I, for one, can't see anybody else . . . . Agarkar never chattered about asceticism. It is true that he was never after money, but that was because he gave more value to certain other things. (July 1945, p. 18)

It's quite certain that Raghunathrao had in his mind, even if unconsciously that like Agarkar, he too had never cared for money.

'Fifty years after Agarkar, there remains a scarcity of true rationalists.'[11]

On Local Trains

He wrote on and off about the changes that were happening in the suburban trains in Bombay and helps us to understand all the changes that have happened over the years. (August 1953, p. 58)

On Dr Ambedkar

He also made a few comments on Dr Ambedkar:

> I don't see any sense in the storm that has descended upon Dr Ambedkar for criticizing the government. But there isn't much truth in the praises he heaped upon the earlier government. The policy of the previous government was to cause as many rifts in the society as was possible; pampering the untouchables by granting them as many concessions as it could was quite helpful for its policy. Any sensible person would agree that caste-discrimination should be removed and the backward castes should be given concessions in the field of education and also be given additional rights in other matters. But Ambedkar doesn't like it. His policy seems to be to separate the untouchables altogether. Otherwise, during the occasion of the laying of the cornerstone in Delhi, why would he have said, "Do not go begging to the upper castes for the completion of this building"? It's clear from this that his estrangement with the caste Hindus remains firmly lodged in his mind, and till such time as this estrangement remains, whatever is done for their upliftment, they shall remain separate. Ambedkar is actually helping the untouchables to remain untouchable, but I don't see any benefit coming out of it. The earlier government had indulged them, but I shall be surprised if he expects the present government to do the same. (May 1951, p. 256)

Nobody has yet talked about the fact that even in his relationship with Ambedkar, his temperament of 'friend and foe alike' remained as before.

Endorsement of Article in Course Book

Gopal Ganesh Agarkar had written an article under the title 'Social Reform and Law' that had been included in a course-book of those times. Since it was impossible during those times for thoughts on sex to be included in an article, there was considerable criticism to it.

During a discussion that was being held in an issue of *Maharashtra* of Nagpur on the books prescribed for schools, a guardian wrote the following with reference to one of Prof. Pendse's books:

Prof. Pendse says, "A number of teachers have said that the passages in my book 'Marathi Abhyaas' are good." But a guardian says, "To give the readers some idea of the facts, I am giving here a sample sentence from the book 'Marathicha Abhyas': 'Till a girl gets to be at least 15-16 years of age and a boy gets to be 20-22 years of age, the two should not be allowed to get into a conjugal relationship'." (Page **57**). Similar such sentences can also be found in the passage 'Social Reform and Law'. Words like 'copulation', 'forced copulation', 'adultery', 'widowing a young daughter', 'a girl beginning her menstruation in her parents' house' and similar such terms can be found in the book. Therefore, no sensible teacher or lady-teacher would ever say that this book is fit for being a course book for 15-16-year-old boys and girls. As the members who decided the Marathi curriculum for High School for three years for 15-16-year-old boys and girls did so with their eyes closed (Who knows how this matter did not come to the attention of

Mrs. Mathurabai Dravid?), so also, perhaps, some teachers would have said the passages were good without having read the book. This lesson deals indirectly with the many hassles related to sexual intercourse. If Professor Saheb has introduced it in his book because he is in agreement with the propaganda that Prof. R. D. Karve has been running of introducing tender-aged boys and girls to sexology, then it is a different matter.

Raghunathrao read the articles that appeared in the daily *Maharashtra* on *Marathicha Abhyaas*, particularly the articles relating to Agarkar's piece, and the objections that the writers had made against them. Arguing in his usual style, he responded as follows:

This gentleman considers 15–16 as tender age and rightly asserts that information at such tender age on such obscene matters as menstruation is improper. Why should it matter that most girls begin to menstruate inside of 14 years? Parents who believe that their daughters should not understand the meaning of 'adultery' perhaps consider the word '*pativrata*' (faithful wife) as obscene too, because if the meaning of '*pativrata*' were to be searched out, the meaning of 'copulation' would also arrive. And then, how would 'forced copulation' not remain understood? Therefore, book writers should keep in mind that they should not write stories related Sita, Draupadi, and others; and if they do write, they should at least not call them '*pativrata*', because it is not possible to elaborate much on such obscene words. Teachers may somehow dodge the issue by defining '*pativrata*' as a woman who does not come into contact with a man who is not her husband; but that would mean that not a single woman would remain '*pativrata*' in a city like Bombay. If a woman wants to avoid contact with an unknown man, she will have to stay confined to her home. The number of such obscene words is so huge that book writers would have a terrible time.

It may be noted that Gopal Krishna Gokhale had married twice. Mama Warerkar had written a play called *Udate Paakharoo* (Flying Birds) and it had also begun being performed on stage. A character in a play had made reference to Gokhale's second marriage, which had triggered a controversy. While reviewing this play, Shakuntala Paranjape had made some statements which Raghunathrao had not liked. He took account of her review in the following words. It actually lays down Raghunathrao's entire position on biographical literature:

> Her (Shakuntalabai's) final complaint is this: "Was there any need for raking up the hassles of these useless people?" I was shocked at reading this. What does 'useless people' mean? Can only those people who have a status in society – extraordinary people like aristocrats and political personages – be the subject matter of plays? . . . These hassles and problems emerge when people's natural desires and expectations do not fit within the framework of society and the law. They can create a storm in the lives of even 'the most useless people'; and out of this storm, attractive stories are created. (February 1943, p. 148)

In short, this was the kind of writing that Raghunathrao did for *Samaaj-swaasthya* under the pseudonym 'Sharada'.

Reviews in *Samaaj-swaasthya*

As the editor of *Samaaj-swaasthya*, Raghunathrao gave a prominent place to literature, music, theatre and cinema. He translated articles from French and wrote on a variety of subjects including birth control, heterosexual relationships, responses to letters from the readers, the 'Sharada's Letters' column, editorials, apart from articles on literature, theatre, and cinema. Shakuntala Paranjape helped by taking over the responsibility of writing book reviews. But even so, Raghunathrao wrote more on literary works than reviews of plays and movies. He did several book reviews, especially those that were highbrow and did all the translations himself. Besides, he also wrote reviews of stories, novels, plays, biographies, etc. It is true, of course, that he did not go by the traditional definition of reviewing. Since *Samaaj-swaasthya* was basically a small magazine, it could allot only a few pages for reviews. Raghunathrao, therefore, took care writing short book reviews.

A good outcome of this policy was that such reviews would dispense with all the frills and get straight to the point. It may be said that he actually laid the foundation of a healthy tradition in Marathi. An excellent example is the review of a volume of selected poems of Vasant Hasabnis titled *Vashya Mhaney* (Vashya Says), and he writes, 'This writer seems to be a follower of Mardhekar and in trying to imitate him, he has littered his writing with English and with street-side words. However, not much poetry is to be found here.'

It can be seen that he was perceptive and made correct assessments of the material under study and reviewed it in précis. In the two-line review given above, he managed to cover so many things. First, he had a dislike for Mardhekar and his poetry; yet it was being imitated in Marathi. He admitted the fact and expressed his unhappiness over it. The free use of English words and abusive language did not escape the reviewer's eyes. He also remarked that poetic qualities were something quite different and they were not to be seen in Hasabnis's poems.

In direct contrast stands this assessment of *Smriti-Chitre*:

It is an excellent book that is extremely readable for young and old alike. Nobody could have dreamt that the journey of the author's life would be over within a few days of the publication of its third part. This extremely entertaining biography of the renowned Christian Marathi poet, the late Narayan Waman Tilak, has been written by his wife. Biographies are mostly quite boring, but this one is not. A biography of this kind cannot be found in Marathi.

Raghunathrao's specialty of using superlatives when talking about the writing of a favourite person or about some linguistic activity is quite evident here. This review is brief, and it gives justice to a literary piece. However, he sees *Smriti-Chitre* as a biography. The autobiographical writings of women in Marathi are generally the 'life spent with' kind; hence there is no expectation of a discussion on how they should be categorized. Raghunathrao's opinion on the biographical writings of those times finds expression here. Basically, he never held a favourable opinion of this category of writing.

Raghunathrao's framework of reviewing is quite evident in his writings. When reviewing a story, novel or play, he first discloses the plot and then comments on the language used. He evaluates the questions raised by the piece from the context of life in society and examines the experiences that could be gained from it. While doing this, he describes them as excellent on the one hand and pretentious on the other. Terms like 'constitution', 'biographical sketch', 'struggle', 'dialogue', 'atmosphere', 'representation' and 'stylistics' had slowly started entering into evaluation, but Raghunathrao does not use them much. Raghunathrao's memorization of Sanskrit was excellent; his study of poetics, particularly of meter and figures of speech, was noteworthy. He had mastery and deep interest in grammar and spelling and translation, of course, was his forte. As a result, we can see that when he reviewed a book, he examined it minutely in all these areas.

Raghunathrao had reviewed a variety of books ranging across various genres including short story collections like *Manaslahari* and *Faraari*; novels like *Garambicha Bapu, Haddpaar, Hindolyawar, Bhartichi Laat, Shaakuntal, Deccan Collejaat, Indu Kale, Sarala Bhole and Balutai Dhada Ghe*; collection of plays like *Andhalyaanchi Shaala, Tilaach tey Kalate, Janmaachey Sobati and Sanyaasaachey Lagn*; biographies like *Lokmanya Tilak Putraanchi Smruti Chitre, Mahatma Gandhi, Arvachin Panchkanya*; a collection of Mahatma Gandhi's letters titled *Vaatsalyaachi Prasad Deeksha*; a research volume titled *Ramayanavareel Prakash* a critical study titled *Kalechi Kshitijey* (The Horizons of Art), a collection of political essays called *Jagaachya Rajkaaranaat*, a book titled *Baatamidaar* that critically examines stories related to the world of journalism.

In the October 1927 issue of *Samaaj-swaasthya*, we see the following note under the title 'Saabhaar Poch' (Grateful Acknowledgement): 'A small book titled *Baaherkhyaaliche Dushparinaam* (The Bad Consequences of Philandering) written by Dr. K.B. Lele has arrived for review. Since the subject is important, it will be reviewed in detail in the next issue.'

The review got published in the next issue, as promised and was the first review published in *Samaaj-swaasthya*. It's not as if reviewing became a regular feature, but there is no doubt that it was an inseparable part of the fare. Even the very last issue of November 1953 carried a review of a book called *Tai Telin*. There was no rule that only books on certain topics would be reviewed. Records show that publishers like Haribhau Motey and author-editors N.C. Phadke would send books to *Samaaj-swaasthya* for reviewing.

Raghunathrao had spent his childhood in Konkan. There is no information on whether he returned there for a visit, but it seems unlikely. Hence, he would often get sentimental when he came across pictures of the Konkan region in novels. He has written very affectionately on S.N. Pendse's *Garambicha Bapu* and *Haddpaar*. 'I feel a special affinity for this region because it is very close to our own village,' he wrote in the early part of his review of *Haddpaar*. 'It is the story of an upright school-teacher and the writer's style is touching. It is rare to find novels of such high quality since the passing away of Haribhau Apte. You can't put it down once you start it, it is so gripping.' It was a glowing review, but here too, he pointed out the wrong use of the word 'netradeep' in the book. The use of unfamiliar words in regional novels create problems for readers; hence he recommended the use of footnotes or endnotes.

While reviewing *Garambicha Bapu*, he wrote, 'The author has displayed the courage of putting across some unfamiliar— but in my opinion very sensible—thoughts. He deserves to be congratulated for it.' He went on to compliment the writer for the picturization of the characters of Anna Khot, Bapu's mother, Bapu and Radha for their extra-marital relationship and for their inter-caste marriage respectively.

While reviewing N.C. Phadke's novel *Bhartichi Laat*, he said that the description of the brother–sister duo who sell guavas does not connect with the core of the novel, adding, 'The author does not seem to have a clear conception of the structure of the novel, because neither the village nor the siblings have any further relevance in the novel'. Writing on N.C. Phadke's *Shaakuntal*, he remarks, 'I, at least, have not been able to understand what is particularly attractive about the novel.' About W.M. Joshi's *Indu Kale, Sarala Bhole*, he wrote, 'This small novel certainly brings credit to the author and gains its attraction for being in the form of letters. It looks like a new way of storytelling in Marathi.' By saying this, he was welcoming a new writing technique. While reviewing Vibhavari Shirurkar's *Hindolyavar*, he wrote, 'Rarely before has this author shown the courage to give an honest picture of women's feelings, and these are prominently present

in both of her books.' While lauding Vibhavari, he also gave
directions on how it could have been possible for the behaviour
of the characters in the story to be in conformity with the law.
He examined Indira Sahasrabuddhe's *Balutai Dhada Ghe* by
the same parameter. He was very happy that women were now
coming forward to forcefully present women's problems; he
also stated his opinion that for social reform, 'plays and novels
present thoughts far more effectively than essays or lectures do'.

While writing on V.V. Joshi's collection of short stories
titled *Faraari*, he stated, 'I too am of the opinion that it is
not true that short stories can be written only along some
prescribed techniques. The only technique is that the story
be told effectively.' He also reviewed Krishnabai's collection
of short stories titled *Manaslahari*. He reviewed Kusumavati
Deshpande's *Deepkali* and wrote, 'This collection of emotional
stories and word-pictures is worth reading. Emotions can be
understood only through emotions. It's best that they are not
examined scientifically.'

While reviewing Madhav Julian's mini-epic *Nakulalankar*,
Raghunathrao did not miss the opportunity of identifying
faults. The other collection of poems he reviewed was Vasant
Hasabnis's *Vashya Mhaney*, this being the second of the two
works on poetry that he reviewed.

When he took N.C. Phadke's *Mahatma Gandhi* written for
children for review, he wrote, 'The opinions of great men gain
currency only on account of their greatness', and remarked on
the one-sided nature of the biography. *Vaatsalyaachi Prasaad
Deeksha* is a collection of Gandhi's letters written to his followers.
Raghunathrao exposed the hollowness of his thoughts on the
basis of what was expressed in the letters. On *Lokmanya Tilak
Putraanchi Smruti-chitre* he wrote, 'It carries the memories
of the author since he was six years of age, and they are very
endearing.' In his review of *Kalaachi Kshitije*, he expressed his

disagreement with Prabhakar Padhye on literary criticism by saying, 'Whatever the purpose of art, in my opinion, if it does not have beauty, it cannot be called art . . . . What does not give delight is hollow art. My definition of beauty is what gives joy to the eyes.'

By writing articles like 'Progressive Literature', 'Glaring Errors in the Staging of Plays' and 'The Marathi of Today', he expressed his opinion on those subjects. He defined progressive literature in the following words, 'All of humankind . . . should acquire contentment and any literature that helps achieve this aim is progressive literature'. Again, 'Any literature that helps in the removal of injustice will have to be called progressive.' For improving the quality of the plays that are staged, he gave important advice on (1) the selection of actors, (2) make-up, (3) costumes, (4) diction and a few other areas. He laid great emphasis on the use of proper Marathi words. He has delved deep into this subject in his article 'The Marathi of Today'.

Summary: The book reviews published in *Samaaj-swaasthya* have so far gone unnoticed. If we keep aside 'Vibhavari's Critics', nobody else has taken cognizance of his critical writings.

Those Who Wrote for *Samaaj-Swaasthya*

The first issue of *Samaaj-swaasthya* was twenty-four pages and was published in July 1927. There was shortage of newsprints during the Second World War, printing ink and other material were expensive, and advertisements were few and so, Raghunathrao could not increase the number of pages despite dearly wanting to do so. An important exception was the issue celebrating ten years of publication in 1937—it carried twice the number of pages, with a number of photographs. From then on, at least for the next three years, the January issue of *Samaaj-swaasthya* would be big. He would write for the issues in the form of independent and translated articles, correspondence with the readers, 'Sharada's Letters', book reviews and the series that were run periodically. He also wrote editorials, fillers and reviews of plays and movies. He checked the proofs, pasted address slips on the bundles sent to subscribers and took them to the post office—he mostly did all the chores himself. Malatibai, of course, would help him with some of these jobs. That is why there are loaded statements like Raghunathrao running *Samaaj-swaasthya* like a 'single-pole tent'.

However true this may be, it wasn't as if *Samaaj-swaasthya* published only Raghunathrao's articles; it would have been impossible for him to manage that. He naturally wanted many contributors for his magazine, but the writing must remain within the intellectual framework of the magazine. It was also his belief that the writers should be paid for their contribution, but he also knew that he did not have the resources for making such payments; hence, he would not reach out to them. The only exception to this resolve was the March 1943 'Two Wives' special issue, when he requested Shankarrao Kirloskar, B.V. Warerkar, Iravati Karve and others to write. Plenty of readers would advise him to increase the number of pages, improve the quality of printing and the paper, change the cover to colour and make it more attractive, continue the pictures of nude women— and bring in Indian women, start new columns, give space to plenty of writers, and many such constructive suggestions. He would always print these suggestions and respond to them to the extent possible.

All this led people to equate *Samaaj-swaasthya* with Raghunathrao and this equation stayed all through the twenty-six years and four months that the magazine remained in existence. Disciplined as he was, he had got the last issue ready just before he passed away and it was published posthumously. His younger brother Bhaskarrao added an editorial to it, announcing the closure of the magazine due to the passing away of its creator.

There were some writers, of course, who so loved the magazine that they wanted it to continue and would write for it without expecting any compensation. R.P. Paranjape, Dinkarrao and Bhaskarrao Karve, Shakuntala Paranjape and his friend Mama Warerkar wrote for the magazine. The writings of such different authors like Damodar Dharmanand Kosambi, Durga Bhagwat, Sahridaya, Mahad, Bhaskarrao Jadhav, Madhavrao Bagal, Dr K.B. Lele and Malatibai Karve were also published in the magazine.

Of the above, Shakuntala Paranjape, besides writing reviews and introductions to books, also wrote stories, poems and farces. The letters of Wrangler R.P. Paranjape and Bhaskarrao Karve have been published. Wrangler Paranjape provides information on a meeting of a Rationalists' Association held in Madras, while Bhaskarrao makes mention of a story related to a German philosopher. Sahridaya Mahad, was actually a Jain who had settled in Maharashtra. (His real name was Chunnilal Motiram Shet.) He published a number of his stories in *Samaaj-swaasthya*. The same applies to Madhavrao Bagal of Kolhapur, but his stories were flippant and subpar in terms of quality. They completely lacked the seriousness one notices in the thought-provoking articles of Raghunathrao on heterosexual relationships and were of the sensual and erotic kind. Bhaskarrao Jadhav was a reformer and thinker of those times and his research on the Ramayana created quite a stir. Setting aside the veil of religion, his research should have been critically examined. His research writings can be found in various magazines of those times, including *Samaaj-swaasthya*.

Dr K.B. Lele was a doctor and a number of his writings on health, hygiene, physiology, psychology, etc., were published in *Samaaj-swaasthya*. Raghunathrao was related to Dr Lele by marriage. Raghunathrao's wife Malatibai's sister was married to D.B. Lele, a headmaster in a Sangamner school; Dr K.B. Lele was his brother. Dr Lele was childless. When he had sent a book to the *Kesari*, its editor S.L. Karandikar had returned it with a letter that such books should not be sent to them. Enraged, Dr Lele had publicly challenged him, and this challenge was published in *Samaaj-swaasthya*. He ran a healthy correspondence with Raghunathrao, which was often published in his magazine.

Damodar Dharmananda Kosambi was a scholar like his father [Dharmananda Damodar Kosambi]. He too was in the habit of sending matter suitable for publication in *Samaaj-swaasthya*. In a way, he was inclined to help Raghunathrao with his writing. An article called 'Shuddh Santati' (Pure Progeny) was published in May 1936. Under the article was written a parenthetic note which read: 'The information provided in this article has been sent by Prof. Da. Dha. Kosambi.'

Mama Warerkar was Raghunathrao's closest friend. Raghunathrao published plenty of his stories in *Samaaj-swaasthya*' but it cannot be said that they were of great quality. (Mama has written for the magazine *Jeevan* too.) The Bombay Marathi Sahitya Sangh had started a periodical called *Sahitya* in 1947 with V.R. Dhavale as its editor and Mama had reviewed the *Sahitya's* special edition, for *Samaaj-swaasthya*.

A box item was published in the September 1939 issue of *Samaaj-swaasthya*:

> Stories are invited for publication in the issue of coming January. The best story in our judgment shall be given an award of Rs. 10/-. The story should not be more than ten pages in length. All the stories will become ours by right. They should be received latest by 1 December.—Editor

The January 1939 issue carried a note that read that a story titled 'Sanatani Mana' (The Ultra-orthodox Mind) written by Anant

Krishna Bapat was adjudged the award-winning story. The story was published in the issue too. Raghunathrao's readers, however, were not told how many stories were received after the advertisement for the award was printed; they also did not know the criteria on which the selection was made or who the judges were. There was just an editorial note that read: 'The characters in the stories published in this issue are imaginary, as they always are.' It is difficult to know why this note was published.

The February 1933 issue carried an article on the subject of 'Birth Control' written by Prof. B.V. Sawardekar. It carried a note right at the beginning that it was a summary of the lecture he had delivered at the Saraswat Brahman Sangh, Mazgaon, in April 1932.

Readers' Appeals That *Samaaj-swaasthya* Should Continue

From its very inception, *Samaaj-swaasthya* was run at a loss and Raghunathrao would repeatedly mention this fact. His relatives, friends, well-wishers and readers gave him as much financial help as they could. Although he had failed in attracting advertisements, there would be some coming from Anantrao Gadre and Appa Pendse. An overt and covert battle would be going on in Maharashtra during this period too between the ultra-orthodox and the reformers. The Ichalkaranjikar–Kirloskar controversy is very revealing in this regard. Looking at the changing circumstances, Shankarrao Kirloskar had been trying to transform the *Kirloskar* magazine. He had taken along renowned writers Phadke and Khandekar, and painters like Sirur and Jadhav, and begun to embellish *Kirloskar* right from the cover to the matter inside with new thoughts and ideas. Some liberal writers of the older generation like Divekar

Shastri had also joined this group. This magazine and its editor had, therefore, become extremely unpopular with the ultra-orthodox people. The Rani Saheb of Ichalkaranji had written an open letter against them in the *Kesari*. But on the strength of his native intelligence and the support of the progressive writers, Shankarrao Kirloskar had successfully pushed back the assault. Actually, Shankarrao was entirely supportive of Raghunathrao's rationalist ideology; in a sense they were co-religionists. Despite this, Raghunathrao had to fight the three cases for obscenity filed against him all by himself. The reason behind this was individual temperamental differences. The reformists needed the work that *Samaaj-swaasthya* was doing and some of them also helped Raghunathrao individually. But financial push and pull forces remained a permanent headache for him. Raghunath writes in the July 1952 issue:

> People often ask me, "Is your magazine still running?" I must tell them that instead of saying that it is running, we should say it is being made to run. If at least the expenditure of bringing out the magazine had been met, we could have said that it was running; but if after doing all the work starting from the editor right up to the peon without any salary, I still find the magazine suffering a yearly loss of about Rs. 800/-, how can I say that it is running?

We have noted that Raghunathrao himself did most of the writing or he translated matter from French to get his articles ready. Monotony, therefore, was bound to creep in. His readers would often write to him, 'The writings in your magazine are mostly done by the same hand. If the help of some other writers can be acquired, the interest level will rise. You may either use your personal connections or make a public appeal through your magazine.'

It is not as if Raghunath did not make these efforts because *Samaaj-swaasthya* was his baby. Whatever reputation it acquired, whatever form it took, the credit for it goes altogether to him. When cases were filed, he fought a lone battle. Hence there was no difference left between the character of the magazine and Raghunathrao's own character. The very existence of *Samaaj-swaasthya* depended upon the existence of Raghunathrao. Responding to a reader, he wrote, 'It [*Samaaj-swaasthya*] has become my addiction. The question is: how long will it last? When it's an addiction, a person stops bothering about the expenditure; which is why it goes on.'

There were some people who dearly wanted the magazine to go on even after Raghunathrao's death. They were few and scattered, but most importantly they were awash in rationalistic thoughts. They were galvanized with the desire to do something about the magazine and would individually write to Raghunathrao about it. In a letter published in the February 1948 issue, one R.L. Naik asked, 'Have you made arrangements for this priceless work you have begun to continue after you?' Raghunathrao responded:

This magazine is a very personal effort, and the chances of its continuing after my passing away are almost nonexistent. It's of course likely that someone may want to continue a magazine with this name, but because of the opinions I hold, I have to run this magazine at an annual loss of Rs. 500-600. Why would someone want to run it after I am gone?

Not satisfied with this response, a reader named Ravi wrote:

Mr. Naik's question – regarding the continuation of your work after you – needs to be considered. The number of intelligent people being so small, it is important to arrange for such magazines as 'Reason' and *Samaaj-swaasthya* to continue publishing. I believe that it is possible to form a group for this purpose. It seems to me that Manohar R. Limaye can learn the skill of clear thinking with some practice. I am a government servant, but I have made a firm decision to go for my pension at the age of 45. That is six years away, but that gives me time to get into a habit. Thus, if about ten such people can get together, they can take a monthly loss of Rs. 50/- each and make it possible for this work of spreading purposeful knowledge to continue unabated. In the same way, this lady (I assume) who writes under the pseudonym of 'Sharada' can also be of great help. It's all right if she doesn't presently desire to make acquaintance with other people, but she can certainly be asked to extend help if required at a future date. The issue of a group of disciples does not arise here because the history of the term 'disciple' has been bad till date; but you may help in the creation of facilities for studying the subjects related to *Samaaj-swaasthya*, giving guidance on these areas and so on. You are therefore requested to tell us your thoughts and publish a plan along these lines and see who step forward.

Raghunathrao responded to this letter as follows:

I am always ready to offer guidance. But people who have faith in rationalism and who are willing to apply it in all aspects of life are extremely few. Therefore, I do not have much hope that this magazine can run after I am gone. It's only lately that I have got acquainted with Mr. Limaye and it is true that his ideology matches with mine. He may, perhaps, be able to run it, but this cannot happen only on the strength of ideology; there has to be readiness to face a number of difficulties. I am not saying that he does not have this readiness, but simply that it is very difficult.

In the issue of February 1950, a reader had asked, 'Why is your magazine so small? Doesn't it have a market? Is it because you do not have business sense? Or is it because people are too puritanical?' Raghunathrao replied:

> Whatever my opinions are, those I write. I do not insist on being called intelligent. Whether I say it or don't, my intelligence does not increase or decrease. It remains what it is. Therefore, I don't care for it. Having business sense is not within somebody's control. Some people are professional, some are not. It is a fault of temperament and there is no remedy for it.

At another place he has written:

> The magazine is going to suffer a loss of some seven or eight hundred rupees this year. Making it bigger will only increase the losses and I am not ready to absorb it. One reason may be that it is too small for the price charged; another reason may be that people do not like my writing. It is true that losses happen because I do not understand business. If I had understood it, I would have written what people like to read; but if that was what I was required to write, I wouldn't have started this magazine at all. It is the same situation everywhere across the world for magazines that proselytize. Businessmen are ultra-orthodox and they do not give advertisements to such magazines, and magazines cannot survive without advertisements. If the magazine belongs to an organization, one can beg for meeting the expenditure. But since my magazine is personal, begging does not look nice. Even so, when help arrives, I do accept.

The above statements show Raghunathrao was unwavering in
his opinions and unwilling to deviate from his stance. Another
point to notice is that except for Mama Warerkar, he did not
call anybody 'nice'. He always laid bare the faults that he saw
in the people around him. Sudhakar Ranade had asked him the
question, 'You easily notice people's faults. Is that a virtue?' He
had responded: 'It's quite true that I notice people's faults quite
fast. But what can I do about it? It may be a fault, but that fault
is in my nature. I cannot change it at will.'

Thus, there were some people who liked the rationalistic
thoughts that Raghunathrao expressed in *Samaaj-swaasthya*
for the progress of society. They seriously believed that the
magazine should continue even after Raghunathrao was no
more. But Raghunathrao had accepted that the magazine was
personal in nature. He was subtly arrogant that he not only
expressed rationalistic thoughts through its medium, but
also conducted himself in a manner that he thought right,
irrespective of its impact upon others. He had therefore very
clearly declared that he would bear losses if he had to, but would
continue bringing out the magazine till as long as he lived and
after him the magazine would probably die. It was thus clear
that although readers like R.L. Naik, Ravi and Limaye, who were
driven by a passion for rationality, were willing to take over the
responsibility of *Samaaj-swaasthya*, Raghunathrao was not
willing to give it over to them.

Shakuntala Paranjape wrote:

> Till such time as the call of Fate arrived, Appa held the single-
> pole tent of *Samaaj-swaasthya* up with great intrepidity.
> After his passing away, a number of people got after me to
> run the magazine, but I know my strength. I did not want
> to make a mess of the comet that was R. D. Karve's *Samaaj-
> swaasthya*.

Bhaskarrao Karve wrote in the last issue:

Looking at the totality of the picture, there is no harm in saying that the incarnation work of *Samaaj-swaasthya* was to a fair degree successful. Therefore, if *Samaaj-swaasthya* has to close down, there is no reason for being grieved about it. If one of Karve's disciples or perhaps an organization steps forward to publish the magazine or his books, that would be welcome. But it is not at all unnatural that a personalized institution like *Samaaj-swaasthya* should move on with its creator. It, however, seems clear that the torch of rationalism that Shri Karve lit will turn brighter as time passes and the health of the society shall go on improving.

Such, therefore, were the efforts launched to keep *Samaaj-swaasthya* going after the passing away of Raghunathrao. But because of the strongly logical position that the Raghunathrao had taken, the magazine had no choice but to shut.

6

Cases and Controversies

Temperament That Attracted Problems

Raghunathrao wrote a ten-page long article titled 'The Question of Adultery' in the September 1931 issue of *Samaaj-swaasthya*. His argument in the article went like this: in our culture, marriage is seen as a sacred institution. The expectation is that a married couple should have a physical relationship with each other, satisfy their sexual urges and thus gain the joy of conjugality. However, there is no assurance of mutual love existing between husband and wife; therefore, there is no assurance of carnal desires being satisfied as per each other's wishes. Also, at some places there can be deviation in sexual preference; there is nothing wrong with that. If a man and a woman get into sexual conjugation with mutual consent, love is present there. The sensual pleasure they derive out of it is of another kind altogether.

That was the reason why he always championed free love. Our great epics like the Ramayana and the Mahabharata keep emphasizing the concept of *pativrata*, that is the faithfulness of the wife towards her husband, yet Lord Krishna enjoys countless *gopis* (group of cowherd women who are devoted to Krishna); Kunti has relationships with the gods of her choice; Bhima has a son from Hidimba; Arjun has marriages in every state he visits;

when Draupadi hears that Karna is Kunti's son out of wedlock, she realizes that Karna desired her. Raghunathrao therefore feels that all of these stories champion freedom of sexual conjugation.

Raghunathrao presented his thesis extremely logically and with gravitas. Even so, with this article as the ostensible reason, a case was filed against *Samaaj-swaasthya*—and by extension, against Raghunathrao—for obscenity. The reasons behind this episode must be examined

The first reason is that although Raghunathrao was educated in Poona, he was not at all influenced by the ultra-orthodox attitude of the city. On the contrary, he was far more influenced by the free and progressive attitude that he found in Bombay. Later, when he went to Paris, he became still more rationalistic. Secondly, from 1921 onwards, he steadily criticized the ultra-orthodox and backward Poonaites, particularly Ahitagni Rajwade.[1] He felt that these ultra-orthodox from Poona who spun all kinds of stories with regard to ancient culture needed to be criticized. He said:

As if the prattle of these Brahmins neutralizes the impiety of copulation! . . . If people can abandon the insane religious notion that conjugation is a sin and that sanction for it can be obtained only through the prattle of the Brahmins, it will benefit all and harm none.'

He added, 'In the same way, who except the religious people can commit the foolishness of holding on to a notion that benefits nobody, and abandoning which everybody gains, except the Brahmins?'

It was, therefore, no surprise that the Poona Brahmins were frothing and seething at these inflammatory statements. They tried relentlessly to bring pressure upon the government of those times and finally succeeded in their efforts. It is quite evident that more than the thoughts he was airing in his writings, it was the manner in which he had been flaying the Brahmins of Poona that had brought their ire crashing down upon his head.

There is, of course, no reason to believe that all this animosity erupted unexpectedly. The cold war between Raghunathrao and the Poona group had been going on since much earlier. Drawing from a Bombay journal called *Mauj*, he informed his readers in an issue after July 1931, 'An organization named Samaajshastra-Charcha-Mandal (Sociology Discussion Club) has been started in Pune to propagate against my thoughts.'

A letter was published later and undersigned by C.S. Bhagwat, which went as follows:

Dear Editor Saheb,

Even though I am not a subscriber of *Samaaj-swaasthya*, I buy it and read it regularly every month. Yesterday I read some criticism on you and your magazine in the *Kesari* under the heading 'Brahmin Vrind Sabha'. I am sending you a cutting of the matter so that you may be able to respond to it in your issue of this month.

I am sure you will disregard the gatherings and criticisms of such Brahmins and continue with the extremely useful and creditable social service that you have been doing. Actually, these resolutions and criticisms only bring publicity for your work and your magazine; people may read it out of curiosity, if for nothing else. It's four years since your magazine began and I cannot understand why these guardians of religion have suddenly woken up to it now. In short, I may say that their gluttonous consumption of food has caused all the blood in their system to gather around the stomach and intestines and their brains have begun to rot. That is, perhaps, why they see obscenity and immorality in *Samaaj-swaasthya*. They have the same calibre as a bullock. Once yoked, a bullock moves round and round in an oil press, while these Brahmins hold their tuft of hair and keep chanting Sanskrit books. Both of them have the same amount of intelligence.

Till as long as such hypocritical, selfish and mischievous protectors of religion exist in society, the health of the society will be difficult to achieve. The surprising thing is that when someone makes an effort at expressing his independent but intellectually agreeable opinion and tries to establish social health, these hypocrites are always itching to pounce upon such efforts. Who can be more damaging to the society than these mischief-makers?

I am certain that all the subscribers of 'Samaaj-swaasthya' will stand up against the resolution of these Brahmins. May your efforts always be met with success and may stay forever.

The May 1948 issue of *Samaaj-swaasthya* carries this note: 'Some troublemakers of Pune filed a case under the Obscenity Law.' The language suggests that it was written by Raghunathrao himself and there was an editorial note right below this item:

There is nothing in the resolution of the '*Brahmin Vrind*' that deserves a response. The Brahmin caste is no different from bedbugs and lice. No benefit comes to the society from them, only bother. If the government gives importance to this insane resolution, it will endorse the complaints of some that this government cannot tolerate any kind of progress in the country, what else?

He later wrote an article titled 'Akaleche Khandak' (The Pit of Intelligence) in which he spewed venom on the ultra-orthodox. The inflammatory language used is worth noting:

Since these old fogies do not have any answer to our argument, they are plotting to bring me down through mouthing abuses and applying to the government for getting my magazine closed. They have thus announced at a number

of places about the bankruptcy of their intelligence. There
is no doubt that my adversaries own powerful weapons.
Tradition has always exercised a strong hold on the common
people. They never have the courage to bring about change
in their behavioural pattern and people are always lazy about
accepting new ideas.

Raghunathrao considered his opponents stupid and would keep
advising them on what they should be doing. That was exactly
what he was doing in 'Akaleche Khandak' and it cannot be
denied that it did not go down well with them. 'You consider us
stupid, do you?' they may have thought. 'You want to dispense
advice to us? Well, all right, you watch out now. Watch how we
take your advice and drag you to court on charges of obscenity.'

The advice Raghunathrao was dispensing to his opponents
goes like this:

> The one satisfying thing here is that my opponents are
> stupid. Otherwise, they would have got into arguments with
> me to defeat me. They would not have resorted to the law.
> Well, finally using the big weapon of the law against me,
> falsely accusing me of obscenity and getting me punished! It
> may perhaps happen because there is no proper definition in
> law of the word 'obscenity', but the question that remains is:
> whether they can find a stupid enough magistrate.

It would not be surprising if the opponents would, perhaps,
have shown this very article to the judge and tried to gain his
sympathy by telling him, 'Let's keep aside the fact that he calls
us foolish; but it is outright insolence that he uses the adjective
"stupid" for the honourable judges of the judicial system!'

The First Case

The people of Poona were victorious. Police Inspector Acharekar marched up Raghunathrao's house on 19 December 1931 and arrested him. He also confiscated copies of the issue that carried the article 'Vyabhichaaraacha Prashn' for which he had been accused of obscenity. The *Vasundhara* issue of 18 June 1932 carried the following news on this subject , 'The High Court has dismissed the appeal that Prof. R.D. Karve, editor of *Samaaj-swaasthya* had made against the penalty of Rs. 100/- that was imposed upon him for the article *Vyabhichaaraacha Prashn*.'

This obviously means that the judgement in the case against him would have been delivered much before 18 June 1932. The case was heard by Justice Indravadan Mehta. Raghunathrao's lawyer was S.E. Shete who had also cross-examined Ahitagni Rajwade and Vishwanath Daware. Riyaasatkaar G.S. Sardesai had stood witness for Raghunathrao. Raghunathrao had presented his own case.

The Second Case

Inspector Acharekar arrested Raghunathrao again on 8 February 1934, for the same offence. On the face of it, however, the responses given by Raghunathrao in the correspondence published in the Gujarati issue of *Samaaj-swaasthya* were presented. Babasaheb Ambedkar and his associate Asaikar fought this case for Raghunathrao. It was again Indravadan Mehta who delivered the judgement and imposed a penalty of Rs. 200.

This is what Raghunathrao has written in this matter:

On the accusation that letters number three, four and twelve of the correspondence published in the December 1933 issue of the Gujarati *Samaaj-swaasthya* were obscene, Inspector Acharekar arrested me as the editor and K. N. Nimkar as the printer and publisher at nine in the morning of February 8. They confiscated some papers, took us to the Lamington Road Police Station and released us on a bail of Rs. 200/- each.

Along with Malatibai, Shakuntala Paranjape and a few other people, K.N. Nimkar helped Raghunathrao. He was a versatile person in the world of journalism of those times. 'We ourselves never came out with a Gujarati edition,' Raghunathrao informs. 'It was done by another person with our permission. He would have closed it after suffering losses.'

Nimkar had an important and valuable role to play in the publication of the Gujarati edition. The concerned persons found obscenity in some matter in the correspondence in this Gujarati edition and filed a case against Raghunathrao. Nimkar was also singed in the bargain. This event was covered in the book *Vrittapatraancha Itihaas* (The History of Newspapers) in the following words:

K. N. Nimkar got associated with the world of newspapers in another unusual manner. He worked as distributor of R. D. Karve's magazine *Samaaj-swaasthya*. During 1933, he also bore the financial responsibility of bringing out the Gujarati edition of *Samaaj-swaasthya*. An obscenity case was filed against this edition too, for which he had to pay a penalty of Rs. 100/-.

The following extract is taken from the book *Nimaale Shabd Hey Ata . . . Hmm, Mee Nimkar, Aata Baatami Ghya*:

He came into contact with the world of newspapers in an extremely unusual manner. It was his job to distribute the late R.D. Karve's magazine *Samaaj-swaasthya* in the town because of which he had close relations with a number of newspaper agents. He was very lax in the matter of recovering money. He not only sold *Samaaj-swaasthya*, but also brought out the Gujarati edition of the magazine. A Maharashtrian gentleman who worked for the Gujarati newspaper *Saanj* helped him in this . . . . A case for the offence of obscenity was filed against the late R. D. Karve for which he was duly penalized. Nimkar was also a co-accused in the case and he too was penalized. As a seller of *Samaaj-swaasthya*, he would also sell material for birth control . . . .

The Third Case

Samaaj-swaasthya used to carry an advertisement for a book titled *Kaam-Kala* (The Art of Lovemaking). In April 1939 he was again arrested for the advertisement that had appeared in the September 1938 issue. The term '*apraakritik sambhog*' (unnatural sex) was considered objectionable there. Vasantrao Karnik was Raghunathrao's lawyer for this case. Mr Bavarekar pronounced the judgement on this case on 24 June 1940. This time, Raghunathrao presented his arguments himself. The court, however, rejected his arguments but he was given the benefit of doubt and released. Thus, he was made to stand in a court of law as an accused.

Yet, it cannot be said that Raghunathrao dragged these controversies upon himself only on account of his argumentative nature. The truth is that society is never ready to quickly accept progressive ideas and Raghunathrao suffered its consequences.

Writings and Thoughts on Obscenity

Raghunathrao was convinced that the magistrate simply indulged his whim and penalized him. As a result, he became permanently indisposed against magistrates and officials. He has recorded extremely bitter opinions in a particularly outspoken manner in 'Ashleeltechya Kaayadyaacha Moorkhapanaa' (The Stupidity of the Law on Obscenity) (*Mauj*, Diwali, 1931), and 'Satya-Vaangmayaateel Nirbandh' (Restrictions on Literature of Truth) (*Jyotsna*, November 1937), as also in what he wrote for *Samaaj-swaasthya*:

> This definition arises in each case related to obscenity. In fact, even after taking this definition, penalizing or not penalizing depends upon the degree of stupidity of the judge. With regard to this law, till date, a number of judges have immortalized their names for their stupidity. Power very often rests in the hands of stupid people, because of which they can behave with any amount of arrogance. The word 'obscene' exists in law; but, till such time as its meaning is decided, this law does not make any clear sense; it can hence be used to mean whatever one wants it to mean. In actual practice, judges find no difficulty in applying a law that does not have meaning. It is true that when a law is new, the responsibility of extracting meaning from it rests with them; but there is nobody to ask them why they gave it a particular meaning. Therefore, whatever they pronounce becomes a precedent. The common practice of herd mentality exists in the judicial system too in that when some smart judge gives the law a certain meaning, all the later judges give the same judgement as the earlier one without applying their minds to it. If there is no pressure working upon them, they consider this policy safer than applying their own minds.

This is a statement of facts, for sure, but it is also a scathing reaction in stentorian words against the injustice done to him. Anybody would know that this piece was written from the context of a hurtful experience. Towards the end of the article, he emphasizes on the need for a serious effort at training, enlightening magistrates. He writes:

> The world bodies that aim to reform man-woman relationship should write articles in various fora and strive as much as they can to get the laws changed in this matter, or at least train the magistrates on this subject. Results can arrive only when all progressive people lend their support here.

Raghunathrao realized that in the matter of obscenity, there was insufficient substance in the prevalent laws and he flung himself body and soul to rectify matters. He had also fielded a renowned lawyer like Dr Bhimrao Ramji Ambedkar in the struggle, but his lot in the end was punishment and defamation. He was now convinced that since the magistrate enjoyed complete freedom, he could deliver judgements according to his whim. Raghunathrao happened to read an article titled 'Vaangmaya-Kshetraateel Niyantrak-Sansthechi Atyaavashyakta' (Dire Need for a Controlling Institution in the Field of Literature) written by Shridhar Vyankatesh Ketkar and published in the weekly *Pratibha* on 16 February 1934. On his own initiative, he wrote the following letter to the editor:

> A discussion has been in progress in your magazine on the possibility of establishing a controlling institution in the field of literature. It is true that you haven't sought my opinion, but I do have a practical suggestion that I am now daring to write about.
>
> It is a general experience that the judgments delivered by government courts and arbitration courts are not always unbiased. However high the calibre of the people who perform this duty, they are bound to be influenced at least a little bit by personal acquaintances and nepotism. As far as obscenity is concerned, it is entirely a personal opinion

and courts can be of no use here. Dr. Ketkar is ready to
tweak Kalidasa's ears for obscenity. Someone will certainly
emerge who will tweak Dr. Ketkar's ears. But untruth is an
altogether different matter. France has an extremely sensible
law in this regard; if we can adopt that law, this question
can be resolved. The law requires that if a person feels that
some statement about him in any write-up is false, he should
send in writing whatever he has to say to the editor. The
editor is compelled by law to print the person's response or
clarification at the exact place where the original piece had
been printed. If the editor does not do so, an appeal can be
filed against him. Obviously, therefore, the editor is bound
by law to print the person's response, giving the reader the
opportunity of reading both sides; thus, there can be no
complaint left on either side. Because of the presence of this
law, this country has never had cases filed for defamation
on account of something appearing in the press. Books, of
course, are a different thing, but this kind of a law will help
matters a long way. Since there is nothing political about
this, the government will not have any objection if such a bill
is presented in the Council.

Dr Ketkar responded to the article in the following words: 'It
can be said that a positive outcome of this controversy is the
suggestion Prof. Karve has made that is different from my
own. Many strategies can be tried for meeting a need. In this
respect, Prof. Karve's suggestion is important and acceptable.'
He, however, added that it was not something that could be
implemented immediately. All said and done, there is little
doubt that a law that had caused him so much anguish and the
magistrate who was instrumental in imposing it upon him, left
Raghunathrao permanently bitter.

Not limiting himself to *Samaaj-swaasthya*, he wrote with abandon wherever he found the opportunity to do so. He wrote:

In my opinion, there is nothing called obscenity. Those who think that it is something should answer the following questions:

1. Why has nobody come up with a comprehensive definition of obscenity?
2. When all other animals happily roam naked on the street and nobody calls them obscene, why, then, is the human body alone obscene? Is this indicative of the superiority of humans?
3. Ordinarily, only those parts of the human body that are not allowed by tradition to be displayed are considered as obscene. A lady from the north of India has lately written that women have started roaming around bare-headed. In different times and regions, different parts of the body have been permitted for display in less or more proportions, including total nakedness. Therefore, why should only some specific parts be considered as obscene?
4. Even so, it appears that people consider the reproductive organs of men and women, women's breasts, the common names of sexual organs and sexual intercourse as obscene. The activity that has brought us into being, the organs that have made it possible and the breasts that provide nourishment—how can all these be considered obscene?
5. Many people consider 'vulgar' as 'obscene'. This only means that the terms that ordinary people can understand are obscene, while those that only the educated can understand are not obscene. Why should it be so?

6. If we think only of opinions, if the opinion that 'adultery may be committed' is obscene, then the opinion that 'it should not be committed' should also be obscene, because both deal with the same thing.

7. If this is not so, which of them is obscene and which is not? Should we then agree that opinions that the ultra-orthodox and the magistrates do not like are obscene?

The subject of obscenity was taken up for discussion in the 1937 Sahitya Sammelan and Madhavrao Patwardhan supported it (the concept of obscenity). Referring to Madhavrao's speech, Raghunathrao took him to task and stated:

He says that there was a woman with a letter in her hand alone in a room in a state of trance. Since she was alone, she had no reason to worry about where her *pallu* lay. In fact, her unconcern about her clothes would underline the state of her trance. Whatever the state of affairs, if he has to say that the showing of bare breasts is obscene, then it's a different matter. But, he would then find obscenity even in the picture of a woman in wet clothes that the chairman liked. How can the body showing through wet clothes be considered decent and an unclothed body be considered as obscene? From the perspective of art, the only question to ask is whether there is any inappropriateness, whether what is shown does not match with the situation that is to be depicted.

Such arguments of Raghunathrao would leave adversaries speechless.

Raghunathrao's Love for Arguments

Raghunathrao called himself a rationalist and conducted himself accordingly. He would launch a merciless attack, uncaring of anybody, on anything that did not agree with reason. For instance, when Dr Babasaheb Ambedkar was his lawyer for the second case, someone asked him his opinion on Dr Ambedkar's change of religion. He responded:

> Ordinarily, I consider a person who changes his religion as either senseless or fraudulent. Changing one's religion for the purpose of getting a job or for some other advantage is a fraudulent act, while doing so in the belief that the other religion is better is senselessness, because all religions contain insane fabrications in large quantities. Therefore, there is no point in leaving one and getting into the other. The matter of the untouchables, however, is different. The fault here lies with the untouchables. Even if we say that the Hindu religion is the best, considering a Hindu untouchable as untouchable while not considering a Musalman as untouchable is foolishness and injustice. Even so, instead of changing religion, it would have been better simply to abandon Hinduism. But there is no legal way of doing so.

Shakuntala Paranjape once declared that 'if someone has to wage a word-battle, it should be Appa.' Although by inclination he was extremely reticent, she was referring to how outspoken, how pungent, how incisive Raghunathrao was in his writings. He doesn't seem to have quarreled with anybody for personal reasons. His entire emphasis was on principles; when somebody fell into his clutches, he would never hesitate to launch a sharp assault on him with his pen. While M.G. Rangnekar was the editor of *Tutaari*, he had run a series under the title 'Maazhya Valdilaanbaddal Malaa Kai Vaatate' (What I Think About My Father). Raghunathrao had not fought shy of writing on Anna in exactly the same manner. He held Anna responsible for unfairly sacrificing Raghunath's prospects for the sake of upholding his own prestige at Fergusson. Whatever arguments that Raghunathrao had, he had them with the editors of various periodicals, writers, associates and readers. Shankarrao Kirloskar, Prabhakar Padhye, Malati Tendulkar and Manoramabai Sabade were editors, while N.C. Phadke, S.K. Ksheersaagar, Dr S.D. Pendse, M.D. Altekar and Appa Pendse were writers; some also journalists.

Mahatma Gandhi

Mahatma Gandhi leads the list of people whom Raghunathrao criticized all his life. On his return from South Africa, Gandhiji visited Pune and met Gopal Krishna Gokhale who publicly took him to be his political guru. Gokhale had been Raghunathrao's Mathematics teacher in Fergusson College and Raghunathrao had held him in great esteem. Despite being disciples in different areas of the same guru, they had sharp differences with each other in the matter of birth control. Raghunathrao understood the importance of this subject from 1901 onwards and had gathered deep knowledge on it over a long period. He read about the subject in progressive western scientific research and was aware of the problem of sexually transmitted diseases in India. Most importantly, he saw it from the rational perspective of practical scientific principles.

From 1920 onwards, after Lokmanya Tilak passed away, Gandhiji became the fastest evolving personality on the Indian political scene. Every word he uttered began gaining worth. He was also aware that the steadily increasing population was a major problem facing the country. However, his thoughts and Raghunathrao's thoughts on birth control were hugely different. Raghunathrao believed that there was need for a strategy that was easy for ordinary people to understand and practice. He had even written to Gandhiji on this matter. In an article he published outside *Samaaj-swaasthya*, he has written:

Gandhi once wrote in his magazine 'Young India' that birth control is desirable; however, it should be done through self-control. Recommending a method for an ordinary individual that he himself has not been able to apply is something that can only suit Gandhi. Some people responded to Gandhi, among whom I was one. The others had written that self-control was an excellent remedy, but if that was not possible, there should be no objection to the use of artificial means. I, however, had written that excessive self-control could only cause harm; people who adopted this method of birth control would barely have five or six opportunities for sexual intercourse in their life; therefore, it would be harmful even for those for whom it was possible.

Gandhiji's opinions on birth control were whimsical. Raghunathrao writes, 'In Gandhiji's opinion, an excellent way of birth control was for women not allowing their husbands near them. He had once advised people not to go for procreation till such time as India gained independence.'

Raghunathrao criticized Gandhiji frequently. He would read his articles in *Young India* and *Harijan* regularly; if he found any note on an event/incident that he needed to grapple with, he would do it either directly or obliquely. See, for instance, his response to an event published in Gandhiji's *Navajeevan*:

Mahatma Gandhi has published certain happenings that occurred in his *aashram*. What emerges from one of them is that a widow lived there three years ago. Mahatmaji recently realized that she was having a relationship with a young man there. This is the outcome of imposing celibacy upon everybody in the *aashram*.

When a reader commented on Raghunathrao's adverse reactions to Gandhiji's opinion, he responded to the reader as follows, 'It's not as if I did not know about Gandhiji when I read his Gujarati autobiography. I would, of course, read about him in the newspapers as and when they appeared. My opinions on Gandhi, therefore, are not based upon misunderstandings.'[2]

Margaret Sanger, the lady who had opened the first clinic for birth control in America had visited India in 1936. She had met Gandhiji and after fully hearing out Gandhiji's opinion on birth control, had expressed her strong opposition to it. Raghunathrao had published the conversation between the two in *Samaaj-swaasthya*. Using excerpts from Gandhiji's autobiography, Raghunathrao had shown the inconsistency that existed between the picture that Gandhi had given of his sex life in his autobiography and the advice he gave to others on this subject. He had also written a letter and sent it to the editor of the *Bombay Chronicle* for publication. But since the letter was scrutinizing Gandhiji's opinion, the editor of the newspaper could not gather the courage to publish it. Raghunathrao had, however, made it available to his own readers.

Gandhiji's opinion that 'people should have sexual intercourse only for the purpose of procreation and at all other times they should exercise self-control' was not in consonance with nature. As Gandhiji had written in his biography, he could not rein in his sexual urge in spite of his father being at the point of death. In Raghunathrao's opinion, for the same Gandhiji to recommend that others should suppress their urge was crazy. Raghunathrao himself believed that a far better option was that people should go ahead and satisfy their sexual urge, but make use of artificial devices so as to prevent child birth. He believed that the use of these artificial devices should be propagated on a large scale; that there was dire need, at least in India, for people to be educated extensively on this matter. The following is the manner in which he expressed his views on Gandhiji's position:

The doltish statements that have been made in the article in the *Harijan* are based upon the principle that as per Gandhiji's imaginary physiology, the best way of maintaining good health is to not use certain parts of the body. There are people who have grown up with the traditional understanding that certain parts of the body are dirty; leave alone using them, even thinking about them is a cardinal sin; these people have no strength to think independently on these matters; Gandhiji is one among such people. God may barely be forgiven for arranging for procreation among non-human animals through the use of such dirty organs. But it is Gandhi's honest opinion that arranging for the same procreation system for human beings—ranging from the vilest of human beings to straight up to those as virtuous as Gandhi himself—is an error for which God cannot be forgiven. It is lucky for God that He cannot be punished, otherwise Gandhiji would have given Him severe chastisement. Why would it have been impossible for the All-Powerful God to arrange for procreation without any physical contact whatsoever, merely through contemplation? At least for the higher class of people? But obviously, the Fellow had no sense of discretion. Well, at least, in His chosen arrangement, he could have arranged for no contentment to arrive from sexual interaction! People like Gandhiji would have collected the merit of doing a dirty, joyless act only out of a sense of duty to procreate. Or, perhaps, after one has had four children (as Gandhi found acceptable), a revulsion could have been created for sexual intercourse! Seen in totality, therefore, God has no sense at all; otherwise, since He did not understand things Himself, he could have consulted Gandhiji.

So it was that Raghunathrao mounted relentless assault on Gandhiji's ideas on birth control. That era belonged to Gandhiji and criticizing him needed an inordinate amount of courage.

People who were totally infatuated by Gandhi were countless and Raghunathrao had drawn the ire of some of them upon himself. One of them wrote to him, 'Even if you blow the horn against Gandhiji across multiple births, his greatness will not reduce even by a mite. Don't you feel ashamed at making such a brainless accusation that Gandhiji has caused harm to Hindustan?'

Responding to this letter, Raghunathrao wrote, 'I have not used the singular person when talking about Gandhi.' Raghunathrao's culture was of an altogether different kind.

Dr K.B. Lele

Rangu, one of Malatibai's sisters, was married to Shri D.B. Lele, headmaster of a high school at Sangamner. There is a one-line mention of this gentleman in Anna's *Aatmavritt*. Raghunathrao's younger brother, Bhaskarrao, informed Prof. M.V. Dhond that D.B. had a brother, Dr K.B. Lele, who wrote several articles for *Samaaj-swaasthya*, 'some supportive of Appa, plenty of them adverse'. Dr Lele has also written a number of books on various subjects. His favourite subject was 'magic'. He also loved writing poems in English. In a letter, he wrote that he knew the Karve family from 1902 onwards.

Raghunathrao was a rationalist and was altogether committed to science. He, therefore, had no place for superstitions, religious concepts, rites and rituals. His entire emphasis was on the rationalistic way of thinking. Consequently, he would come down strongly on gods and goddesses and incarnations. Dr K.B. Lele's ideas were in direct contrast to Raghunathrao's and there was a wide gap between their thoughts. Once this is kept in mind, it is easy to understand why he wrote against Raghunathrao. But Raghunathrao deserves credit and respect for printing Dr

Lele's thoughts in *Samaaj-swaasthya* and responding to them. A lot of intellectual arguments took place between the two in *Samaaj-swaasthya*.

Dr Lele was an opponent of Raghunathrao's concepts. While this was largely true, it is not the complete picture. While he bitterly opposed some of Raghunathrao's thoughts, he was also a vocal admirer of some of his qualities. He, therefore, combined in himself the roles of being both his opponent and his admirer, thus revealing the unusual chemistry of his personality.

Dr Lele wrote an article titled 'Mulaanchya Menduchey Vikaar' (Brain Deformities among Children) and sent it for publication in *Samaaj-swaasthya*. After it was published, he sent the following letter to Raghunathrao in which he praised his commitment, appraised him with a balanced and reasonable eye, and yet recorded his disagreements:

Despite having known you only by word of mouth, when I got in hand the first issue (of the first year), I rushed to you with great excitement. I have met you numerous times after that and enquired about 'Swaasthya' and your own health. There is no aspect of formality here. I do not approve of the manner in which you present your subject. We have had plenty of fisticuffs on this topic and yet never allowed rancour to creep in between us. I shall never ever let go of an editor of this kind .... *Samaaj-swaasthya* has faced plenty of crises till date, but never wavered from its chosen path. This is commitment, even if for a wrong cause, and this is what I have sought.

Raghunathrao not only published the above letter in his magazine, but also gave a brief response to it in a single sentence: 'I am deeply grateful for your sympathy.'

Dr Lele later wrote an article titled 'Mulaanchey Maansik Dosh' (Mental Illness Among Children) in which he discussed the values inculcated in children, the harm they may cause and the consequences they may have on the child's personality during later life. In paragraph seven of the article, he took Raghunath's own personality for analysis, which makes for interesting reading:

> Deficiency in adjusting to circumstances is a ponderous term, but its meaning is quite clear. These children are intelligent, their memory is good too, but a big fault in them is that they do not have the ability to assess circumstances and modify their response accordingly. Hence their personalities are unsuccessful both for their own selves and for society. For example, I have known a professor of Mathematics who has abandoned everything and given himself over to sexology. Not stopping at that, he insists that the adultery (as seen from the perspective of people here) that is prevalent in France should apply to India too under the present circumstances.

Under this article is a note with the subtitle 'My Apologies and Appeal for Forgiveness' which reads, 'I express my gratitude to the editor of *Samaaj-swaasthya* for having printed this unpleasant but beneficial subject.' Below is a note from the editor that reads, 'Readers will understand that I am not in agreement with the doctor's views.'

The next issue of the magazine carried a letter by Dr Lele in the first half of which he expresses his admiration for Raghunathrao and in the latter half he records his adverse opinion on Raghunathrao's article 'Kaarya Saadhale' (Work Accomplished):

> No praise is enough for the manner in which you print articles against your viewpoints. What lesson does your article *'Kaarya Saadhale'* teach our young girls? That they

should spurn the concern of their society and their parents, deceive them and continue with their love episodes, right? This goal will help bring about reform in society and in the country, for sure!

Raghunathrao responded to this letter, with which the doctor was not satisfied. He wrote back and from the blunt language of these letters, it is obvious that there was divergence of opinion between the two. Dr Lele writes:

You have made an effort at responding to my letter. Hence you may clarify the following points:

1. Rationalists can create imaginary stories as per their needs. But these are not real-life characters. In my opinion, you should print pictures of the benefits that come from licentious behaviour. You may start by talking of Shakuntalabai Paranjape.

2. I feel as concerned about the future generation as about parents. You think differently and believe that young people should read 'Swaasthya', even if surreptitiously, and learn sexology from it.

3. My information is that you and Acharya Atre have a thirst for Lord Shri Krishna. But while you want the wantonness, we want the Gita.

4. Even after so many ages have passed away since Shri Krishna, the Gita is read in different countries and in different languages with veneration. How long, do you believe, will your own writing stay alive?

5. In devotional stories and songs, in the Shri Krishna stories it is said that advice was given to the sister to run away. But here, neither the advisor nor the advised considered it as the ideal lesson arising out of sexology.

6. If the Geeta cannot provide deliverance and emancipation
    to the world, let sexology do so.
7. The Gita teaches the lesson of self-control; you are trying
    to become a modern Krishna by teaching licentiousness.
8. In short, however much you scrub coal, it will
    remain black.

In 1927, Dr Lele had many interactions with *Samaaj-swaasthya*. Sometimes his articles were printed, sometimes his correspondence with Raghunathrao got published; other times there would be Raghunathrao's reviews on his books. Once his brochure titled 'Santatiheenaanchi Sanstha—Soochana Va Maahiti' (Organization of the Childless—Advice and Information) was published. In 1937, Dr Lele complained that his letters were being given very evasive responses, to which Raghunathrao replied bluntly that if he thought so, the problem was with his perception. Reviews of Lele's *Aakade-Pandit* and *Jaadooche Maasik* were published in 1951 and 1952 respectively. His association with *Samaaj-swaasthya* stretched for a long period of almost twenty-five years.

In 1942, Lele published his collection of English poems and sent it to Raghunathrao for review. Raghunath's opinion was, 'after looking at your collection of English verse, it appears that God cannot write good poems.' While underlining Dr Lele's enthusiasm for writing English poetry, this terse statement also comments on the paucity of skill in his efforts. Also, by making a reference to God, the rational, atheistic Raghunathrao was taking a dig at a believer like Lele.

Dr Lele admired Raghunathrao and at the same time held strong differences of opinion with him. It would be interesting to know why Raghunathrao made it a point to provide space for Dr Lele's writings in his magazine in spite of knowing Lele's opinions. Dr Lele remarked on Raghunathrao's quality of not feeling offended at the fisticuffs that happened between them on various issues. In a letter, Dr Lele writes:

> I carry a lot of love and pride for *Swaasthya*, which is why I put your name in the articles I write. However, there have been sharp differences of opinion between me and the editors; the reason could be that since I've been in the medical profession for thirty-three years and moved around among young, unmarried students, my brain would have turned mouldy. But there is no remedy for that.

Raghunathrao was much pilloried by people belonging to the medical profession like Dr Manoramabai Thatte, Captain Pillay etc., and Dr Lele was among them.

Captain A.P. Pillay

Reference to Captain Pillay's name and work necessarily finds place in Raghunathrao's biography. Captain Pillay was also working in the area of birth control. He was by profession a doctor, which meant that he possessed medical knowledge, plenty of experience and perhaps a clinic in the city too. It was natural for two people working in the same field in a city like Bombay to run into each other.

But Raghunathrao's peculiar character traits—reclusive and aggressive—left imprints on his personality and his work. In contrast, Captain Pillay was professional and shrewd. He was slick in promoting himself and his work and had entered the exclusive circle of politicians and foreign nationals. He was adept at maintaining relationships and using them to advantage. Whenever Mrs Margaret Sanger (who ran a birth control clinic in America) and Mrs Hough Martin (who did similar work in England) came to Bombay, Captain Pillay would make it a point to meet them. Once, when they were in Bombay, they had

expressed the desire to call Raghunathrao over for dinner, but
Captain Pillay had expertly dodged the request. Captain Pillay
desperately tried to convince people that he was the first to
begin work on birth control in India; however, since the citizens
of Bombay knew otherwise, they would not pay much heed
to his claims. This upset him, and although he wouldn't show
it openly, he held a grudge against Raghunathrao. This is the
reason why Raghunathrao's biographies present Captain Pillay
as cunning, self-centred, exploitative and selfish.[3]

Captain Pillay earlier lived in Solapur where he practiced
as a physician. Birth control was not a part of his practice then,
because he had not studied the subject. Raghunathrao, however
had already made a name for himself in this field. Because of all
the criticism that was being targeted at him, Raghunathrao and
his work had already gained currency, and information about
him had reached Solapur too, which prompted Captain Pillay to
give his practice a new direction. Raghunathrao mentions this
at least twice in *Samaaj-swaasthya*:

> Dr. Pillay, who considers himself as the initiator of work on
> birth control, also says that this work should not be done
> by anybody except a doctor. But when he was in Solapur in
> 1926, he had sent a nurse to us for learning the process. We
> trained her for free, but we hear that he now charges more
> fees for consultation and treatment than we do. If Dr. Pillay
> had possessed knowledge in this area, he would have been
> able to train the nurse himself. It's clear, therefore, that Dr.
> Pillay has acquired this knowledge from me and now he goes
> bragging about himself everywhere.

Clearly, there was no love lost between Captain Pillay and
Raghunathrao. Captain Pillay went on harping on the fact

that Raghunathrao had no medical degree. He also hoped
that by promoting himself as the first in the field, he would
be able to procure business for himself. Raghunathrao's self-
absorbed, reclusive, indifferent nature would have helped
the captain in this venture. In the editorial titled 'Nau
Varshey Poorn' (Nine Years Completed) of the June 1936
issue, Raghunathrao has written about a bitter experience
with Captain Pillay and exposed the vileness of the person.
Here's what he wrote:

> Captain Pillay and some other people opened up a school
> for birth control last month in an organization that has just
> come into being at Parel. While they are offering free advice,
> they are not giving the kit for free . . . . However, when he
> was blowing his trumpet in the inaugural function about his
> being the first organization to offer this facility, he did not
> remember us. Considering that Captain Pillay had himself
> brought Mrs. Hough Martin to our place, it cannot be said
> that he did not know about us. An organization of Gujarati
> ladies in our neighbourhood has also been offering this facility
> and they informed the organizer of the function that their
> Parel organization is not the first in this field, which he had to
> admit. Although I was present for the function, I did not talk
> about my work, because I do not believe it necessary to blow
> my own trumpet.

In short, it may be said that Captain Pillay tried to corner
Raghunathrao's credit for himself.

Dr Manorama Thatte[4]

Raghunathrao was reticent as a conversationalist, but he wrote
with great felicity and power. He would floor his opponents with
logical arguments. His reading was wide and eclectic. He would
sit at the Asiatic Library every day at least for some time, where
he would read newspapers, magazines and books on a variety of
subjects. Whenever he came across articles that ran against his
concepts, he would take account of them in his editorial column
or 'Sharadeche Patr', or through independent articles. A look at
his writings reveals that he would read newspapers from even
the far-flung towns of Greater Maharashtra. Any reader would
rightly assume that he loved disputation. For instance, articles
began being written from December 1937 onwards under the
title 'Ajab Kaifiyat' (Strange Complaint) and this continued
without a break till May 1938. In his editorial titled 'Akraavey
Varsh Sampley' (Eleventh Year Gone) published in the June
1938 issue, Raghunathrao wrote, 'Much of my time this year
went in responding to Dr. Manorama Thatte's hollow articles,
but it cannot be said to have been wasted.' Raghunathrao
obviously considered his battle against Dr Manorama Thatte
and her writings as important.

Manoramabai was the daughter of the well-known reformer
Babasaheb Devdhar. Encouraged by her father, she went to
England and got herself a degree in medicine. After returning
home, she opened a hospital in Sangli and married Mr Thatte.
This was Mr Thatte's second marriage. Like other people in the
medical profession, she too would write in various newspapers
and magazines on her subject. Her articles would get published
in *Yashvant*, an important periodical of those times. Although
Manoramabai was a doctor, she was against the concept of birth
control. While Raghunathrao would bring to the notice of his
readers Manoramabai's inadequate knowledge of her profession,

she would question Raghunathrao's authority to sell articles related to birth control and his running a clinic when he did not possess the necessary degrees for it. She and her husband were convinced that that the government should bring about a law to prohibit such unauthorized people from practicing. It is quite clear, therefore, that the dispute between them was considerable.

Manoramabai wrote in one of her articles, 'People who have said that women should have freedom have committed a terrible crime and women should never ever listen to them.' She further said, 'As if anticipating this movement, P. J. Pradhan had said eighty years ago that what is seen as women's freedom is a kind of prostitution.' Raghunathrao was bitterly against the word 'prostitution'. His stance was, 'A woman who has sexual intercourse for money is a prostitute; a woman who has it for joy is not. Calling her a prostitute is an abuse. When people cannot write rationally, they take recourse to abuses.' He thus got back at Manoramabai by saying that she did not write rationally.

While writing on birth control, Dr Manoramabai had speculated on the possibility of women landing up with cancer. To prop up her contention, she had procured information from related people and had it published in the March 1938 issue of *Samaaj-swaasthya*.

Without naming the person, Raghunathrao wrote about how Manoramabai behaved with women who went to her for advice on birth control:

It is important to give some information here. Since it is impossible in this matter to gather evidence that may stand in court, I am not naming the lady doctor. But this lady who boasts of having taken her education in London collects her fees and prescribes the size of the diaphragm for her patient without even examining her. The size numbers are bound

to go wrong most of the time. However much she may
be opposed to birth control, she has no right to cheat her
patients in this manner.

When Manoramabai remarked upon the absence of any degree
with Raghunathrao, he responded, 'Dr Mrs Thatthe's medical
knowledge may be more than mine, but if ever the need for
medical knowledge arises, instead of giving our own opinion,
we shall take the opinion of a doctor of a far better quality
than her.'

Mrs Hough Martin, who worked on birth control in London,
had visited India around three times. She was curious about how
Raghunathrao ran his clinic and met him a number of times and
satisfied herself with the quality of his work. Raghunathrao has
written, 'Mrs. Hough Martin, who runs a similar organization
in London, had visited us a few times to see what we have been
doing. She asked me several questions and was finally satisfied
that we are doing the same kind of work that she has been doing
in London.'

Dr Manorama had met this Mrs Martin and had posed
to her this question: 'Should people who have no training in
medicine supply birth control devices? Should they give counsel
on it?' These questions were obviously related to Raghunathrao
and Dr Manorama Thatte had expected the lady to reply that it
was wrong of an unqualified person to run a birth control clinic
or to give counsel. If she had received the expected response,
she would have splashed it across all newspapers and made life
difficult for Raghunathrao. She would well have gone beyond
and brought the law down upon the man. But Mrs Martin
knew both Dr Thatte and Raghunathrao very well. Whenever
she visited Bombay, she would always meet Raghunathrao,
take note of the authority that Raghunathrao commanded on
the subject, and the commitment and diligence with which

he conducted his activity. As a result, she was very careful in her response to Dr Thatte. She is reported to have said, 'When I got to know of the stinging response that Prof. R.D. Karve had given to Mrs Thatte's article, I understood why she had posed those questions to me.'

Another accusation that had been laid at the door of Raghunathrao was that he had opened the birth control clinic for the sake of making money. Around the time that Raghunathrao was working in this field, a gentleman named Dr Bhat had been doing the same kind of work too in Bombay. The difference between them was that while Raghunathrao charged a fair fee, Dr Bhat would fleece the patients who visited him. Thus, to clear himself of this accusation, Raghunathrao has written, 'The world knows that if I had wanted to make money, I had many more opportunities to do so than Dr Bhat had.'

When Raghunathrao got to know that Dr Thatte's husband had written a letter to the government on this issue, he was extremely upset. Dr Thatte's interview of Mrs Hough Martin was published in *Dhanurdhari*, 23 April 1938. Clarifying his own position, Raghunathrao wrote a letter to *Dhanurdhari* too, which was duly published. He published the same letter in *Samaaj-swaasthya* too, giving details of the case. It is no surprise that the activities of Dr Thatte and her husband had angered Raghunathrao. His exasperation is reflected in the excerpt that follows:

> Let me also tell Dr. Thatte that even if she manages to stop me from doing this work, she will fail in her effort to destroy the livelihood of her opponent, for the simple reason that I do not make that kind of money from it. Most of my income depends upon my books and on the few devices I sell for birth control. Therefore, till such time as a law is made that prohibits all except doctors from selling these items, I have

no fear. Even if such a law comes into being, I have the spirit
in me to run a tea stall, and I am sure there won't be any law
coming against it.

Dr Thatte's regressive opinion on birth control is evident from her
writings. Mention of it can be found in 'Sharadeche Patr': 'Thattebai
says that every woman should have a child every eighteen months,
which would mean that each woman should finish off with having
eight children, and that nothing can give a woman greater pleasure
than having a child after every eighteen months.' Even if one sets
aside the sarcasm in Raghunathrao's writing, Dr Thatte's attitude
is clearly retrograde. Raghunathrao was left with no choice except
to wield his pen quite stringently against her. A series of articles ran
across six issues of *Samaaj-swaasthya*.

Shankarrao Kirloskar

Raghunathrao's younger brother Bhaskarrao and Madhavrao of
the Kirloskar family were classmates. Raghunathrao, therefore,
was familiar with the Kirloskar family. Shankarrao Kirloskar
was the editor of *Kirloskar Khabar* and had been to England to
learn painting. Shankarrao himself was of a progressive bent of
mind and he transformed the house journal *Kirloskar Khabar*
into a forum for writers, poets, politicians, and social reformers
of those times. He invited writers like N.D. Tamhankar on the
editorial board. He also encouraged freedom fighters like V.D.
Sawarkar and renowned litterateurs of those times like N.S.
Phadke to write. To motivate women to come forward for their
own development, he started a magazine called *Stree*. He held
joint excursions for writers and editors so that they could get to
know each other better and exchange opinions. He would also
print photographs and biographical information of writers in
his magazine.

Shankarrao Kirloskar considered Raghunathrao's work as important and asked him to write an article on it. Raghunathrao's article titled 'Amaryaad Santati' was published in the August 1925 issue of his magazine. However, the Kirloskar factories were in Kirloskarwadi, which fell within the princely state of Oundh, and Shankarrao often had to interact with its ruler Raje Bhawanrao Pantpratinidhi. The king believed in tradition; he had given shelter to Pandit Satwalekar in his principality, who brought out a periodical called *Purushaarth* that propagated ancient traditions and ultra-orthodoxy. This periodical was forever at loggerheads with *Samaaj-swaasthya*; it was natural, therefore, that these people would not have liked Raghunathrao's article. Later, a ban was placed on the distribution of *Samaaj-swaasthya* in the princely state. The 25 June 1932 edition of *Vasundhara* carried this news item: 'It is learnt that some educated people have submitted a signed appeal to the District Magistrate that a ban should be placed on the distribution and publication of *Samaaj-swaasthya* within the princely state of Sangli.'

Shankarrao, therefore, decided not to stand by Raghunathrao and decided to hold his articles. When Raghunathrao sent an article titled 'Vinay Mhanje Kai?' (What is Humility?) to the magazine, the editor returned it to him with a word of gratitude. By doing this, Shankarrao earned the wrath of Raghunath. Since other magazines were refusing to publish his writings, he decided to bring out his own and began publishing *Samaaj-swaasthya* from 15 July 1927 onwards. Through this magazine he began criticizing Shankarrao Kirloskar and the *Kirloskar* magazine whenever he had the opportunity.

A person who considered himself as progressive had refused to stand by him. He had buckled under political pressure from the Aundh principality and refused to print his articles. This grudge that Raghunathrao carried becomes visible over and over again. For instance, he writes in the June 1934 issue of *Samaaj-swaasthya*, 'It was because of the virtuousness of Kirloskar that I was compelled to bring out my own magazine.' When a reader asked him about 'Kirloskar literature' and 'the Kirloskar manner of thought', he replied, 'The Kirloskar magazine sells well because of the backing of plenty of funds and their business policies. The modern ideas that are propagated through the magazine are now termed as 'Kirloskar Literature', particularly because of the patronage of the Vahini Saheb of Ichalkaranji.'[5]

A Progressive Writers' Conference had been organized in Bombay some time in 1938. In 1939, a Marathi Literary Festival was organized in Ahmadnagar under the chairmanship of Prof. Datto Waman Potdar. When someone asked Shankarrao in the festival why he had not attended the Bombay conference, he said, 'I doubted whether there were any really progressive writers in Bombay; hence I did not come.' Raghunathrao responded to this jibe by saying, 'The statement of the editor of *Kirloskar* is as laughable as a labourer of Kirloskarwadi saying, "I wonder if there is electricity in Bombay like we have here!" It is nothing but boorishness.'

When Raghunathrao had decided to bring out a 'Two Wives Special' issue, he had requested Shankarrao to contribute, which he graciously did, setting aside personal differences.

Raghunathrao contributed to *Kirloskar*, *Stree* and *Manohar* that were published under Shankarrao. Below is a paragraph that appeared in *Samaaj-swaasthya* when the *Kirloskar* magazine completed twenty-five years:

The *Kirloskar* magazine: This magazine has completed twenty-five years in 1944. It deserves to be congratulated for not only providing entertainment, but also for performing the important task of awakening thoughts. It began as a house journal that only provided information about the factory and carried the name *Kirloskar Khabar*, but later, its scope increased to carry writings on all kinds of subjects. In terms of intellectual calibre, it steadily kept improving. This magazine has performed the important function of bringing religious chicanery out into the open for discussion. Another special thing about this magazine has been its punctuality. It is the first magazine to have ensured that it reached the hands of the readers on the first day of every month.

It is true that it was *Kirloskar* that brought about this punctuality.

The third part of Raghunathrao's writings on Shankarrao is his articles on the controversy that had flared up between him and Ichalkaranjikar. The background to this conflict is as follows:

The Ranisaheb of Ichalkaranji, Anubaisaheb Ghorpade, wrote for the magazines belonging to the Kirloskar group. The Kirloskar and Ghorpade families had been on friendly terms since much earlier. As it happened, B.S. Paranjape's story 'Abhisaar' was published in *Kirloskar*. The story talks about an impecunious but virtuous woman named Ambu, who, out of compulsion of circumstances, is left with no choice but to put her virtue on sale for the sake of saving her son. Anusayabai found the story obscene. The Diwali 1937 issue of *Manohar* also carried a picture of a heavily clothed lady being carried across a stream in the arms of a gentleman, which too, Anusayabai found objectionable. She had sent a letter to the periodicals of those times to mark her protest. This letter was published in the *Kesari* of 8 December 1937 along with a note from the editor. S.R. Tikekar had written an article in this context in the *Maharashtra Sharada* supporting Anubaisaheb and lambasting Shankarrao. Gita Saney had then written a letter voicing her sharp opposition to Tikekar's stance. Much discussion took place on this issue in the weekly *Chitra*.

Shankarrao responded to Anubaisaheb's criticism in a sixteen-page article that he published in *Kirloskar*. In this article, he talked about a story titled 'Gangubaiche Dharmaantar' (Gangubai's Change of Religion) which Anubai had written for *Stree* under the pseudonym 'Achyutanuja'. It was a heart-rending story of a girl who had defiled herself by converting to Christianity. Driven to desperation by the tyranny of her husband and his mother and sister, she had abandoned her house, though pregnant, and taken shelter with some missionaries. The story describes the delivery of her baby and her conversion to Christianity. This was how Shankarrao had revealed the secret of Anubaisaheb writing under a pseudonym. As a result, Anubaisaheb stopped all *Kirloskar* magazines.

Raghunathrao then wrote an article called 'Dnyaanaavar Nirbandh' (Restrictions on Knowledge) in *Samaaj-swaasthya*, in which he said, 'I understand that two Ranisahebs have stopped (subscribing to) the *Kirloskar* magazine. I know that at least one of these two Ranisahebs attended college where books written by obscene writers like Shakespeare and Kalidasa need to be studied, and these books are selected by extremely traditional people.'

A reader raised the question whether Phadke's novels were obscener than Kalidasa's and wanted to know Raghunathrao's stance. Raghunathrao replied, 'People have raised a pointless storm over *Kirloskar*. Exposing the real name behind a pseudonym is, of course, an unforgiveable offence, but the other points that people have raised against him are meaningless.'

On the surface, it appears that Shankarrao Kirloskar was against R.D. Karve and his magazine. Hence, the absence of any reference to Raghunathrao in the autobiography that Shankarrao wrote makes sense from this perspective. But the fact is that the rivalry between Raghunathrao and Shankarrao Kirloskar was no rivalry at all. When the last issue of the tenth

year of *Samaaj-swaasthya* was published, *Kirloskar* had printed
the following matter under the title 'Paraamarsh' (Assessment):

> The last issue of the tenth year of the monthly *Samaaj-swaasthya* – a magazine that analyzes man-woman relationship from a medical and a psychological perspective – has just been published. Its editor did not care for the criticism of the pretenders of ritual purity and was never fazed by opposition. He sculpted the personality of *Samaaj-swaasthya* by courageously presenting his opinions before the public. We offer our heartfelt compliments to him for this feat and wish him the maximum possible success in his chosen endeavour. This fresh issue is twice as large as usual and also carries a large number of pictures. The articles here like 'Aarogya Mhanjey Kai?' (What is Good Health?) and 'Jyotishi Praamaanik Astaat Kai?' (Are Astrologers Honest?) make for interesting reading. The correspondence that satisfies the curiosities of alert readers and 'Sharadechi Patrey' are two columns of *Samaaj-swaasthya* that have always provided instruction and guidance. (July 1937, page 1016)

Here is another paragraph titled 'Shri Ra. Dhon. Karve' that
appeared in the April 1937 issue of *Kirloskar*. It is a news report
of what Raghunathrao said in a meeting that was organized in
Bombay on 31 January 1937, to support Shankarrao Kirloskar
in the Kirloskar–Anubaisaheb Ghorpade controversy:

> The ultra-orthodox criticize the pictures of women that appear in the magazine as obscene. I ask them whether they keep their eyes shut when they walk up and down the street. If these pictures of women are sexually exciting, the women at least have no reason to worry. Is there any shortage of obscenity

in our *puranas*? There is this story of Kunti having had a son
before she got married. It is said that she conceived by chanting
some *mantras*, but I, at least, don't see how it could have been
possible. A doubt is raised about what libidinous people can do
if the country runs into a crisis. But this doubt may be raised
when the crisis actually arrives. Nobody stops eating out of a
hypothetical fear that a crisis may hit the country sometime in
the future. I want a political revolution too. My opinion is that
all revolutions nourish a political revolution. (Page 773)

Manoramabai Khabade

It was a period when *Satyavaadi*, published from Kolhapur,
was at its peak. *Satyavaadi* carried a special section for women
and Manoramabai Khabade was the editor of this section for a
while. Manoramabai was a Christian and had done her BA. She
married much later to become the second wife of Mr Khabade,
who was the Collector of Kolhapur and had children from his
earlier wife. Manoramabai herself did not have any children.
Their widowed daughter-in-law still lived in Kolhapur.
Manoramabai left *Satyavaadi* and became the headmistress
of a middle school run by the church. She continued with her
writing throughout her life.

Manoramabai had written an article titled 'Aamchya Kaahi
Anisht Chaali' (Some of Our Objectionable Activities) in an
issue of *Satyavaadi*. Raghunathrao attacked some of its points
spiritedly. 'She seems to think that just by being a Christian, she
possesses all modern knowledge. Or, perhaps, she thinks that
there is no need for modern knowledge, religious foolishness
is good enough.' His language was sharp and hurtful when
he assailed her for being a Christian, but what he had really
wanted to criticize was the paucity of scientific temperament
in Manoramabai's writings. People very often bathe in the

open, against which Manoramabai had written in the above-mentioned article, 'A bath is better taken in a closed room.'

Through his magazine, Raghunathrao would familiarize Marathi readers with the progressive thoughts prevalent in Western countries like America, England and France. He would talk to his readers about how 'nudist clubs' were present there and how nudity was beneficial to health. In fact, he had even been mulling over starting a nudist club in Bombay. Therefore, it is quite easy to understand why he took Manoramabai to task. In the context of the bath, Sharada writes:

> I also believe that a bath should be taken in a closed room; but the question is: why? Because there is a law against being naked in public. But the writer doesn't say that a person should bathe naked in a closed room either. What she is saying is, "A person's body becomes quite visible through wet clothes; and however superior wetness may be from the artistic perspective, ordinary people, particularly children, do not possess the artistic vision. Psychologists are of the opinion that the sight of naked bodies leaves a deleterious effect on children's minds." Manoramabai goes further and says, "Children too should not be left naked. Whether it is a boy or a girl, they should always be wearing tunics and briefs . . . . During summer, so many men happily move around bare-chested in their house, with just a *dhoti* wrapped round them. What would a foreigner think if he sees them thus with their hairy chest and massive stomach?"

Sharada (who is Raghunath himself) continues thus:

> This is altogether wrong. This is how the lady would, perhaps, have understood it, so I am not saying that she is lying; but then, what she says sits well with her treasure-house of

ignorance. It no longer remains a matter of opinion. Nudist
Clubs have sprung all over the place.

It is not surprising that Raghunathrao's criticism of
Manoramabai would have hurt her, particularly his jibe about
her being a Christian. She got back at him in equally ferocious
language. Her response, which Raghunathrao published in
Samaaj-swaasthya, reads as follows, 'The customs I have
regarded as improper are applicable to all communities: Hindu,
Christian, Muslim and all others. My thoughts become clear
when one reads all my articles published across three issues of
Satyavaadi.

Going further, she came down heavily upon Raghunathrao's
endorsement of nudity while discussing her statement that it is
better to bathe in a closed room. She said:

> I know of a number of people like Shri Karve who advocate
> nudity but stay clothed before their children so as not to
> display their nudity to them. It is foolish to impose opinions
> upon others that one cannot implement in one's own
> conduct. It seems that these people want that everybody
> should revert to living like human beings lived in the early
> days of the world.

She went further by voicing her belief that Sharadabai was none
other than Raghunathrao himself:

> The language of Sharadabai suggests that it has been written
> by a man . . . . A lot of people believe that it is Shri R.D. Karve
> himself, the editor of this magazine who is notorious for
> using obscene language, who fires these obscenities hiding
> behind the veil of a woman. This letter suggests that their
> suspicion is well placed.

Responding to her diatribe, Raghunathrao said, 'People who have enough sense will understand the advantages of nudity that I talk about.' He challenged Manoramabai by saying, 'Whatever I must write, I do openly. I am always ready to grapple with anyone.'

This entire confrontation was published in the column 'Sharadeche Patr' and Raghunathrao shrewdly side-stepped Manoramabai's accusation of Sharada being his pseudonym.

For the next three or four months there was silence. Then, between January and April 1935, *Satyavaadi* came out with its issue on 'Buvaabaaji' (Religious Charlatanism) and contextualizing Manoramabai's article, he fired a salvo at her:

In the 'Buvabaaji' issue of *Satyavaadi*, Manoramabai Khabade has made an effort to place herself in the front rank of writers who write with total disregard to rationality. She had been very upset with me once earlier.... She has a strong suspicion that the letters are written by a man. Her stance is that men should not write under pseudonyms because people get into misunderstandings and these writings are often quite vulgar. Women alone should have the privilege of writing under a pseudonym because their writings are always clean but men often criticize it. The only reason that men have of writing under a pseudonym is to dump vulgar writings upon the readers, whereas women write under a pseudonym to protect themselves from men's criticism. This unbiased perspective of hers is sure to delight women writers.

She also says that men cannot understand what women want. Women are in a better position to understand other women. She herself says a little further, 'Leaders like Justice Ranade and Mahatma Agarkar gave a fillip to women's education.'

This must have happened, perhaps, because they did not understand women's needs! It's true, of course, that women would understand better, but not all women understand this; particularly, women who are blinded by religion don't understand at all, no matter which religion. For example, the Bible says that a woman has been created for man, man has not been created for woman. Manoramabai is a Christian, therefore she is bound to believe in this. If she does, then what chance does she have of understanding the desires of women? If she does not believe in the Biblical dictum, she should immediately announce abandoning Christianity; otherwise she has no right to talk about women's rights. Just because women know how to read and write, or because Manoramabai is a BA, it cannot be assumed that they understand women's needs. It's only after they abandon the senselessness of their religion that their statements can be given consideration. If the opinions of of religious women are to be taken, Girijabai Kelkar will say that the only appropriate life for a woman is her children and her hearth; however educated a Muslim woman is, she will always say that it is all right for a man to have four wives and countless concubines.[6] Women do understand their rights, but which women? Only women who are adequately educated, who have the ability to think, and those who have the liberty to think because of the absence of religious constraints are likely to understand women's needs; the others cannot. The state of religious women (and men too) is that of small children – they should listen to what the priest says and otherwise stay silent. But since the priests are all men too, they will not let the interests of the men suffer. Therefore, the self-interest of religious men lies in their religion. But all this will hold some meaning only when women can see the damage that religion causes them, right?

Manoramabai finally says, "The society should not bother about who the writer is. It should give encouragement to good literature and editors should bring forward the good writings of men and women writers." If the society and the editor can know good and bad writings without having to know the name of the writer, what remains of Manoramabai's objections against pseudonyms? Neither the society nor the editor deliberately give encouragement to vulgar literature; so why does Manoramabai harbour objections against pseudonyms for men writers? Those men who write under pseudonyms can sort it out for themselves; what have I got to do with it?

The above piece shows how seriously Raghunathrao had taken Manoramabai Khabade's question. He, of course, considered her writing as soaked in dogma, while his own emphasis had always been on rationality.

In her 'Aamchya Kaahi Anisht Chaali', Manoramabai had written that food should be taken at regular intervals otherwise it could lead to problems of digestion. Responding to this suggestion, Raghunathrao replied:

My own experience in this matter is that indigestion happens if one eats without being hungry, irregularity doesn't cause it. For the past eight years I have found it impossible to have my meals regularly; this happened after I had become completely habituated to eat with regularity. I have been able to get by without any sign of indigestion.

Raghunathrao was a hardcore rationalist, and drew on years of experience. It was natural for him, therefore, to expose Manoramabai Khabade's faulty reasoning. But it does appear that he had got personal in his writings about Manoramabai.

Prabhakar Padhye[7]

During the two decades stretching from 1930 to 1950, the magazine *Dhanurdhari* was considered important among Marathi periodicals. Its editor was Prabhakar Padhye. In his autobiography 'Vaateyvarlyaa Saavali' (The Shades on the Road), Kusumagraj has illustrated the kind of sway that Padhye held. Padhye was renowned as the editor of *Dhanurdhari* and *Nava-shakti*. The literary world of those times was rather small: the well-known magazines then were *Pratibha*, *Jyotsna*, *Vasundhara* and *Chitra*, while *Navaa Kaal*, *Lokmaanya* and *Prabhaat* were the popular newspapers. With 'Bombay Marathi Sahitya Sangh' catering to the needs of literature, many of the litterateurs and journalists of widely different persuasions knew each other personally. Raghunathrao had become a well-known name because of his magazine and his rationalistic thoughts. In fact, Prabhakarrao was as intelligent as Raghunathrao, but they did not get along because of differences in nature. The probability exists that the two even exchanged heated words with each other once. Padhye wrote a book titled *Kalechi Kshitijey* (The Horizons of Art). The communist ideology that had begun being seen in Lalji Pendse's book *Sahitya Ani Samaaj-Jeevan* (Literature and Social Life) and P.Y. Deshpande's *Navi Moolye* (New Values) came out strongly in Padhye's *Kalechi Kshitijey*.

Raghunathrao reviewed Padhye's book in the November 1943 issue of *Samaaj-swaasthya*:

It is true that scientific knowledge can be put to use for progress, but there is nothing to suggest that the sensibilities that awaken from a work of art can be put to similar use . . . . Whatever the purpose of art, in my opinion, if it doesn't have beauty, it should not be called art . . . . What doesn't give pleasure is failed art. My definition of beauty is that which gives joy to the sight.

The Bombay Marathi Sahitya Sangh used to give book awards and *Kalechi Kshitije* was taken up for consideration. The September 1945 issue of *Samaaj-swaasthya* carried this information on the issue:

An argument took place in the Discussion Group of the Sahitya Sangh on the words 'lalit' (delicate, lovely, charming) and 'lalit kalaa' (Fine Arts). The five judges expressed their doubts on whether Padhye's *Kalechi Kshitije* fell within the definition of non-*lalit* literature, and in combination with some other factors, declared it as unqualified for the award, giving their reasons for their decision. Padhye created a furore over it. I was only one of the five judges, but there is no harm in saying that the other four, at least, were learned people.

It's not as if the friction between Padhye and Karve was limited to *Kalechi Kshitije* alone. The discord between the two had been happening much earlier. One of the reasons for the conflict was the advertisements related to V. Shantaram's film production company, Prabhaat. During the period 1931 to 1940, Shantaram's Prabhaat Film Company had produced melodramatic films like *Kunku*, *Shejaari* and *Maanoos*. He had made them in Hindi too and earned a name for himself across India. In an effort to give his *Samaaj-swaasthya* a more complete look, Raghunathrao had begun to give reviews of books and movies. He began criticizing Shantaram's films in his magazine. For example, Shantaram had taken a few reels of his movie *Jwaala* to Germany for getting them colourized. The effect, instead of being pleasing to the eyes, was disagreeable. Raghunathrao criticized this penchant of directors of making their movies partly or fully in colour in the following words:

A number of directors now have this addiction of pasting colour on the best parts of their movies and messing them

up. If it had only been the first effort at thus adding colour,
it would have been different, but despite having experienced
a number of times how ugly the colours look, these directors
cannot get rid of their addiction. V. Shantaram had taken
one entire talkie to Germany and brought it back all messed
up. Till such time as they learn to take colour photographs,
they should stay away from dabbling in colours. These
colours floating around all over the place look so ugly that
one doesn't want to look at them.

This conflict between Raghunathrao, Padhye and Shantaram
was therefore triangular. Padhye wrote this in the 1983 Diwali
issue of *Lalit*:

During the time that I was the editor of 'Dhanurdhari',
R. D. Karve had published in his *Samaaj-swaasthya* that,
consumed by the fear of losing advertisements, the owners
of *Dhanurdhari* had got the editor to remove an article
critical of V. Shantaram from the magazine. This was of
course an untruth and had probably been planted into his
head by one of his tale-carrying friends. As soon as this
accusation had come out in print, I had challenged Karve
to prove its veracity; but Karve would neither produce
evidence nor would he withdraw the accusation. After a
good five or six months had drifted, Karve finally wrote,
"It does not happen that all truthful events can be proved."
The moment he made this statement, he got caught in a
saapala – a trap. (It happens that the name of our owner
was also *Saapale*, but there is no pun intended here. While
this controversy was on, Baburao Saapale did not utter
a word about it.) I, then, wrote back: "All this time, our
understanding had been that Prof. Karve was propagating
birth control out of a sense of mission and had made

many sacrifices for this pursuit. But now we have learnt from unimpeachable sources that Karve is an agent for a company in New York that manufactures devices used for family planning and his propagation of birth control is with the intention of making profits. We obviously cannot prove it, but all truths cannot be proved." Karve then fell silent.

Since Padhye was writing this in 1983, it would be impossible for him to remember all the details, but in the editorial of the August 1941 issue of *Samaaj-swaasthya*, Raghunathrao wrote,

> One of Prabhakar Padhye's statements is that I did not resign from my government job out of a sense of self-respect. To prove this falsehood, he manufactured another falsehood and said that the then Director of Public Instruction had set off to file an appeal against me for having made some statements about him and that Dr. R. P. Paranjape had saved me from this danger by accepting my resignation. He (Padhye) had accused me of having made false statements against the then Director; and therefore, it was natural for him [the Director] to want to expel me, it was not within his power to go into an appeal, because we had enough evidence to prove our allegations in court.

It is true that Padhye made this accusation against Raghunathrao in his article in the *Lalit* issue of 1983. Raghunathrao's article in the June 1941 issue under the title 'Dhanurdhaarichi Dhoortata' (The Shrewdness of Dhanurdhari) denies of the accusation that there is plenty of profit to be made from the sale of birth control products. It goes:

> Doing a job or not doing a job or resigning from one – in my opinion there is no glory in any one of these things.

I resigned from my Wilson College job so that I wouldn't
have to stop the propagation of birth control. I had done
it for my own emotional health, not out of philanthropy.
However, the statement of Padhye's lackey that I resigned
from my job because I had more benefit to make out of
selling birth control products is not true.

V. Shantaram

Raghunathrao often criticized V. Shantaram with or without
reason because he did not like his directorial style. In the
November 1951 of *Samaaj-swaasthya*, he casually remarks,
'Doesn't Shantaram indulge in all kinds of improprieties in his
talkies? Take any of his movies. It would be nearly impossible to
find even one in which he has not distorted history.'

Raghunathrao was publishing his magazine at a financial
loss. His well-wishers Anandrao Gadre and Appa Pendse
would try to fetch him advertisements, some of which would
be film advertisements. Among films would also be those of
the Prabhaat movies and the choice of which publications to
patronize always lay with Shantaram. When he found *Samaaj-
swaasthya* criticizing his movies, he stopped advertising there.
It angered Raghunathrao and he seems to have let loose more
criticism in sharp, hurtful language.

In Madras, Shantaram had declared that he welcomed
constructive criticism and yet he could not tolerate the
criticism in *Samaaj-swaasthya*. Raghunathrao got back at him
in these words:

> Shantaram goes to Madras and declares that he wants
> constructive criticism, but when it comes, he issues orders
> for advertisements to be stopped. Therefore, his desire for
> constructive criticism is just a boast . . . that's quite clear. Any

person who has some sense would want to learn from any kind of criticism. This is not humility, it is conceit, arrogance, the intoxication of money. There is no shortage of critics who are willing to sing praises in return for advertisements; therefore, why would he want to give advertisements to real critics? This is business, while art, beauty and the rest are just yarns.

Raghunathrao's anger had boiled over and any alert reader would know that Raghunathrao had gone after Shantaram hammer and tongs. This does not mean that Shantaram was in the right either. However, Raghunathrao's writings are definitely useful in getting an idea of the kinds of movies, the kind of film criticism and the literature–art environment of those times. The story of *Maanoos* and the Hollywood movie *Waterloo Bridge*, and movies like *Kunkoo* (Marathi) and *Duniya Naa Maaney* (Hindi) made on them; the material used in these movies taken from the plays *Shaarada* and *Vidhavakumari*; the production of the movie *Shejari*; the controversy that erupted over Sukhtankar's story 'Mahapurushachi Shikavan', all of these events can be understood better after reading Raghunathrao's writings. His writings also throw light on the strategies that Shantaram used for making his films. We have already seen how Shantaram was not averse to hurting the bottomline of magazines that dared to criticize his films and that was perhaps the reason why Raghunathrao said, 'There are directors who have got used to being praised in return for the advertisements they give. How can they tolerate someone pointing out their faults? But it is important to tell them that their money cannot seal the lips of every single editor.'

To summarize, it is true that Raghunathrao, Prabhakar Padhye and Shantaram were stalwarts in their own fields. But they were conceited and instead of working together, were always adversarial. As a result, Raghunathrao wielded a poisonous pen while writing about them.

N.S. Phadke

Here is the narration of a piece of conversation that happened on 27 March 1925, between the principal of a college and a lecturer:

As I was relaxing in the staff-room after my first lecture, the peon brought a note from Principal Gardiner that read, "Will you please meet me before you leave for home after finishing your work? It's something important.'"

When I went to meet him, Gardiner said, 'Let's go to the library. We'll talk there.'

When we reached the library, even without sitting down, he said to me with a very grave face, 'Have you written a book called *Birth Control*?'

I said, 'Yes, I have.'

'What opinion have you expressed in the book?'

I answered immediately, 'Married men and women of India should exercise birth control, and for doing that, the best guarantee can be when they use artificial means for preventing conception. There is nothing unethical at all in using such facilities.'

When Gardiner heard this, he looked at me steadily, shook his head, clucked his tongue a few times and asked, 'Don't you consider these opinions of an extremely frightening kind?'

I shook my head and said, 'My own understanding is that these opinions of mine should be propagated with great fervour across our country.'

He then asked, 'But you would not consider abandoning these opinions for the sake of convenience?'

(Pause)

'Have you understood? So, what's to be done?'

'By whom?' I counter-questioned.

'By you and me,' he responded.

I replied, 'It's quite clear what we should do. I should submit my resignation and you should accept it.'

The Professor here was N.S. Phadke and this conversation was excerpted from his book *Maazhyaa Sahitya-Seveteel Smriti* (Memories of My Service to Literature). This episode in Phadke's life is eerily similar to the one that happened in Raghunathrao's.

Reference to Margaret Sanger, the promoter of birth control in America, is mostly found in Raghunathrao's biographies and in the articles of *Samaaj-swaasthya*. But Sanger had a correspondence going with Phadke too. In fact, she had also written a foreword for Phadke's book *Sex Problem in India*.

Margaret Sanger had read Phadke's articles on birth control in English periodicals, and had gone on to establish an organization called Indian Birth Control for working in that area. Hence, when a big international conference had been held in Geneva in 1924, she had sent him an invitation to participate as an Indian representative. For some reason, however, Phadke could not make the journey and and yet again, when she invited him to participate in another conference, this time in New York. She even went to the extent of arranging the money required for his travel expenses.

Raghunathrao wrote a review of three of Phadke's books— *Mahatma Gandhi*, *Shakuntala* and *Maazhyaa swaasthya-seveteel Smriti*—in the June 1952 issue of *Samaaj-swaasthya*. With regard to the third book, Raghunathrao says, 'This part contains twenty-eight memories extending from 1923 to 1934. We all suffer delusions about ourselves, and it is equally true

about the author. There's no point in talking about them here; it
is likely to slip into dissensions.'

N.S. Phadke arrived in Bombay in the early days of 1923
where his intellectual horizon expanded. He writes in this regard:

> After arriving in Bombay, while I got the opportunity of
> studying a number of books on socialism, I also got attracted
> to a new subject: birth control. From the time that I realized
> the mutually supportive relationship between progeny
> as desired and the reorganization of society according to
> Communistic principles, I began supporting birth control
> and reading English books on the subject.

This subject had captivated Raghunathrao in 1901 and he
had begun reading on it in Marathi, English and French and
contemplating on and internalizing the concepts. As soon as he
had retired from his government job in 1921, he had begun to
apply his knowledge practically. He had written books in Marathi
and English for propagating the subject. N.S. Phadke veered
into this subject in the period that immediately followed. Based
on his study, he wrote the books *Birth Control*, *Sex Problems in
India* and *Suprajanan-shastra* (Eugenics). During this period,
he would certainly have read Raghunathrao's books too.

It is truly amazing, therefore, that in the decade of 1920 to
1930, professors of two different subjects studied birth control,
wrote books on it, and within a short period of each other,
happily admonished the principals of their respective missionary
colleges and resigned from their jobs. If we look still closer, we
find that neither of them came from prosperous families, which
shows that their driving spirit and resolution was breathtaking.
Both had wanted to bring out their own magazine. Phadke
writes that the structure and scope of his magazine *Ratnaakar*
was ready with him on Christmas day of 1922; with Raghunath,

of course, it was the rejection of his article 'Vinay Mhanje Kai?' by *Kirloskar Khabar* that impelled him to start his magazine. The question that arises is: whose commitment to the cause was absolutely beyond dispute? Phadke's or Raghunathrao's? For the sake of his mission, Raghunathrao threw away the prestigious job of a professor and with that he lost the salary he was being paid regularly. Prof. N.S. Phadke stood his ground and refused to toe the principal's line. He then joined Rajaram College, Kolhapur as professor of Logic and Psychology. As time passed, his writing of Marathi short stories, novels and essays expanded and developed. With his undoubted oratorical skills, he set alight many conferences and forums. He chaired many literary gatherings. His book *Pratibha-Saadhana* on literary criticism gained renown for various other reasons. In the course of time, he garnered prestige, respect, fame and honour in abundance. His talents ensured he acquired both wealth and distinction. But much before all this happened, he had resigned from Hislop College, Nagpur over an issue. What remains to be seen is: what happened to his commitment to that issue.

The fact is that the Phadke who began his story writing in 1912 with 'Menaacha Thasa' (The Wax Stamp) went on to write many novels like *Kulaabyaachi Daandi*, *Daulat* and *Allah-o-Akbar*, which symbolized Phadke. Creative writing of this kind was an internal need with him. It is true that he was enamored by a subject like birth control and did some writing on it. It is also true that his writings on this subject gained recognition by being published in international magazines. But conducting basic research in that area, staking everything for doing practical work in that field, and submerging oneself completely in it, was not Phadke's essential disposition. He was not there by instinct. This was why he didn't spurn all the fame, recognition, scholarship and affluence that would be the envy of many and drag himself away from it all.

Raghunath's case was quite the opposite. His journey down the path he had chosen was not at all comfortable. There were countless difficulties on the way; a series of obstacles that he had to leap over. He had to suffer absurd allegations of obscenity, problems raised by mischief-mongers and the disruptions they caused and the notoriety that came his way. He never valued money, which was why, perhaps, once Lakshmi, the Goddess of Wealth was displeased, she remained displeased. But that never shook his resolve. Being a rationalist, he did not believe in god or in rebirth. But once, when he was asked what he would do if he were to be born again, he had responded without a moment's pause, 'I'll work for birth control with redoubled effort.'

When he turned seventy in 1952, his friends Samatanand Gadre, Appa Pendse and a few others got together to celebrate his birthday. Among those who wrote articles to felicitate him was N.S. Phadke. However, he was not unstintingly generous in his praise. Raghunathrao writes:

N. S. Phadke has written that it is wrong to consider me alone as the original initiator of birth control. He has written a number of things in praise of me, for which I should be grateful to Phadke. But it is also important to record that his above statement is not true. When his own book on this subject was published in 1925, two editions of my Marathi book had been published. Besides, I had already published my English book on this subject in 1921; I had opened up a clinic and begun to train people on the use of birth control devices. Nobody had either written on this subject before nor had anyone begun to train people on it publicly. Such being the situation, on what grounds does he say that it is wrong to consider me as the original initiator?

M.D. Altekar

Prof. M.D. Altekar was his contemporary. Whether it was
a lecture delivered somewhere, or his article published, or a
book released, Raghunathrao would tear into him in *Samaaj-
swaasthya*. This is what Altekar has written about himself:
'I joined Wilson College in July 1924. Later, when Marathi was
introduced as a full-time subject in Bombay University, I joined
to become a Professor from earlier being a lecturer.'

His son writes, 'Father got associated with the international
literary organization PEN from 1940 onwards. Madam Sofia
Wadia was the Indian representative of the organization .
. . . Father was one of the executive members.' Altekar was
Raghunathrao's colleague at Wilson College, but it seems that
they did not get along well. Raghunathrao carried a permanent
grouse against Altekar. Ordinarily, he was not the kind to hold
long-term grudges, but Altekar always remained the target of
his criticism.

Raghunathrao himself was associated with PEN, but his
experience was not particularly pleasant.

Altekar had written a detailed, scholarly essay on modern
literature in an issue of *Paarijaat*. Here is how Raghunathrao
responded to it:

> (Altekar) has tried to write an extremely scholarly essay on
> modern literature . . . . If one can write, one certainly should,
> I have no objection against it; but one should ensure that it
> makes sense. But creating a web of sentences, getting oneself
> entangled in it and trying to get the reader entangled too,
> this is not how it should be. Where there are dissensions,
> they should be presented as dissensions. But if there are
> only assumptions and inferences, they are, perhaps, difficult
> to present rationally. If you are working such subjects, if

somebody asks 'Why so?', one may get away by naming
Panini or Dadoba (Pandurang Tarkhalkar). However, that
is not how it works elsewhere . . . . From his writing, it is
obvious that he does not like modern thoughts on matters of
sex. He seems to consider husband and wife as each other's
property.[8]

That Raghunathrao did not get along with Altekar one can
understand. But Nishaad of *Abhiroochi* also has written against
him. Referring to Altekar's speech in the PEN conference at
Jaipur, he writes, 'It is said that while introducing modern
Marathi literature, Prof. Altekar talked about it in insulting
terms . . . Was Altekar an official representative of Marathi in
that conference? Where did he get the authority from?'[9]

Appa Pendse

Journalist Appa Pendse held Raghunathrao in affection. Through
his advertising agency, he would provide advertisements to
Samaaj-swaasthya. However, once, Appa (Pendse) was late
in sending the payment for the advertising. There was some
misunderstanding somewhere and Raghunathrao placed a box
item in the July 1935 magazine that read:

A Defaulting Advertising Agent
This gentleman has defaulted in paying us twelve rupees. His name is understood to be Appa Pendse.
Right Agency, No. 13 New Bhatwadi, Girgaum, Bombay

The August issue had this:

Despite writing to the person for four months, when we had
not received a response, we had put an advertisement stating

that our money had been purloined; the gentleman issued a notice to us through his lawyer which read, "The statement is untrue. We had no intention of purloining the money. We received the money late from the advertiser. You have defamed us. We shall now give you the money if you issue an apology in the three newspapers *Navaa Kaal*, *Prabhaat* and *Janmabhoomi* within twenty-four hours." We obviously refused to apologize and when (Appa) gave some of the money, we informed (Appa) accordingly through the lawyer. The honest man is still sitting tight on the rest of the money.

An advertisement in the September issue again attracts attention:

After the last issue was published, Shri Appa Pendse, through his lawyer, has given to us on the 11th the money that was due from him towards advertisement. Even if he gave it to us five or six months after it was due, since he has given the money, there is no reason for us to believe that he intended to purloin the money. We had arrived at the suspicion because he had neither informed us anything nor had he been responding to our letter during the intervening months. We now offer our apology for having called him 'a defaulting advertising agent' in our July issue.

The entire episode underlines the integrity with which Raghunathrao worked. It was the same Raghunathrao who, when he realized that a subscriber had paid an extra rupee, had informed him in the July 1936 issue that he should come over and take the money back (p. 351). Again, in 1944, when the shortage of paper had compelled him to bring a joint issue for August–September–October, he had assured the readers that he would compensate by extending their subscription. Here's more: he often visited Rajaramshastri Bhagwat, but he never had tea there because he thought he couldn't return the courtesy. That was the way he lived. No surprise, therefore, that he should have kicked up such a ruckus for a mere Rs. 12 with Appa Pendse.

Appa Pendse does not find much mention in *Samaaj-swaasthya*, but an exception is when a discussion happened in Wasai, where some painters had expressed their displeasure at nude pictures. The magazine mentions that Appa was present there and he opposed them.

Nanasaheb Shinde

In the October 1940 issue, an error has been rectified in the following manner.

On page 165 of the book, *Vaishya-Vyavasaaya*, the meaning of the word 'Shinde' is given as illegitimate boy, followed by a statement that reads: 'it is said that the surname Shinde came in this manner.' It appears that this statement needed clarification. By saying that there is an editorial article in the October issue of the *Maratha* magazine on this topic, Raghunathrao drew the ire of Nanasaheb Shinde of Baroda.

Under the title 'The Shinde Episode Again' in the December 1940 issue, Raghunathrao says, 'The name of Mama Warerkar has been pointlessly sullied In this matter, because even if one assumes that the information on this episode was received mainly from Mama Warerkar, I have nowhere stated so in the book.' He also writes, 'General Nanasaheb Shinde has only lately published the book *The History of Das-Pateechey Shinde Mokashi Inamdar*, thus suggesting that the information could have been extracted from this book.'

V.P. Dandekar

It appears that Raghunathrao was very intolerant of criticism. Whenever a writer criticized him or his magazine, he would be furious. A gentleman by the name V.P. Dandekar had written an article on eugenics in the April–May issue of *Yashvant*. He had written:

> For big people, even books written on this subject are extremely important. Prof. N. S. Phadke's *Santatiniyaman*, Dr. N. M. Bhagwat's *Suprajotpattishastra kivva Daampatya-rahasya* [Eugenics or The Secrets of the Married State] and Prof. R. D. Karve's *Santatiniyaman* examine this subject. A special mention need not be made of Prof. Karve's book because it is very brief and more like an advertisement.

Raghunathrao responded, 'This gentleman is obviously a novice, otherwise he would not have made the error of saying that *Suprajananshastra* can be split into two parts—*suprajanan* and *santatiniyaman*.'

R.M. Athavale

R.M. Athavale was a gentleman from Thane and took a lot of interest in literature-related programmes. In a symposium organized in the Brahman Sabha, he criticized Raghunathrao and though Raghunath himself was present there, he did not counter him, or issue any clarifications. However, in *Samaaj-swaasthya* he wrote:

> Three days of discussion took place in the Brahman Sabha here on periodicals . . . . I felt immense pity for R. M. Athavale. His proposition was that some people carry the conceit of being rational thinkers but they simply cannot manage it, and

he had wanted to prove it by showing Karve as an example. Unfortunately, it got proved with him as an example.

V.M. Joshi

Renowned novelist V.M. Joshi was a lecturer at the Women's University (SNDT) established by Anna. Despite having come into close contact with the Karve family, he disagreed with Raghunathrao. A controversy had erupted between them in *Pratibha* on progressivism. Vamanrao was a lecturer in Philosophy and Ethics. The characters in his novels are often seen discussing philosophical issues, which led to him being identified as the father of the philosophical novel. Raghunathrao did not subscribe to this opinion. He had also written an article titled 'Vamanrao Tattvadnya Navhate' (Vamanrao was Not a Philosopher). However, in the lecture Vamanrao delivered as the chairman in the literary conference held in Mazgaon, he talked of Raghunathrao and his magazine in glowing terms:

> Let me mention Raghunath Dhondoji Karve too. I know that his magazine *Samaaj-swaasthya* publishes some unusual articles, but I strongly believe that all kinds of opinions should be placed before the public. R. Karve has shown here the courage of bringing before the people opinions that they may find unpleasant but in which he himself has faith. I congratulate him for it. Every person should examine his opinion from all perspectives and finally decide whether it should be rejected or accepted.

Raghunathrao has given a favourable review of Vamanrao's book *Indu Kale, Sarala Bhole*. He writes, 'This small novel will match the renown of its author. One of the reasons for its attraction is its narration through letters. This looks like a new technique of storytelling in Marathi.'

But when Acharya Bhagwat mooted the idea of celebrating a memorial day for V.M. Joshi, Raghunathrao reacted with:

Haven't writers of greater intellectual calibre taken birth in Maharashtra? Nowhere do you find a Memorial day celebrated for the great intellectual the late Dr S.V. Ketkar. Writers often have no acquaintance with the late V.K. Rajwade or Mahatma Phule and others. What kind of pretension do the Bombay litterateurs want to get into with a Joshi Memorial Day?

V.S. Khandekar

An article was printed under the column 'Vaangmaya-Bhaktaachi Rojnishi' (The Literature Lover's Diary). Below is an excerpt:

Under the headline 'Aajchya Niyatkaalikaanche Vihangamaavalochan' (An Overview of Today's Periodicals), the October issue of *Paarijaa* has referred to our magazine as "Prof. R.D. Karve's *Samaaj*-swaasthya that is dedicated to discussions on physical pleasure". It further says, "But it is not that every subject discussed in the magazine – particularly a number of other things – stays by this policy." (December 1934, p. 178)

Everybody would have readily agreed with the article. It certainly could not be said that all the stories published in *Samaaj*-swaasthya were in consonance with the magazine's policy. But Raghunathrao found it impossible to agree with the statement.

Raghunathrao never held a positive opinion on V.S. Khandekar's novels. In the book *Bharatiya Prabodhan* felicitating Shankarrao Dev, Khandekar has written the following in the context of India's population problem:

The second example is family planning. In her conversation
with Gandhiji, Margaret Sanger had brought to his notice
the extreme need for the use of artificial devices for birth
control in India. Gandhiji expressed his disapproval of the
use of artificial devices and suggested that the practice of
abstinenceby husband-wife was the superior way. Against the
background of the puritanical Indian culture, it appears to be
an attractive option. But what does the situation on the ground
tell us? To what extent is Gandhiji's admonition going to be
observed? What does the overwhelming population that now
sits calamitously on the country's head suggest? The bitter
truth is that the common man's capacity for contemplation,
forbearance and self-control is woefully inadequate. How does
it make sense to put faith in the ordinary people who are prone
to infatuation and perpetual indulgence in the joyful pleasures
of the senses? Very often it seems that if the country had taken
to heart R. D. Karve's teachings in place of Gandhiji's, their
lives today would have been so different.

The celebrated scholar Durga Bhagwat has said, 'I consider
(R.D.) Karve as the greatest person after Gandhi. He dedicated
his entire life to *Samaaj-swaasthya*. He undertook to teach to
the country the extremely important subject of birth control.'
Durgabai considered Gandhiji great because:

Gandhi proposed the concept of celibacy. Observing celibacy
even after getting married, observing celibacy without getting
married, all these thoughts were in existence, but Gandhi
proposed a sex-free cohabitation of man and woman. But
'proposing a concept' and 'the concept being simple enough
to be observed by ordinary people' are two different things.
Raghunathrao's idea was that people should be able to enjoy

the pleasure of the senses and yet prevent progeny by using
artificial devices. Therefore, his thoughts and remedy were
both based on the firm footing of practicality.

Vibhavari Shirurkar

The book review section in *Samaaj-swaasthya* as well as the
notes and comments on literary events are extremely useful
for understanding the literary tendencies of those times.
One of the important writers of the period 1930 to 1950 was
Vibhavari Shirurkar. As with Raghunathrao, she too created
a storm with her writings during that period. Raghunathrao
has taken frequent note of her writings: July 1931 (pp. 19–21),
November 1931 (pp. 116–119), January 1932 (pp. 155–159) and
January 1934 (pp. 124–125). Fortunately, some part of a 1949
book titled *Vibhavarichey Tikakar* edited by D.B. Karnik and
B.M. Nadkarni has also been included. Although some of her
letters have been published in magazines like *Satyakatha* and
Vishrabdh Sharada, among others, not much cognizance seems
to have been taken of her as literary critic or a literary thinker.

If one wants to examine the development of literary
criticism in Marathi, one needs to take into consideration the
various denominations under which literature was classified;
'decent and indecent', 'modern', 'progressive' were some
important classifications. The social environment of those
times was clearly responsible for all the controversies that had
erupted then. Vibhawari's literature, the controversy relating to
N.S. Phadke's *Pratibha-Saadhan*, the picture titled '*Oleti*' done
by Thakur Singh and published in *Ratnaakar,* the scene in the
movie *Brahmachari* in which the heroine is shown singing in
a bathing-suit, are noteworthy. The court cases that were filed
against Krishnaji Prabhakar Khadilkar for his play *Keechak-
Vadh*, barrister V.D. Savarkar for his book *Maazhi Janmthep,*

Raghunathrao for his writings in *Samaaj-swaasthya*, B.V. Warerkar for his play *Udati Paakhare* and earlier, the publisher of the book *Kraanti-Pooja*, play an important part.

It is clear, therefore, that *Samaaj-swaasthya* played its part in the literary world of its times. Prof. V.H. Kulkarni has described it thus:

> The picture *'Oleti'* in *'Ratnaakar'* caused the controversy of 'Art and Obscenity' to erupt. People regarded *'Kalyaanchey Nihshwaas'* (The Exhalation of Buds) of Vibhawari Shirurkar (now Malati Bedekar) as the spitting of a venomous snake and created a huge furore. R. D. Karve's dedication of his magazine *'Samaaj-swaasthya'* to discussion on sexual matters ruined the peace of mind of the puritans. Divekar Shastri had opened up a front against charlatans in religion. The combined consequence of all these events was the controversies that were created during that period. These controversies were 'Art and Ethics', 'Literature and Obscenity', 'Modernism in Literature', 'Progressive Literature' and 'Marxism'.

R.S. Jog

Raghunathrao would take recourse to various activities to shore up his finances and one of them was participating in literary contests. Even here, minus an exception or two, he does not seem to have met with much success. In 1943, the Maharashtra Literary Awards Committee announced an award of Rs. 500 on books and manuscripts written on literary criticism. Shrimant Phaltankar had sponsored this award. Raghunathrao had also prepared a manuscript and sent it to the committee, but the award was finally conferred on Prof. R.S. Jog for his *Saundarya*

Shodh Ani Anand Bodh (Search for Beauty and the Realization of Joy). Raghunathrao was sure that his work was superior; he felt that he should have got it printed through a publisher or perhaps published it himself and got an opinion on its quality directly from the connoisseur. He did not proceed any further in the matter and his manuscript got lost in due course.

If we keep in mind his extensive reading and his deep interest in art, this manuscript would have at least passed muster as a piece of literature. Also, there was no way it could not have reflected his tendency of looking at literary art from the perspective of life. But, instead of getting the manuscript into public space, he began spewing fire at R.S. Jog and the jury. He wrote:

> My complaint is only that the award was given to R.S. Jog's *Saundarya Shodh Ani Anand Bodh*, because the book is on an altogether different subject. I agree that the book is good. Even if it is Jog who has written it, it is doubtful whether it can be considered as even distantly related to the assigned subject. I do not have an iota of doubt that the award has gone to Jog only because of his image as a great person.

The fact is that the term 'literary criticism' has a wide scope and Prof. Jog's book did fit quite nicely within its definition. Therefore, Raghunathrao had no reason to create such a rumpus. It is interesting to note how Prof. Jog responded to being the recipient of the award. Giving a practical demonstration of his calm and restrained personality, he talked about his inspiration for the book, the circumstances in which he did the writing and the experiences he had when getting it published after receiving the award. Here's an excerpt:

This book came to be written by a coincidence. While the thought of writing something new was twitching in the mind, I came across Richards' book *The Foundations of Aesthetics* in the college library. Believing that I could add something of my own to the subject of the book, I wrote two articles for *Lok-Shikshan* under the title '*Saundarya Shodh Ani Anand Bodh*'. Then the thought arrived that I could expand the thoughts that had arrived in each of the paragraphs, and I began reading and thinking accordingly. Around this time came the information about the award floated by the South Maharashtra Literary Conference, inviting books and manuscripts too. The prize money of Rs. 500/- was a big amount for those times. Whether I got the award or not, I thought this could at least help me write my book and have it examined by experts. This was how I finished the writing within the available time and submitted it. The year was 1942 and blackouts had been imposed on Pune then. So I took as much care as I could and sat through nights and early morning hours to finish my work. Fortunately, the book won the award, but more important than that was the credit that came with it . . . .

The next important task was to find a publisher. A well-known publishing house in Bombay sent a response, effectively saying that it did not publish useless books. Despite his rejection, Prof. Jog did not reveal the name of the firm, nor did he elaborate on the motive behind the use of the hurtful word 'useless'. It was thirty years since the award, but he did not utter a single word on Raghunathrao's criticism of the book, which shows his generosity of spirit.

When *Saundarya Shodh Ani Anand* Bodh was chosen for the award over his own manuscript, Raghunathrao rained fire and brimstone upon the jury, upon R.S. Jog and his book, which, which was quite uncalled for. If he had such confidence in the quality of his own manuscript, he should not have allowed it to remain in a typewritten form but got it published through his own *Right Agency*. Or else, he could have later got it published like he did select articles from *Samaaj*-swaasthya in volumes 1 and 2, *Aadhunik Aahaarshaastra* and *Sangeet Tarala*; or the plays *Guru-baaji* and *Nyaayaacha Shodh* and a number of other books that he published after 1930. If the matter had been published, it could have been evaluated with greater rigour. But it appears that the typewritten manuscript got destroyed after he died.

There were other books too in the competition besides Jog's and Raghunathrao's. Here is some information that could be gathered in this context. The review below of *Saundarya Shodh Ani Anand Bodh* done by Ajit Kumar is quite instructive:

It does not satisfy me enough to learn that the Phaltankar Award considered Jog's book as good. The people who gave the Phaltankar Award were authorities . . . and their judgment on the book does not appear to be acceptable . . . . I hear that plenty of other books were sent to the jury for being considered for the award. I have also heard that B. S. Mardhekar's book *Vaangmayeen Mahaatmata* was among them. I have criticized it severely in my review of it. His principle of beauty is completely unacceptable to me. Yet, I believe that he should have been awarded the Phaltankar award. The South Maharashtra Award Committee had marked this award out for books on Literary Criticism. In my opinion, Jog's book does not fall within this category at all, while Mardhekar's does. This is one reason.

The other reason is that Mardhekar has presented an independent and basic thought on Literary Criticism and his contribution to this field here is original. Mardhekar's book appears quite small, while Jog's book is a tome, but from the perspective of original thought, his book delivers more. My clear opinion is that the jury for the award has made a big mistake. Getting an award is a matter of joy, and I congratulate him for it, but it is equally true that the M. S. Awards Committee has done an injustice to a literary critic who had presented independent, original thoughts.[10]

Curious to know whether Raghunathrao had read Ajit Kumar's review in *Chitra*, I came across his statement that read, 'I cannot accept at all the analysis that Ajit Kumar of *Chitra* has done.'

V.V. Shirvadkar (alias Kusumagraj)

Kusumagraj and P.L. Deshpande may well be regarded as the toast of recent times. But it is interesting to see what Raghunathrao thought of their efforts during their early days. While P.L. received much praise from him, Kusumagraj, however, seems to have been the target of his censure; one doesn't know why. For some unknown reason, Raghunathrao carried a grudge against Kusumagraj. Raghunathrao was an office bearer of the Bombay Marathi Sahitya Sangh and Kusumagraj was a protégé of Dr A.N. Bhalerao. In the first entry of the first act of the play *Nat-Samraat*, Tatyasaheb (Kusumagraj) expressed his gratitude to him (Bhalerao) through the words of the hero, Appasaheb Belwalkar. He has expressed his indebtedness to the doctor even in his memoirs titled *Vaatevarchya Saavalya*.

Raghunathrao writes:

It is still a mystery to me why the Marathi Sahitya Sangh has given a kind of contract to Shirvadkar to supply them with a play every year. His really good play was *Doorche Divey* and that too was a translation. In *Vyjayanti*, the second play he translated, he committed violence upon the original play,

but the actors managed to hold it up. His own first play
Doosra Peshva was not successful and this time's *Kaunteya*
got wiped out.

Vyjayanti was an adaptation of *Monna Vanna*. Raghunathrao
translated the original play into Marathi and published it in
Samaaj-swaasthya.

V.D. Hrishi

Between 1930 and 1940, a person named V.D. Hrishi had become
very popular in Maharashtra, particularly in Bombay and
Poona. He would hold public séances and have 'conversations
with spirits'. People used to attend his programme in large
numbers since superstition and credulity were at their zenith
in those times. Divekar Shastri had pulled up his sleeves against
charlatanism through the *Kirloskar* magazine. Raghunathrao
had written frequently in *Samaaj-swaasthya* against Hrishi
and his acts and made a laughing stock of him for being so far
removed from scientific facts. After all this, Hrishi remained an
attraction for the masses, and they were drawn to him. Hrishi
also tried to invite the attention of prestigious people in society.
Prabodhankaar K.S. Thakare has given information on one of
Hrishi's programmes in the following words:

A huge crowd had assembled for Shri Hrishi's planchette
programme. On a weekday, an assembly of 20–25 people is
considered an overflow; but for this programme, the floor
of Khandke building was packed tight. While introducing
Hrishi, Bhargavrao Vaaman Karlekar, a leader of the
Ashram, said, "Till now, barely 20–25 people would gather
to hear a living man speak, but a huge crowd has assembled
today to talk to people who are dead. This seems to suggest

that people are more attracted towards the dead than towards the living."

The reason for saying that Hrishi invited the attention of the prestigious people of society is that Tatyasaheb Kelkar had met Lokmanya Tilak after he (Tilak) had passed away. This is what Kelkar himself has written:

> Many years ago, when Hrishi had just begun the study of this subject, he had come to me with a request that I watch his show. I saw two or three of his shows, but nothing came of them. After all these efforts at home, one show was staged in the office of *Kesari* where Hrishi summoned the spirit of the late Tilak. We people there asked the spirit two questions. One question was: when Tilak returned from England, how much money he had left behind in the bank there for foreign propaganda. Our estimation was that since three lakh rupees had been collected here in the Tilak Fund and there was the Home Rule League money too, a person not in the know would assume that he would have left a lot of money behind in England; we therefore expected that Hrishi would say that he had left behind a big amount. True to our expectation, Hrishi responded that the money left behind in the bank there was a lakh of rupees.

Raghunathrao described people like Hrishi as 'mischief-makers who exercised power by pretending to be modern kings of ghosts who controlled the imaginary reproductive organ of the succubus'. He had extreme contempt for people who encouraged superstition among the masses. He has twice recounted an incident related to the man in *Samaaj-swaasthya*:

Let me give you another example of Mr. Hrishi's integrity. Once when he was travelling to Europe for his annual trip along with his efficient wife, Dr. Iravati Karve (who works in the new Research Institute of Deccan College) was travelling in the same boat with him. When she heard that this Hrishi and his wife were proposing to hold a few sessions, she requested them fervently that she be informed, because she would like to attend those sessions. The journey takes ten or twelve days and the Hrishi couple held a number of sittings during that period, but not once did they take the risk of inviting her. As the journey was coming to an end, Iravatibai asked them for the reason for being thus ignored, to which he responded, "I could never find you anywhere." It is impossible that a person travelling on a boat to Europe cannot be located . . . . The fact is that the Hrishis don't want questioning people, they want only the blindly trusting ones.

Raghunathrao has written that his persistent assault provoked some of Hrishi's devotees to meet him. A person named Joshirao also published an article titled 'Science of the Afterworld: An Open Letter to Prof. R.D. Karve, Accepting the Challenge to Prove the Existence of Life after Death' in the December 1940 issue of *Praavinya*. To demolish Hrishi, Raghunathrao read up all the available writing on the subject and wrote a number of articles titled 'Hypnotism' in *Samaaj-swaasthya*. He acknowledged right in the beginning 'the inspiration [I] received from Shri Hrishi for making the effort to go to the root of the matter'. It is evident therefore that Hrishi was trying to spread superstition and doing his best to create obstacles in Raghunathrao's work.

7

Other Work

Writings in Other Periodicals

Reason

Once Raghunathrao had decided to publish his own magazine, he would discuss matters with his intimates about what shape it should take. They responded enthusiastically with their ideas and expectations of the proposed magazine. Raghunathrao has himself given information in an article on this subject. He sheds light on the discussion he had with Wrangler Paranjape. 'He suggested a name like *Rationalist* that would indicate its purpose of anti-religion propaganda. But finally we settled on *Samaaj-swaasthya*.' Later, the Rationalist Association of India did start a magazine in Bombay that Wrangler Paranjape had visualized. Paranjape himself was one of its founding members. *Reason* began as a journal but was turned into a monthly magazine. The first issue of *Reason* was published in July 1931, in which the editors laid out the principles the magazine would promote:

> *Reason* is an organ of the Rationalists Association of India. The objects and aims of the Rationalists Association of India may be briefly described as follows:

- To combat the superstitious beliefs and practices of the masses in the country and rescue them from the baneful influence of priestcraft;
- To encourage people to educate themselves so as to cultivate a scientific habit of mind, or at any rate, an inquiring habit so that nothing should be accepted which cannot stand the test of reason and common sense;
- To reject all arbitrary authorities in matters of beliefs, however hoary and venerable they may appear.

Raghunathrao was closely associated with this magazine and this association deepened, to the extent that he would even do editorial work for it. He remained closely connected with it since its inception in 1931 till 1942 when it closed down. He wrote so many articles for the magazine in English on a wide variety of subjects that an independent compilation can be created of them. *Reason* had positioned itself to inculcate a rationalistic attitude among young people; the editors, therefore, strove to publish articles that would be beneficial to the promotion of rational thinking. Raghunath contributed to the magazine through various kinds of writings. He wrote letters on relevant subjects; sometimes he gave his opinion on an article or on some social issue. In the early days of *Reason*, he participated in a contest organized by the editors and even won an award. The award-winning essay was published in the magazine. He wrote essays countering some thoughts expressed by other writers. Some of his articles criticized some undesirable tendencies in Marathi literature. In some of his writings, he has also given an account of the activities of the magazine through a given year and explained the nature of the work done. Here is a note that was published in the March 1931 issue of the magazine:

Prize Essay: We offer our congratulations to Mr. R. D. Karve, M. A., whose essay on 'Saints and Fakirs' has been awarded the fifty rupees prize offered by the Association. Mr. Karve is doing yeoman service in the cause of social reform in this presidency and has suffered many setback(s) in life for holding steadfastly to his mental convictions. We therefore feel very happy that the prize should have gone to him. His essays appear on another page of this issue. The editor will also publish some of the other essays that were submitted, but which failed to get the prize.

The piece under the title 'Obscenity and Law' was published in the same issue:

Mr. R. D. Karve, a member of our Association and [a] staunch social reformer is being prosecuted for publishing obscene literature. The case is sub-judice. Mr. Karve has published books dealing with the [sic] Birth Control in Marathi and is conducting [a] magazine which advocates social reform in Society.

Published in the issue of 5 May 1932:

Religion and Conduct – Prof. R. D. Karve fine[d] for holding wild views. Prof. R. D. Karve, [a] member of our Association and Editor of [the] Marathi magazine Samaajswaasthya, who was charged under Act 292 IPC for having published an obscene article in his paper was convicted by Mr. I. N. Mehta, Presidency Magistrate, Fourth Court, and sentenced by [sic] pay Rs. 100/-. The article to [sic] question was 'व्यभिचाराचा प्रश्न' (The Question of Obscenity).

The following information given in the August 1932 issue of the magazine indicates that a case against him had become a certainty and that Raghunathrao would use every opportunity to state his position in public: 'Substance of the lecture delivered by Prof. R.D. Karve on 6 December 1931 at the Students' Brotherhood Hall under the auspices of the Rationalists' Association . . . .'

The May 1932 issue of the magazine published a letter titled 'The Mentality of [a] Magistrate' under its 'Letters to the Editor' column:

In a recent French novel *un Crime d'Amour* by Jean Auboura [Wikipedia says the author is Paul Bourget], the author emphasizes the fact that in so-called injustice, the mental outlook of the judge is much more important than the law of [the] legal machinery. In the story, the real criminal and an innocent man is [sic] caught. In my recent case, the learned magistrate seemed to be rather riled because *I mentioned in my statement that [the] outlook of the magistrate is the result of heredity and environment like that of everybody else; since my proposition applies not only to human beings, but even to animals and the vegetable world (so far as possible), I do not see how learned magistrates can be excluded.*

In the December 1934 issue, under the title 'Hypocrisy Rampant', Raghunathrao writes:

Another convenient thing in law is what they call 'precedent'; if it happens to agree with the magistrate's view, he quotes it in support, otherwise he coolly ignores it. The Bombay High Court, for instance, in a famous obscenity case, laid down that obscenity is a matter of language, since the same thought could be expressed in decent or in filthy language. Nothing is intrinsically obscene; only the way of expressing it can be obscene. In spite of this, I was convicted on two occasions, though it was admitted even by the prosecution that my language was not obscene.

Thus, it appears that Raghunathrao would supply the readers of *Reason* with information on his case and the editors would treat this information with sympathy. The intention, perhaps, was to use the magazine for propagating information on both birth control and *Samaaj-swaasthya* among English readers and to create a favourable opinion among the public regarding his work. The readership was young, belonged to different religions and, most importantly, believed in rational thinking. Also, highly educated Maharashtrians like Wrangler Paranjape, Dinkar Dhondo Karve, and Rao Bahadur D.L. Sahasrabuddhe contributed their writings to it.

In an article titled 'Population Control in India' published in the March 1935 issue, the author had provided information on Raghunathrao's work. Pointing to the inadequacy of the information provided, Raghunathrao wrote this letter to the magazine:

> In fact, I started my propaganda work with a pamphlet in English fourteen years back, but soon saw that it would not be much good. About the vernaculars your columnist had probably no first-hand knowledge though he mentions my Marathi monthly. I have a small 12 anna book in Marathi on Birth Control, which is now in its sixth edition and was first issued in 1923. It gives all uptodate [sic] information on the subjects. It has also been translated into Hindi and Gujarati.

On the one hand, through *Reason*, Raghunathrao would propagate information about himself and on the other hand he would mount a frontal attack on superstitions, undesirable customs and the bad traditions that were prevalent in our culture and had gained currency in our society across generations. He would also criticize the sadhus, fakeers, priests, charlatans and heads of religious centres of learning called *peeths* who

nurtured and encouraged these tendencies. In fact, the title of
the very first essay that won the *Reason* award was 'Saints and
Fakeers'. In the November 1937 issue of *Reason*, Raghunathrao
wrote about Tukaram, 'While Tukaram preached the futility
of earthly pleasures, it is a fact that when his first wife died,
he married again; and that his second wife was pregnant when
Tukaram died.'

He wrote against Upasani Maharaj of Sakori in the August
1937 issue, against Saibaba in the September 1932 issue and
against Upasani Maharaj and Meherbaba in the September
1933 issue. In an article titled 'The Rishis Know Everything', he
wrote on the concept of *dashaavataar*. In an article published
in the January 1939 issue, while discussing the Bhagwad Gita,
he talked about the natural freedom that Shri Krishna, Kunti
and Draupadi enjoyed in the matter of conjugation. His article
'What Some People Can Believe', he has examined the writings of
rishis that describe rebirth and life after death. From the issue of
February 1937 onwards, he became the editor of *Reason*. He has
written about the circumstances relating to this development in
the June issue of *Samaaj-swaasthya* of the same year:

> 'Reason', the mouthpiece of the 'Rationalists' Association
> of India' here, had been lying closed for a long while. In
> February, the Association decided to revive it and dumped
> the responsibility of its Chief Editor on my shoulder. I used
> the word 'dumped' because I have to work for it without
> getting any remuneration. Also, if there are any court cases
> (as has happened once before), they will be filed against me as
> the editor. But after all that, I well realize that the Association
> has honoured me by appointing me the editor.

The above statements not only show that Raghunathrao's
language was terse, but also suggest that he was content with

the assignment. From the issue of January 1941 onwards, the name of Abraham Solomon began appearing as editor. Raghunathrao, however, continued with his association with the magazine. But five months later, that is from the month of June 1941 onwards, he again became the editor and remained that till the magazine finally closed down. Raghunathrao has himself explained that this change—Raghunathrao as the editor for the early few months changing to Abraham Solomon for the next few editions and then back to Raghunathrao—happened as the outcome of the whim and obstinacy of a wealthy person. He writes:

An organization called the 'Rationalist Society of India' ran a rationalist English magazine called *Reason*. An appeal was filed against its editor Dr. Davine for having published an article that hurt the feelings of Christians. He got away without getting hurt, but resigned from the job, insisting that I should take up the job because I had already had appeals against me. I accepted the responsibility (without any salary, of course). How could the organization pay when it didn't have any money?

Later, a person who called himself a socialist took over the responsibility of financing the magazine on condition that I should be the editor and that some pages should be set aside for social activism. Naturally, since my load of work would increase, I placed my own conditions: only those articles that I approved would be published and that I should be given at least a little bit of compensation. When a few months drifted by without any sign of my salary, I wrote a blunt letter to the sponsor. The letter vexed him so much that he told the organization that he would finance the magazine only if it first removed me from editorship. Both of us were on the Management body. I said there that I would resign to avoid putting the organization to a loss. Another editor was appointed, but he was no writer. He requested me to continue writing as before (to which the financier had no objection) and also read the galley proofs; the byline, however, would not be mine. I agreed to that too. But finally, the organization got fed up with the financier's arrogance and decided to run the magazine on private contributions and to display my name as editor. In the end, however, with nobody to take care of all the other work, the magazine as well as the organization closed down.

Raghunathrao wrote expressly on a number of articles that appeared in the Marathi journals, some of them being: the controversy between Anubaisaheb Ghorpade and Shankarrao Kirloskar, the article of Chiplunkar of Akoli published in *Dharma-Yyoti*, an article written in *Bal-Bodh*, on a Marathi story written by Chinchlikar, on his bitter personal experiences with the office-bearers of the PEN organization in Bombay and many other subjects.

To sum up, Raghunathrao enjoyed a close association with *Reason* and he did extensive writing for it.

Jeevan

During Raghunathrao's times, there was an extremely versatile gentleman by name Ramakant Welde who was also a close friend of Kusumagraj. Tatyasaheb has mentioned him in his autobiography *Vaatevarchya Saavalya*. He had associations with journalism and the world of theatre and cinema. Bringing out journals was with him a hobby and despite the absence of any financial support, he was forever enthusiastic in this regard. His humpback had left him with an inferiority complex, which was why, perhaps, he wrote under the pseudonym 'Kumari

Shailaja'. His writing was of the sensual kind, and he wrote with amazing speed. Around the time that *Samaaj-swaasthya* was at its peak, he came out with his magazine *Jeevan* for which he did various kinds of writing. The paper, the printing and the pictures of naked women were of the better quality; however, the quality of the writing was cheap, pedestrian and sensual. The intention, clearly, was to attract a large clientele.

Writing on Ramakant Welde, Kusumagraj had this to say:

> While he was in Bombay, he published a monthly called *Jeevan* for some time. Given to sexuality, the magazine had a sizeable readership. He wrote under the beautiful name of 'Shailaja'; he would also have published a book or two under this name. If somebody were to be impressed enough by the writing to come to meet Shailaja, he would be disappointed at meeting this short, hump-backed, dark-skinned man. For writing on areas related to sex, he had bought a dozen or so English books, which he would use extensively to fill up the pages of his magazine.

Jeevan did not last for very long, but around 1941, it was quite popular. In the May 1941 issue of *Samaaj-swaasthya*, a reader had asked a question related to *Jeevan* to which Raghunathrao replied, 'We have never looked at *Jeevan* as our enemy. You may, perhaps, not have noticed that my writings are published in that magazine too.' In the September 1942 issue too, he has written, 'The magazine *Jeevan* does not come to us as an exchange arrangement, nor do we buy it.'

Raghunathrao's series of essays titled 'Kaam-Vishayak Swatantra Paaya' (Independent Foundation for Sexology) began being published in *Jeevan* in January 1941 and continued through March to September. In the first of these articles, he dwelt on 'how important the act of sex is from the point of view of physiology'. He points out that the learned men of ancient times had recognized the importance of sex and had got the sexual organs included in religious discourses. He gives the inclusion of Shiva's phallus as an example. The desire for sex is very strongly present in valiant men and has often caused the wheels of history to turn. Literature that deals with sex is limitless. After thus underlining the importance of sex, he proposes that there are two distinct groups of people who hold diametrically opposite views on sex. One group sees sex as an exalted act and the other sees it as base and sinful. Those who consider sex as base include Christian priests, Gandhi and Schopenhauer. Their opposition to sex, however, is not absolute. When a Christian man or woman goes to a priest for confession, the priest queries the person extensively on sex, which is a sign of unmet desires in the priest. While Gandhi did say that a man could have a relationship with a woman for the sake of procreation, he himself was found wanting in keeping his own sexual desires under control. As for Schopenhauer, Raghunathrao reminds us that despite being against sex, he was a married man. Sexual intercourse is an extremely important activity in all life forms and their joys and sorrows depend upon the fulfillment of the sexual urge. If the urge remains unmet, a person tends to turn towards offensive behaviour. As the sexual urge is so strong in all human societies, it follows that there is curiosity about the sexual organs and they are known by various names. There are various things among humans that naturally excite the desire for sex. But after all this, there are plenty of misunderstandings and constraints with regard to sexual desire. In the first essay, Raghunathrao dwelt on the adverse effects these misunderstandings and constraints could have on the development of a society.

In the second essay, Raghunathrao states that the language of sex is universal; man and woman do not need language for communicating with each other, though language can be helpful. Signals for indicating sexual desire and its 'language' are different, in which age, profession and financial status play only a peripheral role. He writes that the appetite for sex is stronger among rational people and they find social constraints vexing. Among some women, the desire for motherhood plays a role, while among some others, the desire for untrammeled sexual pleasure takes charge; they are sometimes willing to go to any extent for its satisfaction. He says the same two kinds may be found among men too, but they shy away from extramarital relations to avoid the ire of the society. Therefore, instead of finding faults with any kind of sexual desire, we should pay attention to how this desire can best be met.

In his third article, he attempts an analysis of Sigmund Freud's theories and examines the Oedipus Complex and the Electra Complex. Stating that Freud's research in these areas had brought about a revolution, he highlighted the salient points of his theory, namely:

1. The desire for sex occupies an important place in the life of every human being.
2. Even young children can be seen to be under its influence.
3. Ethical compulsions in advanced societies require sexual desires to be suppressed.
4. Signs of illness, therefore, can be seen that have emerged from this ignorant suppression of feelings. These suppressed feelings spill out in dreams or in the unconscious rantings during high fever.

V.M. Joshi brought out the dilemma that while the suppression of the sexual urge causes illness, going against the ethical norms of society creates mental tensions. Christianity held sexual desires to be sinful and hence emphasized on the covering of the sexual organs. Raghunathrao believed that this entire area should be examined scientifically. Towards the end of the essay, he states that sexuality is present even during childhood as well as during old age, but the body is not in a position to support it in its entirety.

In the fourth essay, Raghunathrao discusses the influence of sexuality on young children and states that it is different. In the fifth essay, he talks about how the sexuality among 6–8-year-olds is different from those of adults. Among children, there is no conscious awareness, to the extent that they handle even faecal matter without considering it filthy. In contrast, at a later age, as their power of memory as well as their level of awareness grows, social taboos are imposed upon them. During this age, love for parents with a sexual underpinning, homosexuality and masturbation also emerges. The pressure of elders causes these sexual tendencies among the young to get suppressed and they become hypocritical. However, where such suppressions do not exist, they grow happy and content in the matter of sexual desire, sexual excitement and complete sexual intercourse. During this period, a girl is attracted towards her father and a boy is attracted towards his mother and they do not carry any sense of sin for being in their company.

In his seventh essay, Raghunathrao states that societies that are away from the emasculating influence of Christianity carry purer, more natural and more balanced views on sex and examines the reasons for this. He records two points here. The first is that where nakedness is the norm, no distorted curiosity exists among the members of that community; the second is that where there are no taboos with relation to the natural desire for sex, their desire meets with full satiation resulting in a happier and a more contented society.

Thus, it was that Raghunathrao based his essays on Freudian psychology and wrote them for the series 'Kaam-Vishayak Swatantra Paaya' (Independent Foundation for Sexology), quoting extensively from the other books he had read on the subject. Suppression of the desire for sex, either voluntary or imposed by societal restrictions, leads to unhappiness, while its fulfillment leads to contentment. These thoughts of Raghunathrao show that he was miles ahead of his times.

Interest in Institutional Work

PEN

PEN is an international organization of writers, poets and artists (actually, it is an acronym for 'Poets, Editors and Novelists'). Branches are across different parts of the world, including Bombay. The organization believes in freedom of thought and expression. During Raghunathrao's times, a Parsee lady named Mrs Sophia Wadia was its president. Believing that he could do some useful work for it, Raghunathrao became a member of this organization. Although he had done much writing in the areas of stories, poetry, plays, reviews and such like and was also an office-bearer of the Marathi Sahitya Sangh, the question remains whether he was well-known in any of these areas. But this question can be asked of many of the other members of PEN too. He has not written anything anywhere to show what he did for the organization, but he does mention in *Samaaj-swaasthya* and in *Reason* the circumstances under which he was compelled to resign from its membership.

There was a Maharashtrian gentleman named Prof. N.K. Bhagwat who was also a member of this organization. One day,

Raghunathrao received a letter bearing Bhagwat's signature, delivered to him in a sealed envelope, saying that the office-bearers of the organization wanted to have an informal chat with him. He wanted to know when it would be possible for Raghunathrao to visit. By this time, there were cases of obscenity filed against him and a few members of PEN probably disapproved of his writings. Mrs Sophia Wadia was French [she has been mentioned in some places as a Colombian], therefore she had no reason to know of Raghunathrao's writing in *Samaaj-swaasthya* or in his books. She might, perhaps, have read some of his English writings, but that couldn't have created any misunderstandings. It remains likely, however, that some other people could have poisoned her mind. Raghunathrao wrote and spoke French; he had stayed in France for some time; he was quite familiar with French culture; all these together were good reasons why Mrs Wadia should have held Raghunathrao in affection. But what happened was exactly the opposite; neither had faith in the other. They wrote critically against each other in newspapers and magazines, finally leaving Raghunathrao with little choice but to submit his resignation and leave the organization. Raghunath felt it important to inform his readers as to what transpired between the two and he did in Marathi in *Samaaj-swaasthya* and a translation in *Reason*. Mrs Wadia had carried copies of *Samaaj-swaasthya* with her for the meeting and expressed her displeasure at the pictures and the articles inside them.

Raghunathrao has given details of the incident in the March 1931 issue of *Samaaj-swaasthya* under the title 'Aamchey Tikaakaar' (Our Critics). Saying that opposition to him from the ultra-orthodox was quite understandable, he was surprised that people who considered themselves as progressive should do so. Reproduced below is the article that appeared in *Reason*, which is a rough English version of what was published in *Samaaj-swaasthya*:

Readers will forgive me if I cite a personal experience as to how people give effect to their professed opinions, and I am only giving it because it is of some interest to rationalists. For more than a year, I have been a member of a small organization in Bombay whose name I am unable to disclose just yet, but who profess [sic] political, racial and religious tolerance and consider 'freedom as the breath of life of literary expression' and who stand for liberty of expression throughout the world and view with apprehension the continual attempts to encroach upon that liberty in the name of social security and international strategy. This body 'affirms its belief that the necessary advance of the world towards a more highly organized political and economic order renders a free criticism of administrations and institutions imperative from all points of view.' Fine words, which every liberal-minded man will subscribe to. And believing these to be the genuine sentiments of the members, I was very glad to join.

After this, the readers will hardly believe what follows. About two months back, I received a confidential letter from the secretary, saying: 'The Management Committee of the . . . has under consideration the desirability of your continuing as a member of the . . . in view of the quality of certain of your literary activities. They will appreciate your meeting them to discuss the matter privately and confidentially at the office of one of their members and . . . ' The address and the time was mentioned. This letter arrived with a number of seals and doubly enclosed, to emphasize its confidential nature. I did not quite understand at first why all this secrecy was required. I wrote a strong letter to the secretary, protesting against this attempted censorship of my writings, which was diametrically opposed to the principles professed by that body and saying that I considered it rank hypocrisy. However, I agreed to meet them if they still desired it, as

I was myself rather curious to see what fact these people could put upon their conduct. Having received a reply in the affirmative, I went at the appointed time and was confronted with representatives of all the important communities of Bombay: Hindus, Mahomedans, Parsis, Europeans, five members in all including the secretary. One member of the committee was absent.

Under a rather curious rule, the Committee consisting of five persons has the power to expel a member by a two-thirds vote out of the members present at a special meeting called for the purpose. This particular meeting, I was assured, was not for the purpose of expelling me, but just for a friendly talk, which turned out to be a warning to me that if I did not resign of my own accord, they may be compelled to expel me. The rule which gives them this power says: If the conduct of any member shall, in the opinion of the Committee . . . be injurious to the character and interests of the Association, the Committee shall be empowered . . . . The Committee told me that some members found my writing very objectionable and thought it undesirable that I should be a member. Naturally I told them that after all their talk (in print) about liberty of expression and the desirability of free criticism of administrations and institutions, they had no right to sit in judgment on my writings and that their conduct did not at all show that tolerance which they preached. To this, one of them replied that freedom does not mean license and that since I had been tried and convicted for so called obscenity, I had passed the bounds of freedom. I pointed out that several of their members were Congressmen who had not only been convicted, but had been in jail, [of] which I had not had the honour. They argued that political offences were on a different level, to which I replied that for people who advocated freedom of criticism, so-called obscenity should not be a greater crime, since my writings were always couched in decent language and there had never been any suggestion to the contrary, even when I was convicted.

One of the members, a lady, had brought copies of my own Marathi magazine and confronted me with the nude pictures in it asking me whether they were not obscene. Of course I said I would not put them in if I had thought them obscene, and besides, they were reproductions of pictures publicly exhibited in Art and Photographic saloons in the big cities of the world. Besides, in my opinion, there is no such thing as obscenity. It depends on the point of view. Later on, I sent them a quotation from a book reviewed elsewhere in this issue: "Obscenity is always and exclusively a quality of the accusing mind – never a quality that inheres in, or emanates from that which is accused." (Theodore Schroeder)

A Mahomedan member of the Committee, who happens to be a barrister, wanted to trap me in legal fashion by asking me, just for information, he said, whether I advocated pre-marital or extra-marital relations. I naturally refused to submit to a cross-examination and told him he could study my writings if he was anxious to know my views. The implied immorality of my views could certainly not be objectionable to [the] Mahomedan, since his religion allows a man four wives and any number of concubines in addition, and a concubine is certainly extra-marital and may also be pre-marital. Nor can Hindus object to these since Hinduism allows any number of wives and concubines.[1]

The lady member had also brought a cutting from the Bombay Chronicle – a scurrilous attack to which I had replied, but she had not seen the reply. She pointed out that my anonymous assailant had called my writing pornographic. It seems the opinion of a man who dares not sign his name acquires a value when it is printed! Another charge against me was that I advocated birth control and even sold the necessary appliances, which was deprecated as 'commercial'. I pointed out that writing and selling books was equally commercial and that members of the committee themselves would have to plead guilty to that. But obviously no argument could convince such people and I finally left them to take what steps they liked against me, only telling them that I would be obliged to expose their hypocrisy publicly if they thought it fit to expel me.

One can at least understand people who say that there should not be any liberty of expression except for orthodoxy. Religious people may consider their religion as the only way to salvation and try to prevent all counter-propaganda from the best of motives. One may call them bigoted, but when people pretend that they are all for freedom of speech and writing and then try to dictate to others, it is difficult to understand them. Are they merely hypocrites, or are they cheating themselves as well? Slogans have a sort of mystic attraction even for people who have not the slightest intention of acting upon them. It takes some intelligence to analyze one's own thoughts, but people who do not know their own minds can hardly be counted on to carry out any principles that may be laid down for their guidance and such persons certainly do not deserve to be on any committees. It seems to me that if anybody deserves expulsion, it is the members of the Committee who refuse to carry out the principles of the body and take advantage of a law to act arbitrarily. I pointed out to the Committee that, considering the principles laid down as regards freedom of expression, the 'conduct of a member' in the rule quoted above could only refer to his personal conduct, not to his literary activities or his personal views on any subject. Even the lawyers on the Committee seemed incapable of seeing this obvious truth, or perhaps they were willfully blind. One of these lawyers explained the reason of the secrecy they had observed, the double seals and so on. He said that if this question were raised in an open meeting of the members, it would amount to a libel. This shows how sure they were of their own position.

Raghunathrao should have known that he was not a creative writer, or at least he had no reputation for being one. Knowing, therefore, that it was not his cup of tea, he should not have become a member of that organization. Commitment to certain ethical principles was bound to bring about a clash; as a consequence, he had to suffer the pain and humiliation of submitting his resignation.

The second half of Raghunathrao's life was as full of uncertainty and despair, much as the first half was aggressive and lustrous. As a result of this sense of despair, perhaps, he wrote, 'I believed that there were other things more important than money and scoffed at material gains. I regret it now, but that doesn't help.'

Bhaskarrao had formed a good estimate of his elder brother's personality. Here is what he says:

At least in their early days, Appa [Raghunathrao] and Baba (Dr Shankarrao) began with the desire of making sufficient money and settling into a comfortable life. It's a different thing, though, that further on, both abandoned self-interest and got into serving society. Appa forgot himself altogether and got into the great task of disseminating awareness about birth control and bringing out his magazine *Samaaj-swaasthya*.

The 'Nishaad' and 'Shamaa' columns of the magazine *Abhiroochi* upheld Raghunathrao's contention in the PEN episode. Here's what 'Nishaad' writes:

The PEN India had to suffer its mask of hypocrisy to be torn away in its Jaipur Conference. A few European writers had got together to establish this organization to confront tyranny. This lofty ambition attracted to it a number of big names. Many still remember the colourful descriptions and pictures of their grand annual gatherings and banquets; but it is unfortunate that with the shadow of tyranny getting denser, all those delectable morsels and fancy speeches seem to have got stuck somewhere in the throat. The faith, however, had still remained alive that the writer would still have the freedom to express his thoughts and everybody would come together to protect this freedom in a reformed society. The word going round, though, is that PEN India has expelled Karve from the organization by taking objection to the thoughts propagated by *Samaaj*-swaasthya and the nude pictures it carries. It would be interesting to know what impact the pictures of semi-nude starlets had on the Madame Sophia Wadia and the harmless bunch of sycophants that hover around her. Raghunathrao, of course, called these guardians of morality hypocrites to their faces and also let Wadiabai know that PEN India was nothing but a private club. He deserves accolades for his outspokenness.

Relationship with Literary Organizations and the Natya Parishad

In his effort at learning French, Raghunathrao got familiar with its literature. As he began translating and trans-creating from French, his command over the language grew. This increased his interest in literature further. He had written a farcical play titled *Don Bahire* (Two Deaf Persons) from a French play that was published in the *Maasik Manoranjan* in 1915 and another farce titled 'Sangeet Tarala' (Musical Notes) for the same magazine, in 1923. He would go on to contribute stories to *Yashvant*. He also wrote a couple of poems for *Samaaj-swaasthya*. He loved watching plays from an early age. He had published an essay called 'Natya-Kalechi Cheshta' (Ridiculing Drama) in 1928 in *Arun*.

In 1933, he moved to his new address in 13, New Bhatwadi in Girgam and began marking his attendance for different programmes of the Maharashtra Sahitya Sangh. He later became a formal member of the organization and in due course became an office-bearer. The consequence was that he would often be on the selection committee for the various awards that the organization disbursed. He has himself mentioned sitting on the evaluation panels of the Sangh.

He would also be a member of various committees during drama festivals. He has written that once he was on the panel of judges to evaluate fifty-four plays. After he had watched only a few, he fell ill, because of which he had to withdraw from the panel. He writes in the April 1944 issue of *Samaaj-swaasthya* (p. 216), 'I had the opportunity of sitting as judge for thirteen of the plays in the competition organized for amateur groups before the beginning of the hundredth Drama Festival in April.' He would also attend with great enthusiasm the drama festivals at various places as a representative of the Sangh. He records having attended one such festival in Solapur in the company of Mama Warerkar.

He has written about going by a steamboat—*M.L. Madeena*—to the drama festival at Ratnagiri. He also talked about how he had suggested the name of Mama Warerkar for appointment to a committee during the Solapur Drama Festival and how some others had scuttled it.

He mentions how he was helped by a white saheb for getting a seat on the train on his return journey from a literary festival. He was also a member of the Bombay Journalists' Association. At a conference held in Kolhapur he met Madhavrao Bagal for the first time. Because Bagal was among those who had recognized the value of a magazine like *Samaaj-swaasthya* and contributed substantially to it without expecting anything in return, Raghunathrao was particularly gratified at this meeting.

It was during this trip that Master Vinayak had taken him for a round of his studio in Kolhapur. (March 1944, p. 203)

Raghunathrao had written in the magazine *Arun* that the roles of women should be played by women and not by young boys. This being the subject of discussion at the conference held in Jalgaon–Dhule, Raghunathrao informed his readers:

> The topic of discussion was whether the role of women should be performed by men, with particular emphasis on the role of high-caste women. In my speech, I said that if the role was of a high-caste woman, it can be brought to life only by a high-caste woman and not by a prostitute, not even by a loyal, one-man mistress.

It is no surprise, therefore, that he did not like Bal Gandharva's plays. 'The most hideous type of plays is the kind done by Bal Gandharva,' he has written.

Connoisseur Raghunathrao

Knowledge of Classical Music

A constant feature of Raghunathrao's personality was that he was interested in a wide variety of subjects, studied them and acquired competence in them. He loved going for plays at a very early age and he satisfied this desire when he was staying at a hostel during his college days. To add to that, when he was in Solapur, he had the opportunity of attending *tamaasha* programmes too. However, nobody from his family seems to have possessed artistic talents. The best that we

can see is Anna's description in the section titled 'Murudaas
Naatakaachey Prayog' (The Staging of Plays in Murud) in
his *Aatmavritt* of how they enacted plays when they were
very young. Raghunathrao's brother Shankarrao and his wife
Revatibai participated in some plays while they were in Nairobi.
Whenever Anna, Dinkarrao or Bhaskarrao came to Bombay for
work at the university, they would stay with Raghunathrao and
often go to watch a Warerkar play or a *tamaasha*.

After he became an office-bearer in the Marathi Sahitya
Sangh, he would be a judge in drama competitions. Mention
has already been made in Raghunathrao's biography of how
the renowned classical singer Abdul Kareem Khan Saheb
attended Raghunathrao's marriage and chanted a *sloka* and how
Anna had to pay a fine of Rs. 150 imposed by the Brahmins.[2]
There is no specific episode which can throw light on when
Raghunathrao picked up a fancy for plays and music. The fact,
however, remains that along with Mathematics, Raghunathrao
was extraordinarily interested in music. The paragraph below
from *Samaaj-swaasthya* makes for interesting reading.

Mathematics and Music

Raghunathrao has written:

> The famous psychologist William McDougall says on page
> 166 of his book *The Energies of Men*, that the music lover's
> "appreciation and the ground of his pleasure seems to be
> very similar to those of the mathematician reading a well-
> constructed piece of mathematical demonstration. Here
> probably is a partial explanation of the fact that musical and
> mathematical ability are so often combined in one person."
> Now, whether the psychologist's statement is right or
> Mamledar's (Tryambak Narayanrao Sathe)[3] is for the reader

to decide. I am not writing any more because my subject happens to be Mathematics.

Raghunathrao, perhaps, enjoyed declaring his subject to be Mathematics and yet staying silent on his knowledge of music. But although he does not make any specific mention of this knowledge in the above paragraph, he has often written on the subject in *Samaaj-swaasthya*. In this context, Shakuntala Paranjape writes:

> His daily routine too functioned like clockwork. He would set the alarm for five-thirty in the morning. Even if he had stayed up till two in the night in some singing soiree, the time for his waking up would never change. He was extraordinarily fond of songs . . . .

Shakuntalabai makes another mention at some place of a musical soiree that was held in her house at Pune. She writes:

> We had a singing programme of Gajananbuva at our house one morning. The singing was excellent. At about twelve-thirty, Mirashibuva was requested to sing. Both these singers were extremely courteous gentlemen, because otherwise ego issues can often crop up on such occasions. The two were requested to sing together and they both took this request to heart. And the singing! It was nothing short of a contest! R. D. Karve had come specifically from Bombay for this musical programme.

Thus, Raghunathrao had trained his ears for music and expressed his opinions on the subject with authority and conviction.

The use by senior singers of the harmonium as an accompaniment would upset Raghunathrao greatly. *Satyavaadi*

once had a Cinema Special issue which carried an interview
with Abdul Kareem Khan Saheb. Khan Saheb had expressed
his unhappiness at the poor state of music. Raghunathrao
immediately shot back, 'I feel unhappy at this unhappiness
being limited only to words. Isn't it his duty to stay away from
the harmonium?'

A few years later, however, there was a marked difference
in the distance between Khan Saheb's words and deeds. To
highlight this point, Raghunathrao wrote about a musical
programme of Khan Saheb that was held in Poona as follows:

> While Abdul Kareem Khan's programme was in progress,
> a member of the audience (maybe Raghunathrao himself)
> asked him to put away the harmonium, to which Khan
> Saheb responded, "I am delighted to hear that you want the
> harmonium stopped. I don't like the harmonium either."
> Saying this, he immediately removed the instrument. In a
> similar incident in Bombay, he again expressed his dislike for
> the harmonium, but let it continue because people want it . .
> . . In his own school, he would never teach singing to anyone
> on the harmonium. . . .

The last sentence in the above paragraph is, perhaps, in the
context of Indumati Pandit, who will be written about later.

Govindrao Tembe was an ace harmonium player.
Raghunathrao came out against him too, saying, 'Playing the
harmonium is a part of skill with hands, not of music.' He gave
here the example of Abdul Kareem Khan who declared that
the harmonium notes were faulty. Khan Saheb has said that he
gave the twenty-two notes that are needed for Hindustani music
to (Ernest) Clements Saheb, who got a special harmonium
made that produced these twenty-two notes. Later, in 1953,
Raghunathrao praised Tembe by writing, 'Tembe has written
a beautiful series of articles in *Loksatta* on Hindustani music.

But in spite of being a master at playing the harmonium, he has never praised the instrument in these articles.' Drawing on Mahatma Gandhi's opinions on birth control into the argument, Raghunathrao wrote, 'All joys are experienced through the nervous system. The joy derived from music is experienced through the excitation of the nervous system of the ears . . . . One hopes that Gandhiji does not consider music, at least, as cheap. (If he does, then he does not fall within the category of humans.) . . . The joy from music is also physical.' (**203**)

In 1934, a function of (the classical singer) Hirabai Badodekar was to be held in Fergusson College, but, perhaps, the management committee had objected to it. Raghunathrao wrote, 'Even if Hirabai Badodekar's singing was not allowed to be held in Fergusson College, the tradition of considering the joy derived from music as of a high order continues. The question that emerges is, why is the joy derived from eating a favourite dish considered as of a lower order?'

The first Annual Prize Distribution Ceremony of Mahila Sangeet Vidyalaya, Dadar, was organized in December 1934 at Opera House. This was the trigger for Raghunathrao to write his independent comments on music, perhaps, the only one, in 'Sharadechey Patr'. He began by complimenting Indumati Pandit, the principal of the institution for her commendable work but expressed his displeasure at her use of the harmonium in the teaching of music. He said:

I do not at all like the idea of the harmonium being used for the teaching of Hindustani music. All experts on music have agreed that it is impossible for the twelve notes of the harmonium octave to accommodate pure Hindustani classical music. It is a shame that, falling victims to the corrupted tastes of the lay public, music schools should be run on the strength of the harmonium; that even a singing maestro like

Abdul Kareem Khan should hold concerts with harmonium as accompaniment. When he was asked why he did so, Khan Saheb responded that since people wanted the harmonium, he was left helpless. This may be forgivable for those whose livelihood depends on the holding of concerts; but it is also the responsibility of the expert to create good taste among the audience. If schools too show the same attitude, it will become impossible for true training to be imparted to the people. Instead of making empty talks about the development of music, they should then openly declare that it is a matter of their livelihood and that they have no choice. The names of Prof. Devdhar and Prof. Narayan Vyas flutter on the advisory committee of the institution. They, at least, should have given attention to this matter. If they profess helplessness in this matter, all their big talk on the advertisement hand-outs is simply hollow. There is not an iota of doubt that till such time as the harmonium is not altogether thrown out, Hindustani music, instead of progressing, can only get worse.

Raghunathrao's opinion was that 'the harmonium spoils music' and many senior singers of that period were in agreement. Also, he did not believe that merely the ability to identify ragas was good enough to show that one understood classical music. Being able to savour music was the important thing for him. He wrote:

If someone asks me what raga it is, if I can identify the raga, I respond by naming it; . . . but if I cannot identify it, I feel no sense of shame at all. My opinion in this matter is that even if one doesn't know the name of a rose, he can still relish its fragrance. In the same way, one can relish a raga without having to know its name. If, therefore, somebody pulls me up for not identifying a raga, I have no reason to feel small.

In short, even though Raghunathrao did not have formal training in classical music, the knowledge he possessed in the field was phenomenal. He went to the extent of getting into arguments with authorities like Abdul Kareem Khan Saheb, Govindrao Tembe, Krishnarao Phulambrikar and others. Very often, they would admit that he was in the right.

Other Writings

Raghunathrao dabbled in different kinds of writing. He wrote three plays: *Sangeet Tarala* [Waves of Music], *Gurubaji* and *Nyaayaacha Shodh* [Gurubaji and the Search for Justice]; he wrote books on health like *Aadhunik Kaam-Shastra*, [Modern Sexology] *Guptrogaapaasoon Bachaav* [Protection from Venereal Diseases], *Vaishya-Vyavasaaya* [Prostitution as a Profession], *Klaibyaachi Meemaamsa* [An Analysis of Claib], *Aadhunik Aahaar-shastra* [Modern Dietetics] and *Tvachechi Niga* [Skin-care]. He wrote *Birth Control* in English. Besides, he published plenty of stories in *Samaaj-swaasthya*, some his own, some translated from French. He published a selection of these stories in the book *Teraa Goshti*. He also wrote a book called *Parischyaa Paree* (The Fairies of Paris, 1946) that carries sketches of three courtesans of Paris in the seventeenth and eighteenth centuries: Ninon del'Enclos (1620–1705), Yario de Larmes (1611–1650) and Madame de Maintenon (1635–1719).

The volume *Teraa Goshti* contains thirteen stories that were published in *Samaaj-swaasthya* from time to time. In the preface, Raghunathrao mentions that the stories were published in the same chronological order in which they had appeared in the magazines. He adds that all the characters in the stories are imaginary. The thirteen stories are: 'Nanasaheb Takkey', 'Punarvivaah', 'Agnishalaaka Manjusha', 'Sahakaarya', 'Prem', 'Kathin Prasang', 'Vimaleche Sheel', 'Aamchi Kusum', 'Snehaachi Kasoti',

'Zhopeche Aushadh', 'Vivaahaachey Sukh', 'Jagaacha Pravaas' and 'Pechprasang'.

Three of Raghunathrao's books—*Selected Articles of Samaaj-swaasthya* volume 1 and volume 2 and 'Thirteen Stories'—are reprints of material printed in *Samaaj-swaasthya*. One can guess why Raghunathrao would have wanted to compile already published material into book form. One reason would surely have been to make his writings enduring by being bound as books; but perhaps, the bigger reason could have been to generate money. It is beyond dispute that his work in the area of birth control was historical in nature, but it did invite financial dependence on others. Lakshmi, the Goddess of Wealth, remained forever disenchanted with him.

Here's another book that Raghunathrao writes about. 'While I was teaching in Elphinstone College, I wrote a book on a section of Geometry since there was no good book available. It began being used everywhere.'

In *Aadhunik Kaam-Shaastra* (1932, Modern Sexology), Raghunathrao gave detailed and extensive scientific information on different areas of the subject, like: the importance of the sexual urge, ovaries, the reproductive organs of man and woman, menstruation, the natural and artificial excitation of the sexual urge, pre-coital activities, coitus, puberty, postures, sexology from the social perspective, surreptitious sex, spouse selection, difficulties in coitus, sterility, birth control, abortion, heavy bleeding during menstruation, under-or over-indulgence in sex, gonorrhea, syphilis, etc., modern ideas on celibacy, supplements, and so on.

In the preface to the book, Raghunath wrote:

A number of topics discussed in the book have been published in *Samaaj-swaasthya* before, but some of them have been re-written. The desire for sex is an extremely powerful urge and the satisfaction of that urge gives extreme pleasure. Often, this remains the only source of joy for a person seeped in sorrow. Everybody has the right to partake of this joy without causing distress to others. The purpose of Sexology is to teach people how to maximize the joy that sex can give.

Pictures of male and female sexual organs, scientific information and the opinions of authorities like Dr. Havelock Ellis, Prof. Blaschko, Anton Nystrom, Dr. Robinson, Dr. Ravhan Blokh, Dr. Levenfeld, Dr. Schmidt, Dr. Veky, Dr. Aileen Byrne, Dr. Wilhelms, Prof. Freud and Dr. Stanislaus A. G. A. have been given.

In this manner, Raghunathrao introduced a new subject into Marathi and included the scientific findings of European and American authorities. He tried to prove that the one single purpose of the book was the propagation of knowledge.

It was, perhaps, for the first time that the reproductive organs of men and women along with detailed introductions on their functions were published in a Marathi book with such clarity. It can be believed that the ultra-orthodox loved to surreptitiously watch the pictures and read about them.

In *Aadhunik Aahaar-Shaastra* (1938, Modern Dietetics), Raghunathrao examined the following areas related to the subject: the need for dietetics, human diet, how we stay alive, the need for food, the constituents of food, the quantum of food and the parameters for its choice, analytical tables, the digestive process, details on a few food items, compatibility with nature, supplements, purgatives, fasting, intoxicants, and so on. He wrote in the preface:

Appetite and the urge for sex are the two most important needs for humans as well as for a number of other animals. If we try to find the relative importance of one over the other, we will realize that if there is no appetite, a person will not eat anything

and hence will not be able to live; the question for sex, therefore
will never arise. Appetite, therefore is unquestionably the more
important of the two. The sexual urge, however, is not limited to
the individual, it extends to the creation of progeny. But unless
a person stays alive, there can be no progeny; and good health is
not possible without adequate diet. From this perspective, more
importance needs to be given to diet.

The author had long intended to write a book on
dietetics, but the intention remained unfulfilled due to
shortage of time. Meanwhile, I got to know that a gentleman
had announced an award for a book on this subject and had
invited books or handwritten manuscripts before a certain
date. I actually did send a typewritten manuscript. But
because of having fallen ill midway, I myself was not satisfied
with the writing. There may still be a few more months to go
before the deadline for the award, hence I have made some
additions and some improvements and decided to get the
book published before the results are announced. This, then,
is the shape in which the book has been published.

The committee did not find any book deserving of the first
prize. There were two second prizes given and Raghunathrao's
book *Kachchaa Aahaar* (Raw Foods) won one of the two second
prizes. When one enters a competition, the rules laid down by
the organizer become binding and no appeal can be sent against
them. The other point is that one may not always be in the right.
But in this matter, Raghunathrao's extreme self-belief and
egotism welled up and he would refuse to come to terms with
thoughts different from his own. This wasn't true of contests
alone; it applied to all the decisions he took during important
moments of his life and must be accepted as his weakness.

Raghunathrao wrote a number of stories for *Samaaj-
swaasthya*, but it is difficult to say which were original and

which trans-created. With the exception of Aruna Dhere, critics of Marathi stories have not taken much cognizance of his stories, and they can't be blamed for it. From the perspective of literature, his stories do not appear to be of the highest calibre but he should be appreciated for having translated so many of Guy de Maupassant's stories for his magazine.

The first compilation of selected articles from the first three years of *Samaaj-swaasthya* was published in a book for which Raghunathrao wrote a preface. He wrote:

> There is always a demand for the earlier issues of *Samaaj-swaasthya*, and we have received requests that they be printed again. But from the point of view of finances this is an almost impossible task. This book, however, contains selected articles from the first three years of its existence. Most of the important articles have been covered here. Since there is a plan to bring out an independent compilation of articles on sexology, they have not been included here. Correspondence will be compiled in another volume. . . .

This makes it clear that even as the first part was being published, Raghunathrao had plans for a second part in place.

The theatre was very dear to Raghunathrao. He did not have many opportunities to go for plays as a child, but saw a few when he was living in a hostel during his college days. In the articles he wrote on Mama Warerkar, he mentioned that he had wanted to be a playwright. Mama received encouragement from his father by being taken to watch plays even while he was a child. 'Anna, however, did not take me to watch plays,' he writes, 'otherwise I too would have become a good playwright.'

Raghunathrao wrote the play *Gurubaji* in 1923; it was never staged but published as a book in 1937. His *Nyaayaacha Shodh* also remained a book. Though Mama and he were close friends, there is nothing to show that Mama made any effort to have his friend's plays performed on stage. Raghunathrao was himself an office-bearer of the Sahitya Sangh, but even so, no one picked his plays for stage. The reason could be, perhaps, that the way his plays reflected life and the manner in which they were presented were not to the taste of the theatregoers of those times. Besides, those were the days of musical plays, while his were all in prose.

Three Events Post-Independence

1. The Government's Refusal of Permission for Importing Raw Material

The February 1943 issue of *Samaaj-swaasthya* carried a piece under the title 'Sarkaari Adhikaaryaancha Aadmuthepana' (The Folly of Government Officials) which stated that because of the foolishness of government officials during the period of the Second World War, 'there is government control over trade, which necessitates the importing of a jelly required for making Dutch-caps, . . . but even that has become impossible.'

After the Second World War ended, not only had the prices of imported chemicals shot up but heavy import duties had also been imposed upon them. Further, a government license was compulsory for the manufacture of birth control devices and these licenses would be given only to qualified medical practitioners. This obviously hit Raghunathrao quite hard. He made frequent applications but couldn't impress the government at all. He writes, 'It is after a full two months that the government has responded to my application for importing rubber caps (pessaries) from England used for birth control. This is what they have written back: "Since the government does not consider these items to be essential commodities, the permission is denied."'

2. The First Birth Control Conference

The second incident deals with the first Birth Control Conference that took place in Bombay. Raghunathrao was not only invited to the programme but was also requested to deliver a lecture on his long-term experience in the field. He was quite gratified with the honour. It was a welcome change from the vilification he had faced all these years. He would surely have felt that all his work on birth control was finally being applauded. However, he could not say as much as he had wanted in his address. He writes:

> I had been requested to talk of my thirty years of experience in this conference; but since I did not get adequate time, I could not speak about the entire process. When Kashibai Avasare of Santacruz asked me why I hadn't spoken and when I informed her about the inadequacy of time, she requested the chairperson to ask me to talk about the process.

Although the policy of the Congress party on birth control was not satisfactory, S.K. Patil, the Bombay mayor, was favourably inclined towards it. He called over the participants in the conference to the mayor's chamber for tea. Raghunathrao was happy at this gesture. He writes, 'I had this opportunity of sitting in the chamber that I had never seen before. I was given a seat close to the mayor saheb's table.'

When the Congress rule began, Raghunathrao was hopeful that birth control would receive a fillip from the government. But Rajkumari Amrit Kaur, the health minister, was a staunch Gandhian; accordingly, though she did believe in birth control, she wanted it to happen the Gandhian way—through self-control, and not by the use of artificial devices.

3. Felicitation on His Seventieth Birthday

Anantrao Gadre and Appa Pendse remembered that their
friend would be completing seventy years on 14 January 1952
and they began to collect money for presenting to him a purse.
The felicitation programme was held under the chairmanship
of Justice M.C. Chhagla. To celebrate the occasion, N.S. Phadke,
and S.K. Ksheersaagar wrote laudatory articles on him that were
published in various magazines. Raghunathrao acknowledged
these felicitations appropriately, but did not shy away from
voicing his disagreements. The novelist N.S. Phadke wrote a
laudatory article in the *Navabharat*, but expressed regret that
the others had mentioned only Raghunathrao as the progenitor
of birth control.

8

Raghunathrao's Intimates

Mama Warerkar

Raghunathrao did not have many friends, but he did have strong, intimate bonds with people like Mama Warerkar, Shripad Shankar Navare, Anant Hari Gadre and Appa Pendse. Mama Warerkar was especially dear. He was senior to Raghunath by two years and the men were on back-slapping terms with each other and that was perhaps why Annasaheb would go for his plays.

Mama has made no mention at all about Raghunathrao in his autobiography *Maazha Naataki Sansaar* (My Dramatic World), but the article he has written for *Manohar* has been useful to many. Mama wrote for *Samaaj-swaasthya* too; for instance, his article for the 'Two Wives' issue, his article for the 'Literature Special' issue and his letters exchanged in the context of Shakuntala Paranjape's review of the play *Udati Paakhare*.

The grateful reference that Raghunathrao makes of Mama in his *Vaishya Vyavasaaya*, his article in defence of Mama when a case had been filed against *Udati Paakhare* and his criticism against Prabhakar Padhye and others about whom Mama did not carry a good opinion—highlight the friendship between the two.

Raghunath would have been a frequent visitor to Mama's house. Here's a picture drawn by Gangadhar Mhambre:

The one person who Mama would really have wanted visiting his house was his loyal friend R. D. alias Appa Karve. "He doesn't go anywhere these days," would be his groan. He would then give the reason, "The *Samaaj-swaasthya* case has done him in." One day Mama took me to Appa's house, saying, "It's his birthday today, the perfect day to visit him. . . . "

When we reached his house, we found him sitting in a chair . . . . Mama then told him, "Appa, you are younger than me and I am younger than your Anna. But looking at the work Anna has been doing and considering his age, I feel that I have no business cribbing about my age. But as I came up the staircase today, I can tell you that it left me short of breath."

To which Appa responded, "How many more birthdays have I got left? In any case, stop coming for my birthdays now."

"How's that?" said Mama.

"You live on the ground floor," said Appa. "I'll come to you for your birthdays."

Raghunathrao's birthday fell on the 14 January. Since the *Samaaj-swaasthya* case has been mentioned, the episode would have happened somewhere between 1931 and 1939. Again, Raghunath mentions that he does not have many birthdays left in his life. It was in 1937 that he had fallen very ill, to the extent that he had started despairing for life. But then, it is amazing that no mention has been made of Malatibai. She would certainly have been alive when this visit happened. If it had happened after her death, then mention of the court case would have been chronologically incompatible. Be that as it may, this episode does underline the intimacy that existed between the two.

The two of them would visit literary conferences together. They had marked their joint attendance in 1938 at Kolhapur, in 1940 at Ratnagiri and in 1941 at Solapur. Y.D. describes having spotted the two of them together in Solapur in the following words:

> From early childhood I had the hobby of collecting autographs of famous people. In the year 1941 in Solapur I spotted Mama Warerkar and handed my autograph book and a pen to him for his signature. He handed it back to me and pointed to a 'suited-booted' person next to him and said, "*Arey*, take his signature first. He is a very great man. You are very young now. When you grow up, you will understand." I, of course, did not believe what Warerkar was saying, but I also knew that I would not get his signature till I had taken the other person's. I silently handed my autograph book to him and got to know from his signature that his name was R. D. Karve. I was not at all excited at having got his autograph.

We can gather two things from this description: the respect in which Mama held Raghunathrao and Raghunathrao's 'suited-booted' personality. Raghunathrao has written about Mama in other magazines besides *Samaaj-swaasthya*. Ramakant Welde of Nashik had come over to Bombay and started his magazine *Jeevan* in 1941–42, for which, along with Anant Antarkar, Vyankatesh Vakil, Nana Jog and Bhaskarrao Jadhav, Mama and Raghunathrao had also written. While Raghunathrao wrote a seven-part series for it under the title 'Kaam-Vishayak Swaantryaachaa Paaya', Mama wrote for it on some other subject. Raghunathrao had already written books like *Santatiniyaman*, *Guptrog Paasoon Upaay* and plenty of articles in *Samaaj-swaasthya* of this kind, but with Mama, the situation was different. It is likely that Raghunathrao would have persuaded Mama to write for this magazine.

In *Vaishya Vyavasai*, Raghunathrao wrote on the etymology
of the name 'Shinde', which triggered a flurry of correspondence
in *Samaaj-swaasthya*. The controversial statement was this:
'When a woman from a cultured house begins working as a
mistress, she is called "*shindal*" and her son is called "*shinda*".
This is how the surname "*Shinde*" has come into being.' When
General Nanasaheb Shinde of Baroda read this, he was livid. He
demanded an immediate apology from Raghunathrao for this
calumny. 'You have obviously published these remarks on the
advice of Mama Warerkar who is notorious for spreading such
scurrilous gossip. You seem to have no idea how dangerous it is
for a scholarly person like you to place your trust on someone
like Mama Warerkar and put such mischievous, despicable and
humiliating remarks in your book without examining their
veracity,' he wrote.

Raghunathrao, thus, seems to have suffered collateral
damage on account of Mama's notoriety, but their friendship
continued undisrupted. Dr G.Y. Chitnis married Mama's
daughter Mai and thus became a member of Mama's family.
Ramdas Bhatkal has written about the relationship between
Mama, Mai, G.Y. Chitnis and Leela Chitnis, saying:

> Even before she divorced the doctor, Leela Chitnis was going
> through a difficult period when Mama showed her the way.
> On his advice, she got herself a BA degree from Nagpur
> University. It was Mama again who recommended to Master
> Vinayak that she would be able to act in movies. Mai had
> nothing at all to do with the split that happened between the
> doctor and Leelatai.

V.L. Kulkarni, Prabhakar Padhye, R.B. Joshi, Anant Kanekar
and V.H. Kulkarni had a club, which B.S. Mardhekar, Dr A.N.
Bhalerao and V.R. Dhawale often visited. The relationship

between Raghunathrao and Prabhakar Padhye had turned extremely sour. In an article written in 1991, he vilified Raghunathrao in the matter of his friendship with Mama.

Dr G.Y. Chitnis was Mama's son-in-law. Despite this, when the magazine *Chitra*, under the editorship of Chitnis, published a bio-sketch of the proprietor Lotwala Shet, Raghunathrao wrote critically on it as follows:

> When Mama Warerkar saw a fairly detailed bio-sketch of Lotwala Shet in the weekly *Chitra*, he was assailed by doubts. *Chitra* has had many editors before, but now Dr. Chitnis seems to have become the editor. The sense that I can get out of it is that like all other editors before, this editor too has shown the smartness of currying the boss's favour. It may also be possible, perhaps, that looking at the success that *Kirloskar* has gained by publishing biographies, *Chitra* too has decided to emulate it and begun by doing the boss's biography.

In the last sentence, Raghunathrao did not miss the opportunity of taking a swipe at Kirloskar while talking of Chitnis.

Shakuntala Paranjape

Dr Y.D. Phadke's biography of Raghunathrao, titled *R.D. Karve*, has pictures of Raghunathrao and his intimates. One of those pictures is of the renowned writer Shakuntala Paranjape, but the book itself does not talk about her at all. Prof. P.N. Paranjape, who recommended the book in *Lalit*, says that he didn't see the propriety of Shakuntala Paranjape's picture there.

Two women helped him in his mission of propagating birth control—his wife Malatibai and the other—Shakuntalabai, the only daughter of Wrangler R.P. Paranjape. After the early death of his wife, Wrangler Saheb brought up his motherless child devotedly. After returning from England, he had joined Fergusson College as Professor of Mathematics, where he later became principal. Thereafter, he became the minister of education and followed it up by being sent as ambassador to Geneva and then to Australia. He thus had a long and distinguished career in various capacities. While they were in Geneva, Shakuntalabai married a Russian named Youra Steptzoff on 15 February 1935. While she was still in Geneva, she sent £1 to Raghunathrao as contribution towards the starting of *Samaaj-swaasthya*. When she got married, Sharayubai Puntambekar wrote an article titled 'Aamche Ratn Pardeshaat Geley' (Our Jewel has Gone to a Foreign Land) that was published in the March 1935 issue of *Purushaarth*. Unfortunately, their marriage did not last long and they were divorced in Lucknow in August 1937. She wrote a letter in this regard to 'Sharada', asking whether a divorced woman should use '*Sau*' or 'Shrimati' before her name. Not only did Raghunathrao publish this letter, but 'Sharada' responded to it too.

By 1935, the Prabhat Film Company had established itself in Pune. It produced several interesting movies in Marathi and then in Hindi too, thus gaining fame across the entire country. It had produced a movie called *Kunku* based on N.H. Apte's Marathi novel *Patnari Gosht* (An Acceptable Matter). While experienced actors Keshavrao Datey and Shanta Apte played central roles in it, Shakuntalabai played a small role too, but that was the swansong of her acting career. She began writing stories and farces and earned herself a reputation in the world of Marathi literature.

As mentioned earlier, Raghunathrao had been upset with Wrangler Paranjape for not having helped him enough with regard to his professorship after his return from Paris. Since the Karves and the Paranjapes were intimates, they would often be thrown in each other's company, which is when Shakuntalabai would act as the mediator.

The October 1935 issue of *Samaaj-swaasthya* carries an editorial note which read: 'Shakuntala Paranjape has assured us that she will review some books for us. We are grateful.' Shakuntalabai had the wherewithal to endorse her assurance with action. She went ahead and reviewed innumerable books belonging to various genres of literature for the magazine. One among the reviewed books was Vishram Bedekar's *Ranaangan*, which is believed to have been lauded in literary circles from 1965 onwards. Before this belief is taken to be the gospel truth, it is advisable to read the review that was published in the January 1939 issue of *Samaaj-swaasthya*. They would then know that Shakuntalabai had spotted how unusual *Ranaangan* was long ago.

Samaaj-swaasthya is not known for the poetry it published, but one can see there two poems of Shakuntalabai:

Aha, finding the beloved alone,	अहा! एकांती पाहुनी सखीला,
Lust shot through the body	अंगी मदन उसळला,
Love-triggered sport ||	प्रेमलहरी लीला ||
Coy charmer	मुग्ध मोहिनी
Lowering her head	मान मूरडुनी
Smiling soft and bashful	हंसे हळुच लाजुनी
Pallu on head	उभी पदर घेउनी
Delightful damsel! Aha!	रम्य बाला ! अहा! एकांती
Finding her alone . . .	पाहुनी . . .
Ravishing in her nakedness	नग्न कामिनी
Shivering she stood	कम्प पाउनी
Nervously covering her bosom	भये उर झाकुनी
Delightful damsel! Aha!	रम्य बाला ! अहा एकांती . . .
Alone . . .	गाढ मिलनी
The close, close meet	सौख्य तन्मनी
The joy of body and soul	वादुं काय वर्णुनी
Can I describe it	स्वयें याहीं भोगुनी
Even after tasting of it?	एक बाला अहा एकांती . . .
A damsel, aha! Alone . . .	

The above poem does not carry Shakuntala Paranjape's name below it but carries the note 'from an unmarried graduate girl' above the poem. Hence it is believed that Shakuntalabai is the composer. Now, the second poem:

Once, just once our eyes met And at that instance Diverse exchanges | Romance futile ||1|| No knowledge of name nor village How, then, did someone Take charge | Infiltrating the heart ||2|| Not a word made sense, Language strange, Face foreign | The heart beat faster ||3|| Understood by and by those words of love Those desires of the heart In others' presence | Looking at one another |4||	एकदा, एकदा पाहुनी मनी पाहता क्षणी, विविध संचार | देहात मदन बेकार ||१|| ठाउकें ठाउकें नांव नच गांव, घेतला ठाव, कसा कोणी | हृदयात हळुच शिरुनी ||२|| एकही एकही शब्द नच कळे, बोल वेगळे, मूर्ति परकी | छातीत भरली धडकी ||३|| उमजती, उमजती बोल प्रीतिचे, हेतू हृदयिंचे, सर्व लोकी | पाहुनि एकमेकीं ||४||

Shakuntalabai wrote different articles for *Samaaj-swaasthya*. A small play titled *Kumaarikeche Mool* (The Child of an Unwed Woman) was published in the February 1939 issue. A play called *Paangharleli Kaatadi* (The Skin Wrapped Around) was published in the December 1942 issue with the playwright's note: 'Five years ago, while giving his opinion on Marathi plays in a conference, Dajisaheb Tuljapurkar had thrown me the challenge of writing an independent five-act play. *Paangharleli Kaatadi* is being presented in response to that challenge.' Somewhere during 1935–1936, she had written a farce titled *Soyrik* (Intimacy). The *Kesari* reports that it was staged in aid of the Hingane Women's Education Society.

When her review of Mama Warerkar's play *Udati Paakhare* appeared in *Samaaj-swaasthya*, Mama himself wrote a letter that Raghunathrao published. A controversy erupted when 'Sharada' criticized the article that Malatibai Tendulkar, the editor of *Pratod*, had written on Dattu Bandekar's book *Sakhya Hari*. A letter that Shakuntalabai wrote in this context was published in *Samaaj-swaasthya*, where she says point-blank, 'How you love to exaggerate things!'

Raghunathrao had made some adverse remarks on the role that Shakuntalabai had played in *Kunku*, which suggests that the two had got to know each other so well that they could freely criticize each other without causing offence. Their differences were superficial. Shakuntalabai was completely bowled over by Raghunathrao's intellectual prowess, his commitment to his mission and his capacity to sacrifice. Conversely, Shakuntalabai's great artistic talent, her literary skills and her candid behaviour made her get along famously with Raghunathrao. When Raghunathrao felt that facilities should be created for providing birth control devices for women in Pune, Shakuntalabai stood up to help him. Her series of articles under the title 'Sudhaarnechyaa Maargaateel Khaach-khadage' (Obstacles on the Path of Reform) published in *Samaaj-swaasthya* had become quite popular. From 1935 onwards, Raghunathrao's health began to fail. He experimented with a raw diet too and wrote a few articles on the subject. Malatibai passed away in 1944 and Raghunathrao was left lonesome and broken. Shakuntalabai suggested that he should shift to Pune, which he didn't accept.

She had identified herself completely with Raghunathrao's work, so much so that a number of people believed that the 'Sharada' of the column 'Sharadeche Patr' in *Samaaj-swaasthya* was none other than Shakuntalabai herself. After Raghunathrao's passing away, it was suggested that she should keep the magazine going. She has written in this context, 'After his (Raghunathrao's) passing away, several people suggested that I should run the magazine, but I am well aware of my strengths. R.D. Karve came and went like a comet, and I do not want to make a mess of his *Samaaj-swaasthya*.'

Her deep affection for Raghunathrao and a keen understanding of his personality are starkly visible in her writings.

When Prof. M.V. Dhond was collating information on Raghunathrao, he had interviewed Dr Shankarrao, Dinkarrao, Bhaskarrao and Shakuntalabai in 1977 and asked them why Iravati had not written for *Samaaj-swaasthya*.

Shankarrao replied, 'Iravati's areas of contemplation were different from Appa's.'

'Baba, don't try to cover up,' Shakuntalabai interrupted. 'Iravati didn't care at all for Appa's work.'

Prof. Dhond has recorded that he felt a controversy was about to begin. What was obvious, however, was that even twenty-four years after Raghunathrao had died, Shakuntalabai's affection for him was still strong.

People are thrown together either out of circumstances or out of love for each other, but soon they begin to spot each other's faults and begin to drift away from each other—physically and emotionally. Things can become more unpleasant when barbs are thrown at each other. The relationship between Raghunathrao and Shakuntala was quite the opposite. Intellectually, they got to know each other well and they complemented each other at the highest level. It will be interesting to make a balanced and detailed analysis of their internal equation.

Malatibai Karve

Malatibai had become a matriculate in 1908 and, going by what Anna has written, she studied for one year till Previous at Fergusson College. After they had got married, she had stayed in Pune for some time and then moved over to Bombay to live with Raghunathrao. Within a year's time she got herself a job as a teacher at the Chandaramji High School. From there onwards, she was a financial support to Raghunath. Y.D. Phadke writes that she had taken a teachers' training course in Kandivli.

She could not stay for a sustained period working for any institution. From Chandaramji she moved to the Urdu school of the Bombay Municipal Corporation and then to the school run by the N.D. Thackersey University. She reviewed a book on grammar for *Samaaj-swaasthya*, which would suggest that she taught languages at school. She also held physical exercise classes there. There is mention that she worked in a maternity home too. Advertisements for Raghunathrao's birth control centre would carry the message that Malatibai would instruct the women on how to use birth control devices. This spared the women the blushes. Anna has written that she was strong and resilient and that she was particularly interested in household work and orderliness:

> Now she helps her husband in conducting his birth control clinic by giving practical instructions about using birth control appliances to women who go there. She also serves him as his assistant and his clerk . . . . He is fortunate in having got a very sympathetic wife and though somewhat

disabled for the past few years, she is actively helping him. (1933, pp. 173–174).

It is clear that Anna held Malatibai in great affection. The transparency of his writing is also evident here. It is Anna alone who has written that Malatibai would always help Raghunathrao with all kinds of work related to birth control and *Samaaj-swaasthya*. We have already noted Bhaskarrao's affectionate remarks of his stay with Raghunathrao and Malatibai in Bombay.

The last issue of *Samaaj-swaasthya* (although readied for publication by Raghunathrao himself) was edited and published by Bhaskarrao. In the preface he wrote for it, he said:

> *Samaaj-swaasthya* was a single-pole tent. Writing the articles, typing them out, getting them ready for the press, going through the proofs, bringing the printed bundles home, pasting the stamps and the addresses of the subscribers, having them delivered to the post office or to the newspaper agent on the 12th, and all the work at the office would mostly be done single-handedly by R. D. Karve.

This is of course true from the time when Malatibai fell extremely ill and after she died. It is surprising therefore, that Bhaskarrao should have forgotten Malatibai's participation in preparing the magazine for print. He didn't add a single sentence to acknowledge her contribution. This injustice on Malatibai actually began from Raghunathrao himself. When he wrote that he did all the work from 'editor to peon' without remuneration, he never felt that he should appreciate Malatibai's contribution to the cause. As an exception, when he makes mention of the postal arrangement in the March 1936 issue, he writes, 'It is important to tell them that there are just two persons in our office—my wife and I.'

A reader had once written, 'It is nice that you have a woman for helping in the selection of the Dutch Cap. But do you believe that this lady is as competent as you in this matter or, perhaps, you can do it with greater competence?' Raghunath's response to this letter makes for interesting reading: 'This lady has been working under my supervision for the past ten years and there is no harm in believing that she has sufficient experience.' This is Raghunathrao being sardonic. It is no small thing that in an advertisement that was published on the inside cover of *Samaaj-swaasthya*, Malatibai received an emphatic mention:

Facility in Bombay

The work of examining the women, selecting the right size of cap, teaching them how it is put into place and giving them detailed information is done by Shrimati Malatibai Karve.

Morning: 9 to 10; Afternoon: 3 to 4

Raghunathrao was transferred to Dharwad (1917) when he was working for the government; then, he went to Paris for a year-and-a-half (1919) when he returned and worked for some time in Pune and Ahmedabad; he then went to Nairobi on Dr Shankarrao's invitation 'leaving his household behind' for five or six months. During these periods, Malatibai had to stay alone in Bombay working as a teacher: first in the Chandaramji High School, then in the Urdu school of the Municipal Corporation and then in the girls' school run by the N.D. Thackersey University.

The probability exists that she went over to Pune for some time. Y.D. Phadke writes, 'When Raghunathrao was in Pune, Malatibai was in Pune where she worked for the institution of the Hinganes.' But Anna makes no mention of this. Prof. N.M. Patwardhan, who had had a long association with the Hingane Women's Education Society as also with the Karve family, makes no mention of it either. In a supplement that was attached to Anna's *Aatmavritt*, he writes, '(Raghunathrao's) wife Malatibai went for a job and thus supported her husband's household. But when she came down with her disability, that help too did not stay for long.' Patwardhan also wrote a separate piece titled 'Annaanchyaa Sahakaaryaanche Sankshipt Vritt' (Short Information on Anna's Associates), where again he makes no mention of Malatibai working for the Hingane Society. All this puts Y.D. Phadke's assertion under a doubt. Besides, Malatibai herself has written, 'I passed my matriculation in 1909, and all my association with the Society came to an end.'

Malatibai has written about Anna with extreme gratitude:

> I got no degree nor did I get knowledge of any art, but what
> I gained from the good and bad experiences of the time when
> the Society was being established and from the knowledge
> that came my way by being in Anna's company is, in my
> opinion, far greater than any degree.

Malatibai has made repeated mention in this small article of not having acquired any degree. Consciously or unconsciously, this could well be an expression of the deep regret she felt. How was it that Raghunathrao, who went all the way to Paris for higher education in Mathematics, did not sense this regret? He has written:

> No person can become the property of another person, and
> a marriage system that gives a man rights over a woman is

worthy of being discarded. In the law of the jungle, might is always right, but reform is all about giving equal rights to a powerless person, and from this perspective a woman must necessarily be given equal rights.

How could a person who advocated these thoughts have not taken into consideration his wife's distress?

Malatibai carried the regret of not being a graduate because the wives of all the other brothers were highly qualified: Dr Shankarrao's wife Revatibai was a *Gruhitaagama* [Bachelor in Women's Studies], Dinkarrao's wife Iravati was an MA, PhD and Bhaskarrao's wife Kaveribai was a BA. It seems probable that she would have mulled over her own feelings of inadequacy. Let's keep everybody else aside and see what Raghunathrao himself thought in this matter. Responding to a reader's letter, Raghunathrao wrote:

'I received great help from her in the work related to the propagation of birth control. It wasn't as if she liked every one of my opinions. People's opinions are dependent upon genetic factors, education and other circumstances and these things are never common in any two individuals.'

The terms 'genetic factors' and 'education' are worth noting. Raghunathrao seems to be conceited about two factors: one is that he is the son of Maharshi Karve; getting into his extraordinary mission is an outcome of his lineage; the other is that he is an MA with a diploma in Mathematics from Paris. Malatibai, poor soul, had neither of these advantages. There is an unstated, indistinct connection between Raghunathrao's above statement and Malatibai's remark of not being a graduate when she wrote about Anna. It is true that she would go with her husband to the French Club; it is also true that Raghunathrao served her with great devotion during her illness, but the fact remains that they were two independent personalities.

The principled Raghunathrao did not publish the news of his wife's death in *Samaaj-swaasthya*. But he does seem to have put his principles aside when he published the following item in the May 1940 issue of *Samaaj-swaasthya*: 'Lamentable news: One of our well-wisher subscribers V.C. Dev passed away in Pune on April 22, according to information provided by his son.'

When Raghunathrao was forty-three and Malatibai was thirty-five, taking into consideration the circumstances of their life, Raghunathrao had a vasectomy. There is no mention anywhere, however, on whether he had discussed this matter with his wife.

It was in 1928 that ill-health caught up with Malatibai, because of which she had to leave her job. She would now stay at home, but she did her household chores with the help of a crutch. Raghunathrao would help her where he could. 'A lovely aroma—it was vanilla, I learnt later—would come from Malati *kaakoo's* kitchen,' Jai Nimbkar has said, suggesting that Malatibai still did the cooking. Throwing light upon Malatibai's health during those times, Shakuntala Paranjape has written:

> Despite her legs having become useless, she would do all the household work with the help of a crutch. Appa would also help her . . . . She had left her job long ago because of her disability. It is difficult to say how many guests the couple entertained. Quite a number enjoyed their hospitality, I being one of them.

Her illness turned out to be permanent. Raghunathrao wrote to a reader in 1944:

I had such serious problems (when I was in the Bombay-Bahrain company) that I would have resigned from the job, but couldn't because my wife was very anaemic then. Expenditure on her treatment would go up to two or three hundred rupees per month, at least during the early days. She is still unwell. It's now fifteen years since then. (Date of the letter: 26 June 1944)

Sadly, when circumstances worsened, wisdom arrived. Dr Shankarrao informed Prof. M.V. Dhond that the ill Malatibai had told him, 'We should have had a child.'

'How could such a progressive, rationalistic person have had such a backward wife?' some argue. But this question is the outcome of looking at the scenario from today's progressive perspective.

When we take her personality and her conduct together, we notice the aptness of the description that Prof. N.M. Patwardhan gave of her as 'a woman totally devoted to her husband'. Besides, a number of Raghunathrao's regretful notes can be located. The person who resigned from every job because he wanted to retain his self-esteem was later reduced to say, 'If I had known this would happen in the future, I would not have given my resignation.'

'You may find plenty of teachers of Mathematics,' he had said while resigning, 'but nobody is going to come forward to do this work on birth control.' But when he had to face the resultant financial distress, he had been left with no choice but to dismantle his household and go to Nairobi. Wasn't this a compromise? Let's also keep in mind that when Malatibai's health fell, he had become helpless and even tried Ayurvedic drugs on her. On the one hand, he would participate in contests to raise much-needed money, but on the other, he had accepted the editorship of *Reason* with very little remuneration out of a sense of honour. Strangely, he had also accepted the condition that his name would not be displayed as editor.

One way to make sense of these seeming contradictions is to remember that we are talking of human beings with all their inconsistencies. Therefore, it is not fair to look for complete coherence or ignore their shortcomings only to paint them as greats.

Malatibai was, after all, a woman too; there was nothing unusual, therefore, if at that specific moment she felt that they should have had a child. There are some who are surprised at Malatibai making this statement to Dr Shankarrao (who stayed so far away in Africa all his life). But Malatibai would surely have had some reason for voicing this pain to Dr Shankarrao and it may even be a good subject for research.

Even though Dr Shankarrao stayed in Africa, he was always concerned about them. During their days of penury, he had called Raghunathrao over to Nairobi and paid for his travel expenses. He had done all that he could to find a job for him. Since Raghunathrao had wanted to get a vasectomy, he had got the procedure done with the help of his friend. It was good, in a way, that they lived so far away from each other. Distance, as they say, makes the heart grow fonder. Proximity often leads to friction and misunderstandings, and this did not happen between the two brothers. What also needs to be kept in mind is that there wasn't much of an age difference between Shankarrao and Malatibai. They had also known each other since childhood and had even lived in the same house for a fair period.

Malatibai's health had begun to go frail from 1928 onwards and it steadily worsened. A time came when she was confined to bed. It is true that Raghunathrao nursed her with devotion, but surely, so many years of nursing would have begun to tell on his patience? *Samaaj-swaasthya*, meanwhile, was being published with regularity for twenty-six years and four months, except for the break when he had to publish a joint issue for August, September and October 1944. Though Raghunathrao gave the shortage of paper as a reason for the break, Malatibai's ill-health too was a reason. Finally, she had to be shifted to the Sindhaniya Hospital, which was located on the way to Bombay Central from Apsara Theatre on Grant Road, Bombay, where an area called Bharat Nagar now falls. That was where she passed away. Talking about her ill-health, Raghunathrao writes:

The affliction that my wife suffers from is called 'pernicious anaemia'. When it first hit her, the four or five doctors possessing degrees from England could not diagnose it. Some did not even acknowledge their ignorance and subjected her to random medicines. We then took her to Pune, where the treatment of an Ayurveda practitioner brought her to death's door. She was again brought back to Bombay, where we consulted a doctor with a London degree. He got her blood tested and there her problem was located. Not one person had suggested a blood test earlier. Since the diagnosis, the line of treatment has become clear and there has been some improvement. But during this period, the disease seems to have permanently damaged her nerves and tissues. This is evident from the fact that while her health is good in all other respects, her control over has legs has reduced. She cannot lift them readily and has to use a crutch to walk one step at a time. The consequence of all this is that her body cannot produce sufficient hydrochloric acid; hence she has to take liver extracts and stomach sections and such things regularly. Any carelessness here and the disease flares up.

The advertisements in *Samaaj-swaasthya* suggest that in spite of her state of health, she continued to help him in the work of birth control.

The only person who recorded Malatibai's death was the journalist, Appa Pendse. He wrote:

> This story is of the time when his wife passed away. I had
> set off towards Grant Road at around eight in the morning
> to buy vegetables. As I turned the corner, I saw Appa Karve
> there. What was he doing out so early in the morning? His
> wife was being treated in the Sindhaniya Hospital at the
> corner. I went towards him to enquire when I saw a trolley
> for carrying dead bodies about 15-20 steps away with a
> cloth-wrapped corpse on it. He began the conversation by
> saying, "Passed away in the night. Got this corpse-trolley
> from the *Praarthana-Sabha*. Arranged for the man there to
> carry it for five rupees. What can all others do? Why bother
> them so early in the morning? What would they have done
> anyway by coming over? What we can do expeditiously
> we should get done. Well, all right. That trolley man has
> gone ahead, I should move too. I've told him where we
> have to go."

Appa Pendse's word put the event on record. They are actually excerpts from a speech he delivered on *Akashvani*. Malatibai passed away in 1944, while this speech was written many years later, for which Appa had to depend on his memory. He has given plenty of details on the important aspects of the episode in graphic language, but he hasn't mentioned the date. . . .

In an issue of *Samaaj-swaasthya*, Raghunathrao had this to say about Luigi Pirandello[1] with regard to death, 'He had written in his will, "My dead body should be wrapped in extremely ordinary cloth and carried for burial in a jalopy without anybody accompanying". Considering that he had conducted himself on the same principle on Malatibai's death, could Raghunathrao have quoted Pirandello because he had found a soulmate in him?

Two of Malatibai's writings were published in *Samaaj-swaasthya*: one was the review of a book, and the other was on cooking. An excerpt of the book review is given below to give a clearer picture of her concept of a review:

> Mr. S. D. Kulkarni has appended a note in English to this book: ". . . I have tried my best to minimize errors appearing in this book, but some have still remained. The intelligent student will easily identify the errors. If an ordinary student cannot spot them, it will not make much of a difference, because often they are not evident not only to the students but also to their teachers and examiners." Teachers should ponder on this remark. The lecture method of teaching language is in practice these days and the book has tried to apply the same method to the teaching of Sanskrit. There are no clarifications or meanings of difficult words to be found anywhere, which makes the book useless without a teacher. On top of that, there is a possibility of the teachers themselves being confused over some words. For example, the word '*phalak*' has been used to mean a 'bench' in the first lesson, while in the third lesson it means a 'blackboard'. Two separate words should have been used for these two articles. The tenth lesson describes a '*maanjar*' which is the commonplace word for a cat, but the word used for the cat here is '*otu*'. There is nothing wrong with the word, but children should first be given the simpler word and not words that are not commonly used. If a few such errors can be overlooked, the book is good.

This excerpt gives an indication of her perspective in the choice of the book she took for reviewing. Instead of picking up creative literature, she wrote on a book that would be useful for students and something with which she could connect through her years of experience as a teacher. It is obvious that she was well-versed with the subject that she had taken for review. She identified the errors with authority, but did not comment much on the quality of the book, though she endorsed its utility. She expressed her thoughts and differences of opinion with clarity, authority and brevity, a hallmark of the Karve family's style of writing.

Cooking was one of the areas that *Samaaj-swaasthya* covered under the title 'Gruh-Karme' (Household Chores). (A criticism of this had been published in the magazine *Chitra* of those times.) Malatibai has written a piece on the subject of a dish called Paat-wadya.

'Shakuntala Paranjape has assured us that she will review some books for us,' Raghunathrao had written and added, 'we are grateful.' It is regrettable, therefore, that he could not persuade Malatibai to do more writing for his magazine. After all, she did advise and instruct women who came to their clinic on inserting the Dutch Cap and she would certainly have got into a conversation with them. She could so easily have written on her and their experiences and their tales of joys and sorrows. The two reasons why this did not happen are (a) that she would not have received enough encouragement from her husband or (b) that she was not interested in writing.

It is now known and universally acknowledged that Raghunathrao had the vasectomy performed upon himself. Even so, there are writings here and there that hold that it was Malatibai who had undergone the sterilization procedure. Divakar Bapat has written, 'He got the sterilization procedure performed upon Malatibai.' When Bapat was asked where he had got the information from, he said that it was mentioned in *Samaaj-swaasthya*. Prof. J.V. Naik has written, 'His wife Malati, whom he trained and who of her own volition underwent sterilization, fully cooperated with him in the venture.' The interesting thing is that around the same time, he wrote in a Marathi article that Raghunathrao had got the sterilization procedure done upon himself.

Durga Bhagwat writes, 'Because Karve did not want a child, he got an operation performed upon his wife. The skills and facilities for this kind of an operation were limited during those days, because of which his wife became a cripple for life.' Raghunathrao himself has written this on the matter, 'After having left two jobs, the prospect of finding a third one was very low; hence I got the sterilization operated performed upon myself.' (*Samaaj-swaasthya*, June 1949, p. 283) After Dr Shankarrao told Prof. M.V. Dhond that Raghunathrao had undergone vasectomy, there can be no doubt left in the matter.

Whatever the case, the fact remains that in Malatibai, Raghunathrao had found an enthusiastic, happy and like-minded partner.

9

And Finally . . .

Raghunathrao's Death

Raghunathrao was often required to go to the Gulf of Persia along with his boss at the Bombay–Bahrain company. No information could be gathered on how many trips he made, but the saline air there did not suit his constitution. He was very fond of playing tennis in his younger days, and when he moved to Girgam, he would regularly go for morning walks to the beach, to Chaupati. After 1927, when Malatibai's health began worsening, he would look after her as well as he could. He had his own professional work too. He would visit the Asiatic Library and attend the lectures arranged by the Bombay Marathi Granth Sangrahaalaya (Library) without fail. Whenever organizations like the Dakshin Maharashtra Vangmaya Parishad announced writing contests, he would undertake careful study and write books too. And there was always the work at *Samaaj-swaasthya*—writing, printing and posting. He was then beset by blood pressure problems and had even fallen unconscious because of walking in the sun. True to nature, he then did a lot of reading on blood pressure and even wrote pieces on the subject in *Samaaj-swaasthya*. When he began writing on dietetics, he wrote to his brother-in-law Prof. D.L. Sahasrabuddhe and called over some books from him. To take care of his own failing health, he switched over for some time to raw food. He was not very fond of eating meat; he had, however, tasted it while he was in Paris. He had tried out port wine too.

Raghunathrao's wife passed away on 14 October 1944 and the rest of his life was spent in solitude. He turned seventy on 14 January 1952. During the last years of his life, he was served by a lady named Pirojbai Naik.

His fierce idealism drove him to stretch himself to the limits in his chosen endeavour: selling birth control devices at reasonable prices, propagating information on sexually transmitted diseases and bringing out *Samaaj-swaasthya* under the most testing of circumstances. His love for reading voraciously and going to plays, movies, lectures and conferences never waned. He had never enjoyed robust health since childhood. He has written that during the time that Malatibai was unwell there would be occasions when he didn't get his two meals on time. Whatever photographs have been printed of him along with his biographies and other writings on him are generally of his younger days, which make it impossible to know how he looked in his fifties and particularly in his seventies, when his health had taken a severe knock. The rare photographs and sketches that were published on Anna's centenary show Raghunath to be weak and unwell.

During the last decade of his life, the country gained Independence and concern began to be felt in some quarters over the burgeoning population. The salutary effect of this concern was that Raghunathrao's prescience and his unrelenting efforts in the area came to public notice. While opposition still remained in some sections, its severity had certainly turned blunter.

Some of his friends like Samatanand Gadre and Appa Pendse decided to celebrate his seventieth birthday and collected funds to present a purse to him. He was felicitated in a function that was chaired by Justice M.C. Chhagla. Since Raghunathrao had been closely associated with *Reason*, it is quite likely that Justice Chhagla and he would have known each other even before this event. He has even reviewed a book written by Chhagla. Writers like S.K. Ksheersaagar, H.R. Mahajani and Prof. N.S. Phadke wrote articles in praise of him. He has acknowledged his gratitude to them in an article called 'Aamchi Sattari' published in *Samaaj-swaasthya*. Raghunathrao is now referred to as the first propagator of birth control. Certain kinds of jellies and other material required for producing birth devices control devices were required to be imported then, which could only be done under government license. This rule continued to stay even after Independence and Raghunathrao had applied to the government for the required permission. He was terribly disappointed when he was informed that he did not qualify to be granted the import license.

The Brahmin community of Girgam had organized a question–answer session with Raghunathrao on 10 October 1953. Towards the end of the programme, he started feeling unwell. Dr A.N. Bhalerao checked him for blood pressure and found it unacceptably high. By the time he was rushed to Bhatia Hospital, he had lost consciousness. After four days of struggle, on October 14, he lost his battle with death. A note by him read that he had borrowed Rs. 25 from Anna on the fourth of that month and gave details of the expenses. He, therefore, died in debt.

From October 10 onwards, Dinkarrao, Iravatibai and Bhaskarrao would take turns to look after him. It was Bhaskarrao who wound up Raghunathrao's household after his death. Anna was then ninety-five years of age and he had already been informed of his son's critical state. He heard the news of his son's death with his usual stoicism. Members of the Karve family were known for not getting rattled on such occasions, and even if they did, they never wore their grief on their sleeves for public display. This was seen by many as impassivivity. *Kesari* covered the news of his death in the following words: 'Prof. Raghunath Dhondo Karve, the editor of *Samaaj-swaasthya*, passed away on Tuesday. His passing away has deeply grieved his aged father Annasaheb Karve. We share the grief of the Karve family.'

People would visit Anna to commiserate with him on his bereavement. The response that Anna gave to one such person has been reported by Iravatibai in an article called 'Aajoba' (Grandfather): 'Well, he had grown old and he was not keeping well either. Man is destined to die one day.' This dry statement shocked a number of people. With Iravatibai as his reference, Dr. Y.D. Phadke has stated thus:

> After Raghunathrao's passing away, his friends like Anantrao Gadre, Shripad Shankar Navare, Appa Pendse and others held a condolence meeting to express their admiration for the departed soul. Anna, however, could not come over from Pune to take a last look because of his extreme age. People had been queuing up at Anna's house to offer their condolences. To one such person, he said, "It's because I have lived so long that I've had to face the death of my wife as well as my son. Well, he had grown old and he was not keeping well either. Man is destined to die one day." It was a trait with the Karves to resort to fortitude on such occasions. It, however, came as a jolt to the person to whom this response was addressed. His sensitive, emotional daughter-in-law Iravatibai was also deeply affected.

This entire episode was given a different account in what N.M. Patwardhan wrote:

> His eldest son Raghunathrao passed away at age seventy-three in 1953. Fearing that this news would grievously impact Anna, nobody could gather the courage to bring it to him. However, when Anna heard it in Pune, all that he is reported to have said is this: "He had reached his age. It is I who have lived too long. What can one do about it?" Another old man would have made an emotion-charged statement like: "Why didn't I die in his place?" These are matters that do not depend upon a person's whim.

During his declining years, Anna was living with Dinkarrao and Iravatibai, which gave Iravatibai the privilege of spending time with him. This should have helped her know even the smallest aspects of the great man's personality. This is not to suggest that she didn't know them. But the singularity of the article 'Aajoba' is that while Anna is at the centre of the article, he isn't the only one there.

When a biography is written, the personality of the subject is captured in words. Even if it is written from the biographer's perspective, the biographer's own personality is required to be kept at bay. Importance needs to be given exclusively to the subject of the biography. The case of biographies written in the Marathi language is, however, different. Instead of being one-person centred, they become dual-centred. The other centre is occupied by the author, who projects herself as much as she projects the subject, if not more; her own likes, dislikes and prejudices get to occupy greater space. From the very beginning of the article 'Aajoba', it is Iravatibai, the agent, the narrator who comes out more prominently; she is seen commenting on Anna's nature, thoughts and ideologies, and his words and deeds. The last few sentences of the book make this dual-centrism very evident.

Writing done with a clear, unbiased perspective in the reportage fashion, however, comes out as more credible. If the narration of someone close to the family could be found that gives an intimate account of Anna's state of mind during Raghunathrao's last days—how son and daughter-in-law took care of the old man, what his initial reaction was on hearing of his son's death etc.—it would endorse Iravatibai's narrative and strengthen its authenticity. If it happens to differ from Iravatibai's presentation, the reader gains by having another perspective for consideration.

In this context, G.L. Chandavarkar wrote an English biography of Anna in 1958, which was launched at the hands of Pandit Jawaharlal Nehru at the Brabourne Stadium, Bombay. It was translated into Marathi in 1974. Chandavarkar writes:

> Annasaheb's eldest son Prof. R. D. Karve died after a short illness on October 14, 1953. He was seventy-two years old at the time. As he lay on his deathbed in a hospital, his brothers were cautiously preparing their father's mind for what was coming. A little before dawn on the 14th, news came by a long distance call from Bombay. The message was sent by Dinkar who was at the bedside of his brother when the end came. Bhaskar broke the news to his father. Dr. Karve received it without a sigh. There was silence for a few seconds. It was broken by Dr. Karve himself.
>
> "Here I am, an old man of ninety-five!," he said. "It was my time to quit. Instead, the call came for my son! It is a queer world!"[1]

The above description brings to mind Iravatibai's harsher version of Anna's response. It could well have been how it happened, but his children seem to have exercised caution before the news reached him. Anna's mental strength for accepting facts and his pain at his son's passing away seem to be clear in Chandavarkar's words.

Five days after Raghunathrao's death on 19 October 1953, a condolence meeting was held at the Marathi Sahitya Sangh. The information below occurs in the eighteen Annual report of the organization:

> The late R. D. Karve: We are grieved to place on record that Prof. R. D. Karve, Vice-President, life member, social worker, editor of the monthly *Samaaj-swaasthya*, passed away on October 14, 1953. A condolence meeting was held on October 19, 1953 under the auspices of the Sangh and the Bombay Marathi Patrakar Sangh, with the participation of other literary organizations, to mourn his death. The second Vice-President of the Sangh, Prin. K. R. Gunjikar, was in the chair. A number of speakers delved on the late R. D. Karve's great qualities. A resolution of condolence was later passed.

Because of the differences of opinion with regard to Raghunathrao's personality and work, and as newer and newer information and details keep emerging, a strong possibility exists of disagreements continuing to happen among scholars and biographers. But there will be one point on which all of them will be unanimous—his integrity. Durga Bhagwat has written, 'What kind of a person was R.D. Karve? When he went to people's houses, he never had tea there. He would come to our house to visit grandfather, but he never had tea, because he could not return the courtesy on account of his poverty. This was the Karve culture.'

Raghunathrao was a rationalist and was proud of being one. Gopal Ganesh Agarkar was the first to hold the torch for rationalism in modern times and he spoke and behaved accordingly. Raghunathrao was well aware of that, but he rejected being referred to as his intellectual heir or solitary heir. He never fought shy of talking of Agarkar dryly. Here's what he has written:

> Rationalism is not something that emerged out of Agarkar's head. He merely advocated it. A number of rationalists regard Agarkar as the extreme limit of rationalism and that it is not possible to go beyond him. In my opinion it is very possible and I have made efforts in that direction.

The above statement reveals his conceit that in the matter of rationalism and the conduct that went with it, he independently, vigorously and selflessly took it to its next level. He, perhaps, disliked occupying the secondary position that is indicated in being considered as 'Agarkar's heir', because he was a fiercely independent person. Prof. J.V. Naik's assertion below, therefore, needs to be taken with discretion:

> The principal object in all his literary and social activity, as stated by him, was to spread the gospel of rationalism preached by Agarkar, the first pure rationalist of Maharashtra. It was left to Karve, who regarded himself as the only true disciple of Agarkar, to give a practical shape to the cause espoused by the master four decades earlier.

The Demise of *Samaaj-swaasthya*

Samaaj-swaasthya never received adequate advertisements, nor were there enough subscribers. The price of paper had shot up during the Second World War and because of the quota system that too would not be available in sufficient quantity. Running a magazine under such conditions, therefore, was a difficult task and the number of its pages would be impacted. Raghunathrao can be seen to have expressed his despair to his readers and alerted them to the possibility of bringing the publication to a halt. He would appeal for donations; he would acknowledge these donations; publish the letters of the donors and express his gratitude to them.

He was sixty-six when *Samaaj-swaasthya* completed twenty-one years of its existence. The knowledgeable readers who had been won over by the magazine and its editor and who appreciated Raghunathrao's work were keen that the magazine should continue for a long time. His intimates, however, knew well the kind of work it entailed. Dr Shankarrao Karve, Dr Bhaskarrao Karve, Dr Iravati Karve, Wrangler R.P. Paranjape, Shakuntalabai Paranjape, Malatibai Karve and Dr K.B. Lele wrote for the magazine to the extent that they could. But writing for a magazine is one thing; getting the selected articles printed and posted so that subscribers got it on time is another thing altogether. Raghunathrao did the work beginning from an editor and ending with a peon. When he died on 14 October 1953, the November issue, true to form, was ready for publishing. The issue that the subscribers received on 15 October would have been the October issue. The November issue that had already been sent to the printer was finally published with an editorial written by Bhaskarrao. That was the last issue of *Samaaj-swaasthya*. Bhaskarrao wrote in the editorial:

'*Samaaj-swaasthya*' was a single-pole tent. Writing the articles, typing them out, getting them ready for the press, going through the proofs, bringing the printed bundles home, pasting the stamps and the addresses of the subscribers, having them delivered to the post office or to the newspaper agent on the 12th, and all the work at the office would mostly be done single-handedly by R. D. Karve. Due to the paucity

of public patronage, the magazine was being run at a loss. He
was everything – from its office to its staff. With his death,
the single-pole tent has collapsed. It is in the fitness of things.

Everything related to the publishing of this last issue was
in readiness, as was his custom. It is being presented to the
readers with the request that they may kindly accept it and bid
it goodbye. Arrangements are being made to return the balance
amount of the subscribers so as to free ourselves of the debt.

> Looking at the totality of the picture, there is no harm in
> saying that the *raison d'etre* of *Samaaj-swaasthya* was to a
> fair degree successful. Therefore, if *Samaaj-swaasthya* has
> to close down, there is no reason for being grieved about it.
> If one of Karve's disciples or perhaps an organization steps
> forward to publish the magazine or his books, that would
> be welcome. But it is not at all unnatural that a personalized
> institution like *Samaaj-swaasthya* should move on with its
> creator. It, however, seems clear that the torch of rationalism
> that Shri Karve lit will turn brighter as time passes and the
> health of the society shall go on improving.

This, then, was how the demise of *Samaaj-swaasthya* was
announced. The announcement of the return of the balance
money to subscribers was also in step with Raghunathrao's
principle of keeping accounts clear.

There wasn't much money left with him at the time of his
death. His hospital expenses seem to have been borne by his
brothers. The announcement of returning the balance, therefore,
throws a sharp light on the ethics of the Karve family. Here is
a box item that was printed on the back cover of the last issue:

The monthly 'Samaaj-swaasthya' is now being closed. A subscriber could have joined from any month, which means that many subscribers would have received only a few of the issues for which they had paid their subscription. It is our duty to return the money for the undelivered issues. This money will be returned by money-order. If there has been an address change for any subscriber, it may kindly be intimated at the following address:

Right Agency
C/o. Shakuntala Paranjape,
Wrangler Paranjape Road,
Pune – 411004.

Samaaj-swaasthya thus died along with its progenitor, but its pages carry various aspects of his personality and signals of his foresightedness that will continue to be useful to scholars. Of this there is not an iota of doubt.

Glossary

1. **Agarkar, Gopal Ganesh** (1856–1895): Social reformer, educationist, and thinker from Pune. At one time a close associate of Bal Gangadhar Tilak, he co-founded educational institutes such as the New English School, the Deccan Education Society, and Fergusson College along with Tilak, Vishnushastri Chiplunkar, and others. He was the first editor of the weekly *Kesari* newspaper and founder and editor of the periodical *Sudharak*.

2. **Apte, Narayan Hari** (1889–1971): Freedom fighter, Marathi popular novelist, publisher, and editor of *Kirloskar Khabar* for a few years.

3. **Atre, Prahlad Keshav** (1898–1969): Popularly known as Āchārya Atre, he was a prominent Marathi writer, poet, educationist, orator, and founder-editor of the newspaper *Maratha* (a Marathi-language newspaper).

4. **Badodekar, Hirabai** (1905–1989): Indian Hindustani classical singer. She was the daughter of Ustad Abdul Karim Khan, founder of the Kirana Gharana, and Tarabai Mane, a princess of the princely state of Baroda.

5. **Bagal, Madhavrao** (1895–1986): Also called Bhai Madhavrao Bagal, he was a noted writer, artist, journalist, social reformer, political activist, orator, and freedom fighter from Kolhapur.

6. **Balgandharva** (1888–1967): Narayan Shripad Rajhans, popularly known as Bal Gandharva, was a famous Marathi singer and stage actor. He was known for his portrayal of female characters in Marathi plays, as women were not allowed to act on stage during his time.

7. **Bapat, Divakar**: Prominent Marathi writer. He wrote numerous books, notable among them being works on Dr S. Radhakrishnan and Dhirubhai Ambani.

265

8. **Bapat, Senapati** (1880–1967): Pandurang Mahadev Bapat, popularly known as Senapati Bapat, was a freedom fighter. He was given the title 'Senapati,' meaning commander, for his leadership during the Mulshi Satyagraha.

9. **Bapuji, Jacob** (1863–1933): Jacob Bapuji Israel (Wargharkar) was born in Ahmednagar, India, to a Bene Israel subedar in the Bombay Presidency Army of British India. He wrote a number of articles for David Erulkar's *Israelite* in Marathi and English, where he worked as an editor.

10. **Bedekar, Malatibai** (1905–2001): Marathi writer and the first prominent feminist writer in Marathi literature. She also wrote under the pseudonym Vibhavari Shirurkar.

11. **Bhagwat, Durga** (1910–2002): Marathi scholar, socialist, and writer. She studied Sanskrit and Buddhist literature and spent time in the jungles of Madhya Pradesh to study tribal life. She was among the prominent writers who opposed the Emergency. She also declined institutional and civilian honours such as the Padma Shri and the Jnanpith Award.

12. **Bhagwat, Rajaramshastri** (1851–1908): Eminent scholar and social reformer. Worked until his last breath for women's education and the eradication of untouchability.

13. **Bhandarkar, R.G.**: Sir Ramakrishna Gopal Bhandarkar (6 July 183 –24 August 1925) was an Indian scholar, orientalist, educationist, and social reformer. He retired as the Vice-Chancellor of the University of Bombay in 1894.

14. *Bhishagavilas* **(periodical)**: A magazine that published articles criticizing R.D. Karve and his writings.

15. **Chhagla, M.C.** (1900–1981): Chief Justice of the Bombay High Court, Union Minister of Education, and later, Minister of External Affairs.

16. **Chitnis, Leela** (1909–2003): Indian actress in the Hindi film industry, active from the 1930s up to the 1980s. She is best remembered for playing virtuous and upright motherly roles opposite leading stars.

17. *Chitra* **(periodical)**: A weekly magazine in Maharashtra owned by Marathi author Anant Kanekar. It featured cartoons by prominent Indian illustrator Dinanath Dalal, who satirized the British Raj and its policies.

18. **Chitre, Dilip**: Dilip Purushottam Chitre (1938–2009) was one of the foremost Indian poets and critics to emerge in post-independence India. Apart from being a notable bilingual writer (in Marathi and English), he was also a teacher, painter, filmmaker, and magazine columnist.

19. **Deodhar, Manohar** (1928–2006): Author and journalist with *Loksatta* and *Maharashtra Times*. **Dhavale, W.R. (1909–1984):** He wrote poetry under the nom-de-plume of Balshahir. Resha is one of his better-known collections. At different times, he was the editor of newspapers, magazines and sundry journals. He was closely associated with the Mumbai Marathi Sahitya Sangha

20. **Deshpande, P.L.**: Purushottam Laxman Deshpande (1919–2000) was a Marathi writer and humorist. He was also an accomplished film and stage actor, scriptwriter, composer, musician, singer, and orator.

21. **Deshpande, Prof. Kusumavati** (1904–1961): Marathi writer from Maharashtra. From 1931 for over twenty-five years, she taught English literature at Nagpur University. She also served as Chief Producer of Women and Children's Programmes at All India Radio, and as the Convenor of the Advisory Board for the Sahitya Akademi on Marathi literature.

22. **Dev, Shankarrao** (1895–1974): Indian freedom fighter born in Bombay, British India. A member of the Indian National Congress, he participated in several movements including the Bombay Home Rule Movement, Salt Satyagraha, and the Quit India Movement.

23. *Dhanurdhari* **(Marathi periodical)**: A literary magazine edited by S. R. Tikekar. Prominent contributors included D. B. Karnik, Kusumagraj, and Roy Kinikar.

24. **Dhond, M.V.**: Madhukar Vasudev Dhond (1914–2007) was a literary and art critic from Maharashtra, India. He wrote on numerous topics in Marathi and received the Sahitya Akademi Award in 1997 for his book *Jnaneshwaritil Laukik Srushti*.

25. **Ellis, Havelock** (1859–1939): An English physician, eugenicist, writer, progressive intellectual, and social reformer who studied human sexuality. Ellis was among the pioneering investigators of psychedelic drugs.

26. **Frazer, Nelson**: Principal of a training college in Mumbai.

27. **Freud, Dr Sigmund** (1856–1939): A prominent Austrian neurologist and social scientist who founded psychoanalysis, a clinical method for evaluating and treating psychological pathologies rooted in inner psychic conflict.

28. **Gadkari, Ram Ganesh** (1885–1919): A Marathi poet, playwright, and humorist from the Bombay Presidency, British India. He wrote poetry under the pen name *Govindagraj* and humorous articles under *Balakram*, playing a significant role in transforming Marathi literature.

29. **Gadre, Anantrao**: Also known as *Samatananda*, he was a journalist, novelist, and playwright. He initiated the *Satyanarayan Pooja* for untouchables.

30. **Gajendragadkar, P.B.**: Pralhad Balacharya Gajendragadkar (1901–1981), born in Satara, Bombay Presidency, served as the seventh Chief Justice of India, from 1964 to 1966.

31. **Ghorpade, Anubaisaheb**: The queen of the Ichalkaranji state. She was the daughter of Kashibai and Govindarao Kanitkar, a prominent writer of the time. She wrote short stories.

32. **Gokhale, Gopal Krishna** (1866–1915): An Indian political leader and social reformer during the Indian Independence Movement. He was also the political mentor of Mahatma Gandhi.

33. **Haire, Dr Norman (1892–1952):** Born Norman Zions was an Australian medical practitioner and sexologist. He arrived in London in December 1919 and gained fame for his lectures and books on birth control and sexology

34. **Apate, Haribhau** (1864–1919): A noted novelist of his time and editor of the journal *Karamanuk*.

35. **Harshe, R.G.** (1900–1974): A critic known for his works on *Govindagraj*, *Tukaram*, and *Dnyaneshwari*.

36. **Hasabnis, Vasant** (1923–1967): A journalist and poet from Gwalior. His collection of poems was titled *Vashy Mhane*.

37. **Jadhav, Bhaskarrao**: Bhaskarrao Vithojirao Jadhav (1867–1950) was an Indian politician, social reformer, and a leader of the *Satyashodhak Samaj*, the Non-Brahmin movement, and the co-operative movement.

38. **Jambhekar, Balshastri**: Bal Gangadhar Shastri Jambhekar (1812–1846), also known as Balshastri Jambhekar, was an Indian journalist from the Bombay Presidency. Known as the 'Father of Marathi

Journalism', he launched the first Marathi-language newspaper, *Darpan*, during the early years of British rule in India.

39. ***Jeevan* (periodical)**: A magazine mainly devoted to popular fiction, mostly on themes related to sex. Ramakant Welade was the editor and wrote under the pseudonym *Ku. Shailaja*. The magazine ran for nearly 14 months between 1940 and 1942.

40. **Jog, R.S.**: Ramchandra Shripad Jog (1903–1977) was a renowned Marathi critic and poet who edited and analysed ancient Sanskrit literature. He also edited three volumes of the Marathi Sahitya Parishad's *Literary History* and presided over the All-India Marathi Literary Conference held in Thane in 1960.

40. **Joshi, Narhar B.**: Brother-in-law of R.D. Karve.

41. **Joshi, Vamanrao M. (1882–1943)**: Novelist and critic. He was a Professor in Hingane Stee Shikshan Sanstha, Pune. He was President, Marathi Sahitya Sammelan, Madgaon,Goa (1930). Novels: *Ashramharini, Indu Kale, Sarala Bhole, Nalini, Ragini athawa KavyaShastra Vinod*.

42. **Joshi, W.M.**: A novelist and teacher at Hingane Stree Shikshan Sanstha.

43. **Julian, Madhav** (1894–1939): A prominent Marathi poet from Maharashtra, India. His real name was Madhav Tryambak Patwardhan, and he wrote under the pen name *Madhav Julian*.

44. ***Jyotsna* (magazine, 1936–1941)**: A literary magazine edited by V.S. Khandekar and W.R. Dhavale. Renowned poet Kusumagraj published his poems in it.

45. **Karve, Anandibai (Baya)** (1866–1950): A Brahmin woman who was widowed young and later married social reformer Annasaheb Karve, assisting him in his work for the Hindu Widows' Home Association. She was also the first widowed pupil at Sharada Sadan, the residential school founded by social reformer Pandita Ramabai.

46. **Karve, Bhaskar**: The youngest son of Dhondo Keshav Karve and younger half-brother of R.D. Karve. He was a life member of Hingane Stree Shikshan Sanstha. He cared for R.D. Karve in his final days and wrote the last editorial for *Samajswasthya*.

47. **Karve, Dhondo Keshav (Maharshi, aka Anna)** (1858–1962): A social reformer dedicated to women's welfare in India. He founded India's first women's university, SNDT Women's University, in 1916. He was popularly known as *Maharshi Karve*. He was awarded India's highest civilian award, the Bharat Ratna, in 1958.

48. **Karve, Dinkarrao Dhondo** (1899–1980): A renowned Marathi chemist and rationalist, known for his significant publications. He was the third son of educator and social reformer Dhondo Keshav Karve.

49. **Karve, Iravati** (1905–1970): An Indian sociologist, anthropologist, educationist, and writer from Maharashtra. She is widely regarded as India's first female sociologist.

50. **Karve, Malatibai**: A Marathi social reformer and the wife of prominent Marathi educationist and social reformer R.D. Karve (1882–1953), actively assisting in his cause.

51. **Karve, Radhabai Dhondo**: The wife of renowned women's welfare activist Dhondo Keshav Karve (1858–1962).

52. **Karve, Revatibai Shankarrao**: The wife of Dr Shankarrao Karve, the younger half-brother of R.D. Karve.

53. **Karve, Shankarrao Dhondo**: A pioneering doctor in Mombasa, Kenya, during the twentieth century. One of the three sons of noted Marathi educationist Dhondo Keshav Karve, he established the Pandya Memorial Clinic in 1947—the first clinic in East Africa open to all religions and races.

54. **Kashalkar, Shantabai**: A prominent social worker from Bombay Province in the twentieth century. She played a key role in establishing the Ramabai Paranjape Balmandir, an educational institution in Mumbai. She was also a member of the Social Service League, founded in 1911 in Maharashtra.

55. **Kaur, Rajkumari Amrit** (1887–1964): An Indian activist and politician who actively participated in the Indian Independence Movement. She was appointed as independent India's first Health Minister in 1947.

56. **Kelkar, Narasimha Chintaman (N.C.)** (1872–1947): A lawyer from Miraj, Maharashtra, as well as a dramatist, novelist, short story writer, poet, biographer, critic, historian, and writer on philosophical and political themes. He served twice as the editor of the notable Marathi newspaper *Kesari* when Bal Gangadhar Tilak was imprisoned in 1897 and 1908.

57. *Kesari* (periodical): A Marathi newspaper founded in 1881 by Bal Gangadhar Tilak, a prominent leader of the Indian Independence Movement. It served as a mouthpiece for the freedom struggle and continues to be published by the Kesari Maratha Trust and Tilak's descendants.

58. **Ketkar, Dr A.V.**: A physician who strongly opposed family planning and actively wrote articles against it in magazines to propagate his views.

59. **Ketkar, Shridhar Vyankatesh** (1884–1937): A Marathi sociologist, historian, and novelist from Maharashtra. He is best known as the chief editor of *Maharashtriya Jnanakosha*, the first-ever encyclopedia in the Marathi language.

60. **Khan, Abdul Kareem** (1872–1937): An Indian classical singer who founded the *Kirana Gharana*, one of the most prominent traditions of Hindustani classical music.

61. **Khandekar, Vishnu Sakharam (V.S.)** (1898–1976): A Marathi writer from Maharashtra and the first Marathi author to win the prestigious Jnanpith Award in 1974.

62. *Kirloskar Khabar* (periodical): The house journal of the Kirloskar industrial group, launched in 1916. Shankarrao Kirloskar served as its editor. The journal primarily propagated the company's activities. In 1929, the word *Khabar* was removed from its title.

63. **Kirloskar, Shankarrao**: A twentieth-century Marathi visionary who played a key role in the success of Kirloskar Brothers Limited (KBL), a multinational company specializing in pumps. He also contributed to the Maratha Chamber of Commerce and Industries and helped establish the Deccan Manufacturers' Association.

64. **Kolhatkar, Shripad Krushna (S.K.)** (1871–1934): A Marathi writer from British India's Bombay Presidency. He was a pioneer in humor writing and literary criticism in Marathi and presided over the Marathi Sahitya Sammelan in Pune in 1913.

65. **Kosambi, Damodar Dharmanand** (1907–1966): An Indian polymath with contributions to mathematics, statistics, philology, history, and genetics. He is also recognized for his work in numismatics and for compiling critical editions of ancient Sanskrit texts. His seminal book, *An Introduction to the Study of Indian History*, remains highly regarded.

66. **Ksheersagar, S.K.** (1901–1980): A Marathi writer, thinker, and critic. He once headed the Marathi department at the Maharashtra Education Society's College of Arts and Science.

67. **Kulkarni, Vitthal Hari (V.H.)** (1902–1982): A Marathi writer, critic, and biographer who wrote under various pen names, including *Chandrahas*, *Ratnaparkhi*, *Sharadchandra*, and *Suhas*.

68. **Kusumagraj** (Vishnu Vaman Shirwadkar) (1912–1999): A renowned Marathi poet, playwright, novelist, and short story writer, Kusumagraj wrote extensively on themes of freedom, justice, and social emancipation. He received the Sahitya Akademi Award in 1974 for *Natsamrat*, the Jnanpith Award in 1987, and the Padma Bhushan in 1991.

69. **Lele, Dr K.B.**: Dr Keshav Bhashav Lele was a pioneering Indian magician who played a key role in the development of modern magic in India. He authored books on magic, founded and edited *The Indian Magician*, and helped establish the Society of Indian Magicians in 1932.

70. *Loksatta* (newspaper): An Indian daily newspaper established in 1948, *Loksatta* gained prominence for its coverage of Mahatma Gandhi's assassination and related developments. It remained the largest circulated Marathi daily for many years.

71. **Madkholkar, Gajanan Tryambak (G.T.)** (1900–1976): A Marathi novelist and literary critic from Maharashtra. He presided over the Marathi Sahitya Sammelan in Belgaum in 1946.

72. **Sahridaya, Mahad**: The pseudonym of Chunilal Jain, a writer who contributed stories to the periodical *Samaajswaasthya*.

73. **Mahajani, Hanmant Ramchandra (H.R.)** (1907–1969): A Marathi journalist and writer with socialist leanings, known for his contributions to literature during the Indian freedom movement.

74. *Manoranjan* (periodical): A prominent Marathi monthly founded by Kashinath Raghunath Mitra in 1885. It published its first *Diwali Issue* in 1909 and frequently featured works by social reformers and writers. Highly regarded in its time, the periodical ceased publication in 1935.

75. *Marathi Sahitya Sangh, Mumbai*: A literary association established in 1935 with the goal of promoting the Marathi language and literature within Mumbai and its suburbs.

76. **Mardhekar, Bal Sitaram (B.S.)** (1909–1956): A Marathi writer and poet who revolutionized Marathi poetry with a modernist approach. He won the Sahitya Akademi Award in 1956 for *Saundarya ani Sahitya* (*A Study of Aesthetics*).

77. **Master Vinayak** (Vinayak Damodar Karnataki) (1906–1947): An Indian actor and film director of the 1930s and 1940s, best remembered for directing the 1938 Marathi film *Brahmachari*.

78. *Mauj* (periodical): A weekly publication started in 1922 by Anant Hari Gadre, with D.R. Sarolkar and P. M. Bhahwat as editors. Under the same publishing house, *Satyakatha* (a monthly) and *Prabhat* (a daily) were also released.

79. **Mhambre, Gangadhar** (1931–2008): A Marathi writer, poet, and lyricist. In addition to poetry and songwriting, he wrote extensively about businesses in the Konkan region and provided guidance on related ventures.

80. **Naik, Prof. J.V.** (1934–2019): A historian and former head of the Department of History at the University of Mumbai. He also served as Chairman of the Asiatic Society of Mumbai's Board of Trustees.

81. *Navaa Kaal* (periodical): A Marathi daily newspaper based in Mumbai, founded by Krushnaji Prabhakar Khadilkar in 1923. It strongly supported Gandhi's philosophy during the Indian Independence Movement.

82. **Navare, Shripad Shankar**: A writer, journalist, and editor of the Marathi daily *Prabhat*. He also founded the Mumbai Journalists' Association.

83. **Padhye, Prabhakar** (1909–1984): A renowned Marathi writer who won the Sahitya Akademi Award in 1982 for his book *Saundaryanubhaav.*

84. **Pantpratinidhi, Raja Bhawanrao** (Bhawanrao Shriniwasrao Pant Pratinidhi, CBE) (1868–1951): Also known as Balasaheb Pant Pratinidhi, he was the ruler of the princely state of Aundh from 1909 to 1947.

85. **Paranjape, Shakuntala** (1906–2000): A writer, actress, and social worker, she contributed significantly to Marathi literature through plays, sketches, and novels. She served as a nominated member of the Rajya Sabha (1964–70) and was awarded the Padma Bhushan in 1991 for her pioneering work in family planning.

86. **Paranjape, B.S.**: A short story writer known for his collection *Vasantachya Khuna.* He also wrote *Marathi Sameeksheche Aadiparva*, a collection of literary essays.

87. **Paranjape, Raghunath P. (Wrangler Paranjpye)** (1876–1966): A distinguished Indian mathematician and diplomat, he was the first Indian to achieve the prestigious title of Senior Wrangler at the University of Cambridge. He later served as India's first High Commissioner to Australia (1945–47).

88. **Patil, Karmaveer Bhaurao** (1887–1959): A social reformer and educator in Maharashtra, he championed mass education and founded the Rayat Education Society. He was associated with the Satyashodhak Samaj and was honored with the title *Karmaveer* (King of Actions) by the people of Maharashtra.

89. **Patil, P.C.** (1905–1978): Traveled to England for higher education and was closely associated with the Maharaja of Kolhapur. His agricultural research gained significant recognition.

90. **Patil, S.K.** (Sadashiv Kanoji Patil) (1898–1981): A veteran freedom fighter, Congress leader, journalist, scholar, and orator from Maharashtra.

91. **Patwardhan, Madhavrao** (Raja Madhavrao Hariharrao Patwardhan) (1889–1950): The fifth Raja of the princely state of Miraj Jr. in British India. He signed the Instrument of Accession on 8 March 1948, integrating Miraj Jr. with independent India.

92. **Peltier**: A French lecturer at Elphinstone College who taught R.D. Karve in private classes.

93. **Pendse, Dr Vinayak Vishvanath (Appasaheb Pendse)** (1916–1983): A visionary Marathi educationist who founded *Jnana Prabodhini* in 1962, a social organization aimed at promoting education in India.

94. **Pendse, S.N.** (Shripad Narayan Pendse) (1913–2007): A prominent Marathi writer whose novel *Rathachakra* (*The Chariot Wheel*) won the Sahitya Akademi Award in 1963.

95. **Phadke, N.S.** (Narayan Sitaram Phadke) (1894–1978): A writer who wrote in both Marathi and English. He worked as an assistant editor of *The Maratha* newspaper (1919–1920) and was awarded the Padma Bhushan in 1962 for his literary achievements.

96. **Phadke, Y.D.** (Yashawant Dinkar Phadke) (1931–2008): A historian and political activist from Maharashtra who wrote extensively on historical events and personalities from the last two centuries. He served as the President of the 73rd Marathi Sahitya Sammelan in Belgaum (2000).

97. **Phadnis, Nana** (Balaji Janardan Bhanu) (1742–1800): A Marathi minister and statesman during the Peshwa administration in Pune. British historian James Grant Duff referred to him as 'the Maratha Machiavelli.'

98. **Phulambrikar, Krishnarao** (Krishnaji Ganesh Phulambrikar) (1898–1974): Also known as Master Krishnarao, he was an eminent

Hindustani classical vocalist, composer, and musicologist. He created three Hindustani ragas and several *bandishes*. He was honored with the Padma Bhushan in 1971 for his contributions to music.

99. **Phule, Jyotiba** (Jyotirao Phule) (1827–1890): A pioneering Indian social reformer, writer, and anti-caste activist from Maharashtra. He championed women's education and fought against untouchability. In 1873, he founded the Satyashodhak Samaj (*Society of Truth Seekers*) to promote social equality.

100. **Pillai, Capt.**: A physician from Sholapur who later moved to Mumbai. He developed a strong interest in family planning and met Margaret Sanger during her visit to Mumbai. He founded the magazine *Marriage Hygiene*.

101. *Prabhaat* (periodical): A Marathi daily newspaper founded on 21 November 1929 by P. M. Bhagwat. S. S. Navare later became its editor.

102. *Pratibha* (periodical) (1932–1937): A Marathi weekly that primarily focused on literary discussions. Key contributors included G. D. Khanolkar, K. Narayan Kale, V. A. Kulkarni, and Daundkar.

103. **Priyolkar, A.K.** (Anant Kakba Priolkar) (1895–1973): An Indian polemicist, author, and political activist. He served as the President of the Akhil Bharatiya Marathi Sahitya Sammelan in Karwar, Karnataka, in 1951.

104. **Rajwade, Ahitagni** (Shankar Ramchandra Rajwade) (1879–1952): A Marathi philosopher and lecturer who extensively researched ancient Sanskrit knowledge and independently explored philosophical questions. He was later conferred the title *Ahitagni*.

105. **Rangnekar, M.G.** (Motiram Gajanan Rangnekar) (1907–1995): A Marathi playwright and writer from Maharashtra. He received the Sangeet Natak Akademi Award in 1982 for his contributions to playwriting.

106. *Ratnakar* (periodical): Founded by S. A. Gokhale on 14 October 1925, this periodical featured articles on music, dance, sculpture, painting, and literature. Prof. N. S. Phadke was a key contributor, writing in various literary forms.

107. *Reason* (1930–1942): A magazine started by the youths of the Rationalist Society of India in Mumbai. It featured debates, articles, and discussions promoting a rationalist perspective. Editors included Mr. Abraham, Mr. Erunkar, and R.D. Karve. Chief

Justice M. C. Chagla and Wrangler R. P. Paranjpye were closely associated with it.

108. **Robinson, Dr William J.** (1867–1936): An American physician, sexologist, and birth control advocate. He was an influential figure in the early 20th-century Birth Control Movement in the United States.

109. **Russell, Bertrand** (1872–1970): A British philosopher, logician, mathematician, and public intellectual. His contributions influenced mathematics, logic, set theory, and analytic philosophy. He was awarded the Nobel Prize in Literature in 1950.

110. **Khabade, Manoramabai**: A writer from Kolhapur who managed the children's section of the Marathi newspaper *Satyawadi* for some time before dedicating her life to Christianity.

111. **Sahasrabuddhe, DRD. L.**: An agricultural scientist and professor at Pune's Agriculture College. He was related to R.D. Karve and authored books on agriculture.

112. **Sahasrabuddhe, Indira** (1894–1959): A Marathi-language author who wrote numerous books during her lifetime.

113. **Sanger, Margaret** (1879–1966): An American birth control activist, sex educator, writer, and nurse. She founded the first birth control clinic in the United States and played a key role in developing the first birth control pill. She is regarded as a leader of the Birth Control Movement in the U.S.

114. *Sanjeevani* (magazine): A women's magazine edited by P. S. Kolhatkar. Contributors included Anant Kanekar, Indira Sant, and Kusumagraj.

115. **Sardesai, Govind Sakharam,** *Riyasatkar* (1865–1959): A historian from the Bombay Presidency, popularly known as *Riyasatkar Sardesai*. He was awarded the Padma Bhushan in 1957 for his contributions to Indian historical research.

116. *Satyawadi* (Marathi magazine): A publication catering to Marathi readers, covering local and political issues.

117. **Savarkar, V.D.** (Vinayak Damodar Savarkar) (1883–1966): A prominent Indian politician, activist, and writer. He developed the Hindu nationalist ideology of Hindutva and was a leading figure in the Hindu Mahasabha.

118. **Shantaram, Rajaram Vankudre** (1901–1990): Also known as V. Shantaram or Shantaram Bapu, he was an acclaimed Indian film director, producer, screenwriter, and actor known for his contributions to Hindi and Marathi cinema.

119. **Shirurkar, Vibhavari**: Malati Vishram Bedekar (1905–2001) was a Marathi writer from Maharashtra, India. Writing under the pseudonym *Vibhavari Shirurkar*, she is considered the first prominent feminist writer in Marathi literature.

120. **Sinnarkar, V.**: A painter of that era.

121. **Stopes, Marie** (1880–1958): A British author, palaeobotanist, and campaigner for eugenics and women's rights. She played a critical role in bringing birth control into public discourse and founded the first birth control clinic in Britain.

122. **Tambe, Ramabai**: A member of the women's club in Nagpur.

123. **Tamhankar, Bhagirathibai**: A member of the women's club in Nagpur. She participated in debates on *Samaaj Swaasthya*.

124. **Tembe, Govindrao** (1881–1955): Govind Sadashiv Tembe, popularly known as *Govindrao Tembe*, was a prominent Marathi harmonium player, stage actor, and music composer.

125. **Tendulkar, Malatibai**: Editor of the Marathi weekly *Pratod* (1937–1949).

126. **Tikekar, S.R.** (1901–1979): A journalist and writer who served as a correspondent for *Kesari*. He traveled extensively in Arab countries and co-authored the well-known book *Aaj Kalacha Maharashtra*. He was also the editor of the magazine *Maharashtra Sanjeevani*.

127. **Tilak, Narayan Waman** (1861–1919): A Marathi poet from the Konkan region of the Bombay Presidency. He was a well-known convert to Christianity from the Chitpavan Brahmin community.

128. **Trilokekar, Khanderao**: A Marathi poet.

129. **Sant Tukaram** (1608–1650, contested): A seventeenth century Hindu Marathi saint and poet, devoted to Lord Vithoba (Vitthal) of Pandharpur. He is best known for his *Abhanga* devotional poetry, which often addressed themes of social reform.

130. **Tulajapurkar, Dajisaheb**: A lawyer by profession, he wrote *Maharashtra Bhupali* and the popular fact-based novel *Maze Ramayan*.

131. **Varerkar, B.V.** (1883–1964): Bhargavaram Viththal Varerkar was a Marathi writer who translated several novels into Marathi. He presided over the Marathi Sahitya Sammelan in Dhule (1944) and was later nominated to the Rajya Sabha.

132. *Vasundhara* (magazine): A fortnightly publication (1930–1940) edited by M.G. Rangnekar. It was particularly popular among college students.

133. **Weade, Ramakant**: A writer from Nashik who assisted Acharya P. K. Atre. He started the magazine *Jeevan*, of which 14 issues are available. His articles were known for their controversial and vulgar tone. He wrote under the pseudonym *Ku. Shailaja*.

134. **Vyas, Narayan** (1902–1984): A Hindustani classical singer from Maharashtra, associated with the *Gwalior gharana*. He was renowned for his *khayal*, *bhajan*, and *thumri* singing.

135. *Yashvant* (magazine): A periodical (1938–1950) mainly dedicated to Marathi short stories. Published by G.M. Veerkar, it was widely read by Marathi-speaking audiences.

136. **Yashvant, Rajkavi** (1899–1985): Yashwant Dinkar Pendharkar, a renowned Marathi poet, wrote under the pen name *Yashwant*. In 1940, Maharaja Pratap Singh Gaekwad of Baroda honored him with the title *Raj Kavi* (State Poet). He also presided over the Marathi Sahitya Sammelan in Mumbai (1950).

1. Early Days

1 Four-class or four-caste.
2 All quotations from *Aatmavritt* are direct translations from Marathi.
3 In the beginning, Narharpant Joshi, Anna Karve and Moreshvar Ramchandra Kale lived together along with their wives. Wrangler R.P. Paranjape has written that Kale left them soon.
4 'Jaalyaateel Chandra', Mauj Publications, 1998, pp. 93–173.
5 He later became the registrar of the SNDT University.
6 This subject has appeared in *Atmvritt* on pages 138–139 in more or less the same form.
7 *Samaaj-swaasthya*, November 1930.
8 How Anna looked after the girls can be estimated from the paragraph that Malatibai has written:
'This story is of two and a half years ago. My elder sister was running temperature. Since I was too young, I didn't understand the nature of this fever. As always, I wrote a letter to my father and handed it over to Gu. Anna for posting. Anna wrote something more and posted it. The next day, when we were having our meals, my sister's limbs turned cold. We were all panic-stricken. We fomented her hands and feet and used some household remedies; after some while, she regained consciousness and began feeling better. Anna wrote another letter to my father the next day, telling him that there was no need for him to come over, since the girl's fever had subsided. During prayer time, he distributed sweets as thanks-giving for the girl's recovery. That was when I understood what responsibility for someone else's daughter means.'
9 Shankarrao told Dhond that the wedding took place in 1910.
10 Nobody has made a clear mention of the date of their marriage.

2. Professor R.D. Karve

1   In a letter to Ravindra Kelekar, Raghunathrao has written, 'The college was up till Intermediate. Two years later, when the World War got over, I took leave and went for further studies to France. If I had known that during my absence the college would grow up to BA, I would not have gone.'

2   *Samaaj-swaasthya*, editorial, June 1930.

3   To be pronounced the English way. Not to be confused with 'Anna', the honorific with which Dhondo Karve was addressed.

3. Jobs in Other Areas

1   In this deputation, leaders like Mohammad Ali, Suleman Nadvi, Abdul Kasam, Bashir Bidwai had gone to Paris. They had sent information by telegram that was published in the 3 August 1920 issue of *Kesari*.

2   'Prof. Peltier's son was working in a French company. He recommended my name there ... doing shorthand and typing for eight hours every day on a lesser salary than before had made life very difficult, but there was no choice. Hence I gave my acceptance,' Raghunathrao has written.

4. *Samaaj-swaasthya:* Earlier Life and Writings

1   'Anna ordinarily does not watch movies. While he was with Raghunath in Bombay, he received four passes. There is mention that for the sake of keeping the Manager's heart, the foursome of he, Raghunathrao, Iravatibai and Bhaskarrao went for the movie.' *Aatmavritt*, 1958, p. 595.

2   'What is not to happen will never happen; what is bound to happen will happen.'

5. Launching *Samaaj-swaasthya*

1   Sanskrit drama attributed to Sudraka, perhaps of fifth century CE. The word means 'a little clay cart'.

2   Folk-dance of Maharashtra.

3   An article written by Leela Patil published in the book *Baap-Leki* is important in this context.

4   *Samaaj-swaasthya*, May 1944, pp. 184–185.

5   *Pratibha* 4 A, 1935, p. 148).

6   '*Jaalyaacha Chandra*', D.A., p. 88.

7   February 1949, p.186.
8   December 1950, p. 142.
9   October 1951, pp. 78–79.
10 October 1951, p. 79.
11 *Samaaj-swaasthya*, July 1945, p. 16.

6. Cases and Controversies

1   For example: 'A certain person who during his younger days defined circles around girls on his bicycle and teased them has now taken up the pretence of getting into religious work. He now delivers lectures in such meetings for the sake of gaining popularity. It is perhaps true that he may not have given trouble to women of other religions; therefore he may look holy to ultra-orthodox eyes. (*Samaaj-swaasthya*, June 1935, p. 376)

2   Gandhiji had written the following letter to Raghunathrao, 'Received your letter. As long as I believe that the measures suggested by you are morally harmful, I shall not support them. But if you send me literature on this subject, I am ready to study it. You have written about Holland. (Raghunathrao had sent him his book on birth control.) I wish to know the figures and the circumstances related to it. You haven't responded to the questions I had raised. Will the use of the devices loosen marriage-bonds or not?'

3   Phadke, Y. D., 'Ra. Dhon. Karve', *H. Motey Prakashan*, 1981, p. 96.

4   Dr. Manoramabai Thatte's article titled 'Santatiniyaman' was published in *Jeevan* (March 1942). The degrees printed under her name were 'I.C.P.S. (Bombay) L.M. (Rotunda)'. Mr. Narayan Parshuram Thatte helped her.

5   A humorous piece was published in the 20 March 1937 issue of the weekly *Chitra* titled 'April Fool' (Letters to be sent on the April 1)
    'Dear Vahini Saheb,
    We Kirloskar brothers are extremely grateful to you for having provided us with immense publicity by writing a letter against *Kirloskar*. For the purpose of ever remaining grateful, we have hung an enlarged photograph of yours in our office. Please send us a story for the next issue of *Kirloskar*.
    Awaiting your response,
    Yours faithfully,
    S.V. Kirloskar.'

6   This is a passing reference that R. D. Karve had made. Girijabai Kelkar
        was a writer and one of the social activists of that time. Raghunathrao
        has referred to her one of the general talks on this issue.

7   Prabhakar Padhye had made the following comment on
        Raghunathrao in 1981: '. . . I sometimes suspect that this gentleman
        suffers from a split personality.'

8   *Samaaj-swaasthya*, March 1934.

9   Rajadhyaksh, M. V. (as Nishaad), 'Vad-Samvaad', *Mauj Prakashan*,
        2003, pp. 67–69, edited by Gr. R. Kamat and Meena Gokhale.

10   ('*Chitra*', 1943, p. 57).

7. Other Work

1   'Samaaj-swaasthya', March, 1934.

2   Dr Shankarrao Karve mentioned this episode to M.V. Dhond
        during an interview. He, however, made no mention of the fine that
        was imposed.

3   Sathe obviously believed that there was no link between mathematics
        and music.

8. Raghunathrao's Intimates

1   Luigi Pirandello's play *Six Characters in Search of an Author* was
        translated into Marathi under the title 'Naatakkaaraachya Shodhaat
        Sahaa Paatrey'.

9. And Finally . . .

1   [*Mahsarshi Karve*, Ganesh L. Chandavarkar; p. 204; Popular Book
        Depot, Bombay; April 18, 1958]

Scan QR code to
access the Penguin
Random House
India website